America and the Misshaping of a New World Order

America and the Misshaping of a New World Order

EDITED BY GILES GUNN
AND CARL GUTIÉRREZ-JONES

Global, Area, and International Archive
University of California Press
BERKELEY LOS ANGELES LONDON

The Global, Area, and International Archive (GAIA) is an initiative of International and Area Studies, University of California, Berkeley, in partnership with the University of California Press, the California Digital Library, and international research programs across the UC system. GAIA volumes, which are published in both print and open-access digital editions, represent the best traditions of regional studies, reconfigured through fresh global, transnational, and thematic perspectives.

University of California Press, one of the most distinguished university presses in the United States, enriches lives around the world by advancing scholarship in the humanities, social sciences, and natural sciences. Its activities are supported by the UC Press Foundation and by philanthropic contributions from individuals and institutions. For more information, visit www.ucpress.edu.

University of California Press
Berkeley and Los Angeles, California

University of California Press, Ltd.
London, England

Library of Congress Cataloging-in-Publication Data

America and the misshaping of a new world order / edited by Giles Gunn and Carl Gutiérrez-Jones.
p. cm. (Global, area, and international archive)
Includes bibliographical references and index.
ISBN: 978-0-520-09870-1 (pbk. : alk. paper) 1. United States—Foreign relations—2001–2009. 2. War on Terrorism, 2001-—Political aspects—United States. 3. Terrorism—Government policy—United States. I. Gunn, Giles B. II. Gutiérrez-Jones, Carl Scott.

E902.A46 2010
973.93—dc22 2009023257

© Manufactured in the United States of America

19 18 17 16 15 14 13 12 11 10
10 9 8 7 6 5 4 3 2 1

The paper used in this publication meets the minimum requirements of ANSI/NISO Z39.48–1992 (R 1997) *(Permanence of Paper).*

Contents

Acknowledgments

The editors gratefully acknowledge a "Critical Issues in America" grant from the College of Letters and Science of the University of California, Santa Barbara, which supported the yearlong set of activities, culminating in a national conference, that inspired this volume.

We dedicate this book to our wives, Barbra and Leslie, who, like our contributors, have borne the wait for its appearance with patience and good cheer, and to all the students who become more sensitive every day to the impact of culture and cultural values on the formation of international policy and global governance.

1. Introduction

The Place of Culture in the Play of International Politics

Giles Gunn

This book is organized around the belief that cultural assumptions, principles, and aspirations have played a much larger role in international politics than is often conceded. In the American academy as well as the public arena, there has until fairly recently been considerable skepticism about, if not resistance to, such an idea. Not that anyone has considered international affairs immune to the influence of ideologies, values, or even symbols, but only that the conventional orthodoxy in international relations has tended either to downplay the effects of such factors or, more likely, to presume that the best way of understanding their importance is by determining how they have been expressed within the terms and constraints of the state system. In much of the scholarship devoted to the study of international relations, "culture talk" has often been held to be at best a diversion or distraction, at worst a distortion or even a delusion, and given some of its recurrent exaggerations one can rather easily see why. It is scarcely necessary to cite the notoriety of something like Samuel Huntington's "clash of cultures" thesis, much less the more widespread obsession in the United States and elsewhere with "culture wars," to realize that the term *culture* has been as susceptible to misrepresentation and deformation as the word *politics*. Where culture is held to explain everything, it illumines almost nothing. And yet the cultural component has worked its way back into the discourse of international politics not simply as a necessary way of accounting for the temper, tension, and force of particular policies and practices but also as a way of comprehending the political itself. One can no more divorce political interests from cultural prejudices than one can separate the history of institutions, diplomacy, and war from the history of consciousness.

Such elemental linkages have, of course, long been acknowledged in the writings of everyone from Adam Smith, David Ricardo, and Karl Marx to Max Weber, Hannah Arendt, Karl Polanyi, and Immanuel Wallerstein, but they have been given new applications in the work of, among many others, Judith Sklar, Robert Cox, and, now, Samantha Power. Culture in their work is not simply a tool kit but a template, a blueprint and road map for how people think and act and, above all, interpret their world to themselves and to others. In this sense, cultural systems as they operate in the international sphere are neither simply framed nor delimited by politics; as Edmund Burke knew as well as Antonio Gramsci, not to mention Sayyid Qutb, they generate the emotional and cognitive weather of which at various levels politics is both the consequence and sometimes the corrective.

This assumption has not been lost on a series of scholars who are particularly interested in which cultural system or set of values is to be preferred if one wants to promote "human progress." By "progress" they mean such things as democratic participation and economic development. "Culture matters," as one collection has been titled, because it establishes the horizon of expectations and the grammar of motives that enable people to act in behalf of their own, and perhaps of others', well-being.[1] This is by no means an idle ambition but it tends to restrict the case to be made here for why culture counts for so much. *Culture* as the term is employed in this book will not be confined to those values, assumptions, beliefs, perspectives, and dispositions conducive to the creation of economic advancement and political democratization, but will be widened to include all the practices, subjective as well as empirical, by which people make their lives not simply productive (according to some economic or political calculus) but meaningful.

This wider understanding of the place and play of culture in international affairs has become increasingly self-evident since the end of the Cold War, which caught so many students of global politics by surprise. Itself a battle between ideological mindsets and their many variations projected onto the field of superpower rivalry, the end of the Cold War suddenly revealed many international structures to be ineffective and outworn, others surprisingly resilient, and everyone scrambling to define the different ordering of the world that might take its place. James Rosenau spoke for many when he suggested that the Cold War now appeared "more a collage of perceptions than a confrontation of powers, . . . more a shadow play than a stark drama." If, as he continued, "weapons build-ups and arms races were perpetuated more by unwarranted perceptions and distorted intelligence reports than by actual plans for military offences," one was now compelled "to realize how fully the course of events are fictions of convergent imaginations, of inter-subjectivities rather than objective conditions."[2]

The language here is telling. The Cold War turns out not only to have been represented by figurative forms but also in some profound sense to have been fictive in its conduct. This perception merely underlines what international relations scholars, like members of the informed public generally, have now relearned from the current wars in Iraq and Afghanistan, not to say the eastern Congo: that global politics are threaded with cultural assumptions that profoundly affect not only how we conceive and enact our relations with others but also how we imagine that the world should be reshaped. Constructing images of world order and models of global governance is not an exercise reserved for the select few. It is rather rooted in what might be called the telos of culture itself, which tends to make imperialists of us all, and nowhere is this more obvious than in the United States.

The genealogy of America's own imperial destiny goes back to a time long before there was a nation or a people. It begins, one could argue, with the founding of the ill-fated Roanoke colony in 1584, but conventional histories of American adventurism usually associate its origins, if very tardily, with the Spanish-American War of 1898. A fairly naked grab for territory and trade in the Caribbean and the Pacific, the Spanish-American War drew some of its sharpest criticism from America's then most internationally renowned author. Writing in the *New York Herald* on October 15, 1900, Mark Twain's response was characteristically prescient:

> I left these shores, at Vancouver, a red-hot imperialist. I wanted the American eagle to go screaming into the Pacific. It seemed tiresome and tame for it to content itself with the Rockies. Why not spread its wings over the Philippines, I asked myself? And I said to myself, here are a people who have suffered for three centuries. We can make them as free as ourselves, give them a government and country of their own, put a miniature of the American constitution afloat in the Pacific, start a brand new republic to take its place among the free nations of the world. It seemed to me a great task to which we had addressed ourselves. But I have thought some more, since then, and I have read carefully the treaty of Paris, and I have seen that we do not intend to free, but to subjugate the people of the Philippines. We have gone there to conquer, not to redeem . . . It should, it seems to me, be our pleasure and duty to make those people free, and let them deal with their own domestic questions in their own way. And so I am an anti-imperialist. I am opposed to having the eagle put its talons on any other land.[3]

Others, like President William McKinley, saw this pre-emptive move rather differently. Insistent that the Philippine people could not be left to themselves, as "they were unfit for self-government—and would soon have anarchy and misrule over there worse than Spain's was,"[4] McKinley was incredulous and outraged that detractors [presumably like Twain] could challenge the "virtue," "capacity," "high purpose," and "good faith" which qualified "this free people as a civilizing agency." Believing that a century and more of "free government" has uniquely qualified the people of the United States "for the great task of lifting up and assisting to better conditions and large liberty those distant peoples who, through the issue of battle, have become our wards," McKinley embraced colonialism, like so many of his imperialist kinsmen throughout the nineteenth and twentieth centuries, as a moral challenge.[5] McKinley did not think of himself as patronizing but rather as large-minded and patriotic, yet his kind of condescension is so often merely another mask for coercion of the sort that has guided much American thinking and behavior ever since. Referring to Kant's notion of radical evil, Lionel Trilling warned in the 1950s that there is no moral danger greater than the process by which, "when once we have made our fellow men the objects of our enlightened interest, [we] . . . go on to make them the objects of our pity, then of our wisdom, ultimately of our coercion."[6]

There is, nevertheless, another school of thought, now most vigorously defended by the British historian Niall Ferguson, which suggests that America has long been an imperial power and should not be ashamed of admitting it. Ferguson contends that America's centrality to the stability and well-being of international order has been an accepted truth for well over a century, and now in the face of what Thomas E. Hicks has described as the "fiasco of the American military adventure in Iraq"[7] and the threatened destabilization of the entire Middle East, the United States cannot allow its reluctance to be perceived as an empire to prevent it from fulfilling its global responsibilities. The only real issue, say the defenders of what they view as a too-hesitant American imperialism, is how to do it well. And doing it well requires acting multilaterally when we can and unilaterally when we must.

The most recent challenge to global governance and America's hand in guiding it comes from the attacks on the Twin Towers and the Pentagon on September 11, 2001. Those attacks, which were perceived by the American administration and, at least in the beginning, a considerable percentage of Americans and indeed the world as assaults on not just the United States but some of the supports of the world system itself, set in motion a massive, far-reaching counterresponse whose purpose, it has become all too apparent, was not only to preserve world order as it was constructed on September 10, 2001, but to reconfigure it. One can speculate about whether al-Qaeda actually believed that its targeting of some of the symbolic foundations of world order could be so successful, much less foresee the reaction that those attacks would subsequently generate, but there is little doubt that the counteraction they produced by the "Coalition of the Willing" led to consequences that were the very opposite of its intention. Actions taken by the United States and its allies have thus far succeeded not in strengthening world order but in further endangering it, at once destabilizing the Middle East, bringing new and terrible suffering to millions of people displaced by the violence, weakening if not crippling the American military, alienating many of its allies and potential new partners, and discrediting the United States for at least a generation.

This paradox might seem obvious, but reducing its global meaning to the self-contradiction of failed American policies clearly misses the role that cultural forms played in producing it. It effaces the way the symbolic in our so-called postmodern world has taken over much of the definition of the real by compelling us to see the real through images of itself. This is not to imply that simulacra necessarily go all the way down, but it is to suggest that the terror of which 9/11 was the expression, and the terror it unleashed, cannot be comprehended without understanding their function as cultural representations of a very special sort. On 9/11, it is often said, life was rendered as spectacle, as cinema, as theater, as horror film, as indeed the movie *The Towering Inferno,* but this gets less than half of it. The larger truth is that this simulation of the real was actually shadowed by the reality of which it was a copy, a spectre turned corporeal, palpable, personal, catastrophic, deadly, and almost, but not quite, inconceivable. What made the event so frightening is that the Baudrillardian hyperreal had suddenly been transformed into a kind of global surreal, where the terror of the symbolic made real almost overwhelmed the terror of the real made symbolic.

But the meaning of the word *terror* is in fact extremely difficult to pin down. While states have used spectacular violence as a political strategy to spread fear and panic among their own citizens from the time of the French Revolution, if not before, the first "global" attempt to define terror sought to decouple the practice of terrorism from the policies of states. Hence the League of Nations restricted terrorism to "criminal acts directed against a state and intended or calculated to create a state of terror in the minds of particular persons, or a group of persons, or a general public," and this definition is echoed more than a half-century later in an FBI publication which defined terrorism as "unlawful use of force and violence against persons or property to intimidate or coerce a government, the civilian population, or any segment thereof in furtherance of political and social objectives."[8] Although "one person's terrorist is," as the old adage has it, "another person's freedom-fighter," such definitions have helped reinforce the mistaken view now widely held by the American public that terrorism involves no more than the illegitimate violence directed by disenfranchised groups at innocent civilians.

The problem with this view is that it erases too much of the past. While it is not the purpose of this introduction to detail the full history of such matters, it is essential to remember that the United States, along with other world powers and, to be sure, numerous dissident groups, bears responsibility during the postwar period for the creation of an international climate favorable to the use of terror.[9] This occurred most dramatically during the administration of Ronald Reagan, when, in response to the overthrow of friendly dictatorships in places like Iran and Nicaragua, the United States began to view various forms of militant nationalism as proxies for Soviet communism and thus determined to employ "all means necessary," as the phrase went, not merely to contain Soviet expansionism but to reverse it. Terror became the weapon of choice both for the Contras in Nicaragua and for the *mujahideen* in Afghanistan, and the justification of its covert use coincided with the labeling of all nations suspected of sponsoring terrorism—Iran, Libya, Sudan, Cuba, North Korea—as "rogue states."

This is not for a moment to pretend that all terrorism and terrorists are the same—there are crucial distinctions between the genocidal murders of the Khmer Rouge in Cambodia and ethnic cleansing in Bosnia and Kosovo, mass murder in Central Africa and now Darfur and separatist terrorism in Chechnya, the "shock and awe" employed by the American military in the invasion of Iraq and the bombing of abortion clinics in the United States—but rather to claim that this most recent global expansion of the use of terror, by state and nonstate actors alike, probably had its origins in the later phases of Cold War and thus did not, as many people like to think, arise suddenly with the emergence of Islamic jihadism. Terror was used by Timothy McVeigh, Theodore Kaczynski, and the nameless perpetrator (or perpetrators) of the anthrax attack on members of the United States Congress, no less than by, say, Kurdish nationalists in Turkey, the Tamil Tigers in Sri Lanka, or the Revolutionary Armed Forces of Colombia (FARC), and this should caution us against the use of any discourse that associates terror only with non-Western others and rarely if ever with states.[10]

Nonetheless, terror has now acquired various new sponsors, adopted different methods, and developed altered (if far from uniform), enhanced ambitions.[11] The terror we now face as what could be, and certainly feels like, a recurrent condition of global life, may have its most immediate roots in the Cold War era, but it is now different not only in scale but also in scope, purpose, and, perhaps, in nature from what preceded it. If terror is at bottom no more than a strategy for using excessive, seemingly gratuitous violence to gain attention and intimidate populations, it has become infinitely more lethal, disruptive, and psychically disabling as terrorists have learned how to exploit the tools of the modern media, availed themselves of more destructive weapons, and exploited tactics in the service of causes that are not only ethnic and national but also religious.

This has led some experts to differentiate between the "old terrorism" of the Cold War era—where the goal was the expulsion of colonialist regimes, the overthrow of capitalist imperialism, or the desire for ethnic or regional separatism, and the object was to ensure that many people watched while only a comparatively few died—and the "new terrorism" of the post–Cold War period, which is more often but by no means always linked, as Mark Juergensmeyer has written, to vague religious or apocalyptic aims and seeks to inflict as much pain as possible. At least until 9/11, the new terrorism seemed to be best represented by Aum Shinrikyo, the sect led by Shoko Asahara that first employed weapons of mass destruction in March 1995, when it released sarin gas into the Tokyo subway system. Miraculously killing only twelve people while injuring several thousand, Aum Shinrikyo actually possessed enough sarin gas to cause hundreds of thousands of deaths and aimed to destroy entire major cities.[12]

But the full impact of the difference between the new terrorism and the old was not fully absorbed worldwide until the attacks on the World Trade Center and the Pentagon. Here, it became clear, terror by nonstate actors had escalated to a new level where the symbolic, if not also substantial, harm inflicted was meant to equal or surpass the kinds of social injury once associated with large-scale military attacks by state actors. "Megaterrorism," as Richard Falk calls this newest form of violence, operates outside the legal framework of states (thus remaining to a certain extent "invisible" or only partially visible), indiscriminately targets entire populations, and measures success chiefly in terms of the destabilization caused both by the fear it inspires and by the excessive, defensive counterreaction it is intended to create.[13] Hence megaterror transforms the assailant from a sovereign state or dissident community or group into a global network and turns the assailed into any and all who are rendered vulnerable by its stratagems of cruelty and carnage.

In the process, the atrocities of 9/11 brought something still more dreadful into play. This new element was a result not only of the world stage on which these actions were performed but of the world, or rather conception of the world itself, that their performance sought to menace. 9/11 changed the rules and strategies of war by seeking to place the structural supports of world order itself under assault. Though the attacks of 9/11 did not, like Aum Shinrikyo's assault in the Tokyo subway system, rely on weapons of mass destruction, the abyss they opened was just as potentially bottomless. It was the abyss revealed when terror becomes more than a violent instrument of intimidation and coercion and is converted into a technology devoted to disrupting, indeed disabling, mentality itself and the affective circuits that make it work. Far from merely shocking the mind, megaterror seeks utterly to enfeeble it; and with that enfeeblement is threatened the possibility of imagining much of any future at all beyond the present of its own ravages. In this new era, terror seems at times, especially with the threat of the use of weapons of mass destruction, to open onto a futureless present bereft of the hope of any other destiny but the one defined by its own mechanisms of unpredictable mayhem.

The late Jacques Derrida went still further, arguing that 9/11 became uniquely lethal because of its perverse autoimmunitary effects. Operating like an organism seeking to protect itself from a perceived threat by suicidally destroying its own system of defense, the United States after 9/11 actually succeeded in reproducing aspects of the very evil it was seeking to resist. This was revealed, first of all, when the United States found itself on 9/11 being attacked from within, as it were, by militants associated none too distantly from the forces it had itself helped train and supply to fight the Soviet Union before the end of the Cold War. Moreover, that earlier training of the mujahideen in Afghanistan not only created many of the conditions that supported the development of al-Qaeda but may have, in turn, helped focus al-Qaeda's interest in targeting two of the most potent symbolic expressions of American might.

Second, this autoimmunitary logic enabled 9/11 to acquire the status of a calamity worse than the Cold War itself by threatening Americans and others with the loss of something less tangible but almost more irreplaceable than the world of institutions and structures and even individual lives that were preserved for more than forty years by the nuclear balance of terror. What was put at risk by this autoimmunitary logic was, as Derrida described it, "nothing less than the existence of the world . . . [or the] worldwide itself," that process, by turns legal, economic, linguistic, ethical, and spiritual, through which we seek to extend the world's meaning as well as materiality by bringing ever widening spheres of experience both here on earth and beyond within its range of significance. Derrida referred to this multidisciplinary process of world-making and world-extending as *mondialization,* and assumed that there is no more crucial component of the global than this.[14]

Third and finally, this autoimmunitary logic suggested that repression might be circular, that revenge may quite possibly become insatiable, that reprisings and reprisals could feed off of each other ad infinitum. Were this to occur—and he believed that the repressed always returns to unsettle constructions whose exclusions compel and enforce it—Derrida was fearful that the relationship "between earth, *terra,* territory, and terror" might be permanently altered, further blurring distinctions between combatant and noncombatant, civilian and soldier, insurgent, citizen, occupier, and peace keeper.[15]

Whether the potentially suicidal logics of autoimmunology can be extended, as Baudrillard maintains, to the entire global system—megaterror is merely the global system under attack by its own antibodies—they demonstrate, with all the modern technological and nanotechnological resources available, that death is not simply the source and sign of the global system's power, but also—and emphatically—its nemesis. That is, the sacrificial violence of the terrorist attacks the system at the one point where the system cannot defend itself. By rendering death preferable to life, death gains dominion in the very act in which it simultaneously displays itself, like life itself, as disposable. Such logics pose a series of hard questions: Where, beyond the wars in Afghanistan and Iraq, in Chechnya, Somalia, Baluchistan, and possibly Iran, may these actions and counteractions potentially take us? What in the way of costs to international structures and practices will they, or could they, exact? Who among the world's people are likely to bear the largest burdens in paying for them? What will they do to our senses of ourselves as members of a global and not just a national community? How can these actions be explained and justified in relation to international covenants, global understandings, and widely shared human standards? All this, and a great deal more, is very far from clear.

By contrast, there is less of a mystery about what is meant by *world order.* This term is most often associated with the international architecture that began to take form in the century-and-a-half after the Peace of Westphalia, when the Thirty Years' War that effectively brought to an end the Holy Roman Empire and devastated most of Europe was concluded in 1648. The new international system of governance that slowly emerged—and that was eventually to replace, in a location like the future Germany, the 300 independent states as well as hundreds of semi-independent principalities that existed previously—was organized around territorially bounded states whose sovereignty within their own realms encouraged a disposition to advance their own interests at the expense of other states. This potential for conflict meant that the Westphalian system of state-based sovereignty was inherently precarious and unequal. While the sovereign statism on which it was premised was intended to provide a measure of parity among its participants, the hegemonic nature of their relations created striking imbalances that rendered the existence of the system itself dependent on the maintenance, through alliances, treaties, and other compacts, of a tolerable but always shaky balance of power.[16]

This "realist" description of international order was originally articulated in the United States in the Cold War writings of George F. Kennan and Hans Morgenthau and is currently linked with a wide array of figures from Henry Kissinger and Zbigniew Brzezinski to John Mearsheimer and Kenneth Waltz. Defining global governance as a process of managing potential and actual international conflicts between sovereign states seeking to extend their own power and influence with the help of transnational agreements and juridical practices, as well as through the use of brute force, has made it appear as though world order was almost solely dependent on political, legal, and military determinants. But this portrayal of world order was already becoming outdated by the early nineteenth century when the international order defined by state-based sovereignty began to be influenced by the rise of ideologies like nationalism, imperialism, colonialism, racism, communism, and fascism, ideologies which spread like wildfire due to revolutions in everything from communications to armaments. Suddenly it became apparent that political factors alone, even when coupled with economic and social factors, were not capable by themselves of explaining the dynamics of global change. Transformation and innovation in the international arena were also the result of forces, often long at work in the interstices of global architecture, that affected everything from the establishment and transmission of belief systems and normative regimes to the shaping of symbolic systems of feeling and desire.

Nowhere has this been demonstrated more clearly than in the United States itself, where a predisposition to define its own place within the Westphalian system has always found expression in terms that were as semiotic as they were geopolitical, religious as they were strategic. Indeed, from the time of its earliest messianic beginnings in the theocratic aspirations of some of its first European settlers, America has rather consistently exhibited a tendency to define its own political ambitions in a language heavily laden with cultural premises and has recurrently conceived of those ambitions as constituting a model, an archetype, a paradigm that others might well emulate. The Puritan John Winthrop may have been the first of his kind to call upon his prospective fellow voyagers to think of themselves as building an exemplary "City upon a Hill," but he was certainly far from the last. Just as Americans have always tended to treat their own view of themselves and their "New World" experiment as normative and prescriptive, so do they believe in a world where that model has been turned into a replicable, not to say exportable, commodity.

But this in turn has created, at least in the United States, a discursive environment where it has currently become nearly impossible to distinguish between putative recommendations for revising world order in light of the threats posed by the new "War on Terror," as the last U.S. administration insisted on misnaming it, and the forms that American exceptionalism now takes in the global reshaping of the Middle East and elsewhere. The neo-Wilsonian ambition to spread democracy to the Middle East and perhaps beyond—in the thinking of some, all the way to East Asia—is still seen by many neoconservative (if not also neoliberal) apologists and defenders to possess its idealistic precedent in Thomas Jefferson's dream to couple freedom with national expansion by constructing, as Jefferson termed it, an "empire of liberty." Such imperialist rhetoric in fact goes back still further to the spiritual impulses that activated the first colonists in tidewater Virginia. Never ones, like Herman Melville's Captain Peleg in *Moby-Dick,* to resist the opportunity for commerce, conquest, and conversion, these colonists observed as early as 1610 that if the Indians would not submit to Christian conversion "apostolically, without the helpe of man," they would have to be compelled "imperiallie, [as] when a Prince, hath conquered their bodies, that the Preachers may feede their souls."[17] Physical domination, then, both economic and political, along with ideological control, would henceforth tend to be yoked together as the two components most indispensable for fashioning what American Protestants actually liked to imagine as a "righteous empire," and this utopian ambition, geo-religious as well as political, continues to inform what, for many citizens and policy makers alike, is their international imaginary.[18]

Recent discussion of a "new world order" did not originate with George W. Bush but rather, as it happens, with his father, George H. W. Bush. The senior Bush revived a phrase first associated with Woodrow Wilson's "Fourteen Points" speech and then later applied it himself to the fashioning of the Bretton Woods agreements and the founding of the United Nations.

Bush *père* again retrieved it to describe the new world both he and Mikhail Gorbachev hoped would emerge after the Cold War from collaboration between the U.S. and the Soviet Union. Bush specifically used the phrase in a speech he delivered to a joint session of Congress on September 11, 1990, almost immediately following Saddam Hussein's invasion of Kuwait the preceding month, which he titled "Toward a New World Order." Nonetheless, the vagueness of the phrase's reference—was this about the restoration of the rule of law, U.S. military leadership, a more active U.N.?—wasn't finally resolved until it came to be identified with what George H.W. Bush in particular thought would emerge from the collective international response to Iraqi aggression during the first Gulf War.

In the aftermath of that war, there was considerable public commentary about whether such a new world order had in fact already emerged, or had been replaced by enduring elements of the old post–World War II world order that had preceded it, or had been overwhelmed by the forces of globalization. Two among a number of books that kept alive the belief in a newly emergent world order were Samuel P. Huntington's *The Clash of Civilizations and the Remaking of World Order* and Francis Fukuyama's *End of History and the Last Man*, but the real work of reprising this phrase had been going on elsewhere for a number of years. It was actually set in motion as far back as the late 1960s, when a group of conservatives in both parties associated with Washington's Senator Henry "Scoop" Jackson began to argue that America was losing its backbone abroad. In the 1970s, neoconservative alarm only increased following America's humiliating defeat in Vietnam, the Iranian Revolution in 1979, and the Soviet invasion of Afghanistan the same year; all this led to the creation of the Committee on the Present Danger, which was designed to broadcast concerns about American infirmity of purpose and further commitment to the spread of democracy.

When Ronald Reagan was elected president in 1980, neoconservative ideas immediately found their way into policies that within a decade (or so neoconservatives would argue) were to lead to the surprising collapse of the Soviet Union. While that collapse emboldened some, like Fukuyama, to argue that history in its previous bipolar form was now in effect coming to a close with the victory of the capitalist order, it soon encouraged others, such as Robert Kagan and Paul Wolfowitz, to wonder if the time had not now finally arrived for America to begin more aggressively to spread the Good News of democracy throughout the world. To insure the protection and support of this all-important mission alongside other American "assets," then–Secretary of Defense Dick Cheney, with support from Paul Wolfowitz, commissioned the creation of a policy statement in 1992 entitled the "Defense Planning Guidance" (its authors were Zalmay Khalilzad, America's eventual Ambassador to the United Nations and former Ambassador to Iraq, and Abram Shulsky), which proclaimed America's need to remain preeminent as a beacon of democracy in an unstable world.

This doctrine seemed to be confirmed by the first Gulf War, but it also left a number of its most ardent supporters (many of whom were now affiliated with the swelling number of conservative think tanks that had grown up in Washington in the 1970s and 1980s) more convinced than ever that the United States should have gone all the way to Baghdad to overthrow Saddam Hussein and to secure the country and its oil. But regime change and the pursuit of U.S. economic designs in the region were merely several among a number of agendas associated with America's global interests and ambitions that by 1997 would be systematically articulated in the creation of the Project of the New American Century. Here Wolfowitz and other neoconservatives like Richard Perle, Elliott Abrams, and fellow traveler Donald Rumsfeld began to consolidate their convictions about America's simultaneous need to expand its global governance and solidify its global dominance.

As early as 1996, in fact, Perle and some of his friends had begun to bruit about the possibility of removing Saddam Hussein from Iraq, but it was not until 9/11 that they and others found the rationale for such a mission. That rationale was more than a policy objective; it was what Robert Kagan described as "a ready-made approach to the world."[19] Indeed, by March 2001, nearly six months before the attack on the Twin Towers and the Pentagon, Charles Krauthammer, the conservative columnist for *The Washington Post,* had found the terms to define it when he declared that "America is in a position to reshape norms, alter expectations and create new realities."[20]

That world order had in various ways already passed this monopolar global moment by spring 2001 would not dawn on Krauthammer and others of his persuasion for several more years, but there was no mistaking the changes that would in time confound such confidence. With such self-assurance about the shape of global architecture, the United States was to embark upon a series of policies myopically indifferent to the way the world was already rearranging itself. New centers of power were emerging not only among states but also above and below them. Regions like South America, the Middle East, East Asia, Southeast Asia, and Africa were reorganizing themselves around local states; states within states like California and global cities like Tokyo, London, and Shanghai were taking on larger roles in the global economy; global organizations such as the United Nations, the International Monetary Fund, OPEC, and the World Bank were establishing guidelines for the operations of everything from international finance and energy production to development; NGOs from Human Rights Watch, Oxfam, and the International Red Cross to the Bill and Melinda Gates Foundation were addressing issues everywhere that transcended state power; terrorist organizations like al-Qaeda and militias like Hezbollah and the Taliban were pursuing agendas that owed allegiance to religions and ideologies rather than nationalisms and states. Power in the vacuum caused by the end of the Cold War and the erosion of communism was redistributing itself in ways that would prevent what many thought of as the strongest state the world has ever known either from acting in its own self-interest or being able to impose its will on the world. Even before George H. W. Bush was elected, a new world order was in the process of emerging that looked and would eventually begin to operate in a very different way than was assumed in the White House.

What the administration of George W. Bush did or didn't do in relation to these developments is almost less important than why and how it went about it. Assuming itself to be the world's only real hegemon and thus able after 9/11 to dictate to allied world powers the course of action it wished to take, the United States acted as though all other nations would, in the other sense of hegemony, accept its values and priorities as their own. Thus the United States immediately set out to invade Afghanistan for the purpose of destroying the Taliban and capturing Osama bin Ladin but only succeeded for a time in preventing the return and resurgence of the Taliban, who now control increasing sections of the country and are firmly established in parts of Pakistan (and may or may not be the primary object of the Obama administration's military designs, as the war continues to unfold), and it conspicuously failed to capture bin Ladin by refusing to pursue him with, as the phrase goes, "all means necessary." The Bush administration then, according to the famous "Downing Street memo" of July 23, 2002, cooked the evidence in order to justify its predetermined decision to invade Iraq, falsely alleging in the process that there was a connection between Saddam Hussein and al-Qaeda.[21] The initial success of the invasion itself, which employed terror tactics of "shock and awe," was supposed to produce a grateful and compliant populace, but when the ensuing occupation proved incapable of providing even minimal security or essential services, the mood of the population quickly began to sour and within a matter of months produced suspicion, fear, dread, resentment, and eventually insurgency, militias, assassinations, and chaos.

As is well known, the creation of the insurgency was made almost inevitable by the recklessness of L. Paul Bremer, the head of the Provisional Coalition Authority, when he fired all the members of the Ba'ath party and at the same time disbanded the entire armed forces. With two strokes of the pen Bremer not only created the conditions which would lead now unemployed and increasingly desperate men to resort to violence and terror to redress grievances and eventually begin settling scores but also turned over the promised reconstruction of a shattered Iraq to cohorts of American bureaucrats completely inexperienced at nation rebuilding and whose ranks were supplemented by tens of thousands of almost always American private contractors and security personnel. The latter, along with members of the American military acting on orders from the very top of the chain of command, then compounded the catastrophic bungling of the Iraqi occupation by committing the outrages associated with places like Abu Ghraib, Bagram air base, and Guantánamo, and practices like rendition and extreme forms of physical and psychological torture. Initially excused by the administration as the inappropriate behavior of a few "bad apples," these egregious violations of America's own laws were accompanied by a suspension of many other legal protections affecting the treatment of prisoners, creating a climate for extending this abuse not only to other foreign nationals but also to American citizens.

If governmental authorization of warrantless wiretapping and other threats to civil liberties have now brought home to the American people (and not just to those who have suffered the loss or fearful wounding of loved ones) some of the domestic "unintended consequences" of the Iraq War, it has as yet done surprisingly little, beyond generating among a majority of the populace a desire to end the war and bring home the troops as soon as is reasonable, the kind of massive resistance one would expect from those who consider themselves a "free people." Suspending the rule of habeas corpus for anyone suspected of a connection with terrorist sentiments or groups, refusing except under extreme pressure to investigate human rights violations, narrowing the terms of legitimate dissent by viewing almost any act of criticism of the government as "aiding and abetting the enemy," employing vast numbers of "signing statements" to protect the president's right to disregard congressional legislation if it conflicts with his interpretation of the law, and exploiting the "fear card" while defending secrecy, profiling, and the spying on fellow citizens—in all these ways the federal government has continuously appealed to and exploited America's weakness rather than its strength.

One of the more flagrant such examples occurred on September 14,

2006—in its lead editorial the next day *The Washington Post* described it as "A Defining Moment for America"—when the president made a personal journey to Congress to lobby for the use of torture in the interests of protecting national security. Scarcely more than a week later, on September 24, 2006, a classified National Intelligence Estimate entitled "Trends in Global Terrorism: Implications for the United States" came to light—it was completed in April 2006—which confirmed that all sixteen federal spy agencies agreed that America had been made *more* vulnerable to terrorism by the invasion and occupation of Iraq. Nonetheless, on September 29, 2006, the Bush administration won a major legislative victory with the passage of a Senate bill (echoing a similar bill previously passed by the House) that stripped detainees of the right of habeas corpus—this was barely mentioned in the debates on the Senate floor!—and gave the president broad powers to conduct military tribunals for terrorism suspects and determine permissible techniques for interrogation. A year later many of those powers, broadly challenged in the courts, were still in use and were being defended by the executive branch. A series of articles, again published in *The Washington Post,* revealed that the chief sponsor of many of these and other secret proposals and policies was the vice president's office, clearly acting on President Bush's behalf.[22]

It thus became obvious that the utopianism underlying the rhetoric of the Bush administration ultimately promoted something considerably more dangerous, possibly even more feral, than the conquest of the real by the representational, of the actual by the imaginary. Because this discourse is frequently justified by recourse to terms that are by turns incipiently religious and militantly absolutist, it reinforces—and is reinforced by—America's recurrent tendency to conceive itself, albeit sometimes grudgingly, as a warrior state whose calling is to convert as much of the rest of the world as possible—by force if necessary, by persuasion if possible—to its own salvific theology of democratic liberty and free enterprise. That this theology often masks the meretricious politics that frequently informs and expresses it is part of its purpose. Spreading democracy in a world seen through Manichean lenses that divide the world into good and evil, virtuous and iniquitous, light and dark, then becomes a license to turn the empire of liberty into an imperium of reckless power and arrogant privilege.

Nor has the new American administration, while clearly disinclined to invoke any of this crude triumphalism, been able to shed some of its exceptionalist bias. Despite the sobering experience of an almost catastrophic financial meltdown in the global marketplace, and the discouraging realities of one war that is currently being lost to the Taliban in Afghanistan and another that may reawaken when the United States withdraws the bulk of its forces from Iraq, President Obama, like his predecessor, continues to allow, if with less appetite, the discursive fashions of today's politics to shape the conduct, and sometimes the conscience, of his policies. Despite widespread evidence that the economic stimulus package of 2009 is largely assisting those same individuals and institutions that put the international market at risk, he insists on defending it, or permitting others to defend it, with arguments that are still basically neoliberal. Or again, even where he separates himself from practices such as torture and the unilateral policies of the last administration, he persists in violating Pakistan's sovereignty through the undeclared war he is waging with Special Forces and predator drones against the Taliban and al-Qaeda in the tribal territories of North and South Waziristan, outraging ordinary Pakistanis and Pashtuns alike, and he justifies the continued operation of interrogation facilities at Bagram air base, and who knows where else, as, against all evidence, an indispensible instrument in America's fight against terror. While President Obama prides himself on the putative difference between his policies and those of his predecessor, there is a disconcerting overlap in the questionable assumptions on which they are based—the United States is in a global struggle with radical jihadism; if the world cannot count on American consistency in the economic as in the military sphere, who can it trust?; American preeminence in world affairs is the surest guarantee of international security—and the myths used to support them.

Hence the current debate about global governance, and more precisely the argument about America's role and rights in its future reframing, has been awash with language that is decidedly, as well as disconcertingly, metaphorical. The verbal atmosphere in the United States has been full of talk about "old Europe" and "young America," "rogue states," "axes of evil," "the clash of civilizations," "the War against Terror," "winning in Iraq," distinctions between "those for us" and "those against us," nuclear weapons composing with conventional ordinance a "boutique of armaments," "regime change" reimagined as a form of home renovation or a facial makeover—after a surgical invasion and three months of difficult but tolerable rehabilitation, we can produce a wholly "new you"—democracy conflated with American virtues, and American virtues conceived as universals, as unconditionals.

Not least among the symbolic constructions on view is the idea of world order itself. While no one would seriously dispute the historical provenance, power, and validity of such a notion, it carries large imaginative freight. For one, it conveys a sense of stability and coherence that is belied by the last hundred years of world history. For another, it lends to those who use the term an impression of authority and control that is often illusory. More significant is the fact that it discounts all that tends to fall outside its presumed range of governance and now, given its identification with the Westphalian model of state-based sovereignty and international relations, obstructs a comprehension that global design and governance is currently being refashioned and sometimes very seriously threatened by nonstate actors of various kinds. The term "world order" can easily blind one to the actual decentering and disorder that it seeks, often only provisionally, haphazardly, and intermittently, to contain and manage. Hence the idea of the world, both as a philosophical concept and political construct, is more fragile and fluid than it sounds and is also more plural in its formations and dispositions than is portrayed. Just ask President Obama.

The danger in all this is not simply, or even chiefly, that such discourse is figurative through and through. The danger is rather that, far from representing mere verbal embellishments in debates about global governance, such figures, and the tropes on which they depend, are now part and parcel of what is at issue in its revision and reform. This danger is far from new. In response to the recurrent penchant in the United States to prefer reproductions to originals, imitations to realities, fakes to the genuine article, the historian Daniel Boorstin subtitled his 1961 book, *The Image*, as "A Guide to Pseudo-Events in America." While this was scarcely a new disability in American social and political life even then, it is now markedly more pervasive, perverse, and potentially fateful. One critical intellectual challenge therefore becomes how to penetrate this fog of words, images, metaphors, and tropes before we drown in them. A second challenge is where to find the conceptual and moral leverage to bring this nearly impenetrable fog under intellectual scrutiny. Still a third is what to make of the new imperiums that continuously and consciously confuse simulations with facts, symbols with sentiments, artifice with the actual. And finally, how is one to conduct a conversation in political cultures even still so indifferent to nuance, so resistant to alternative perspectives, so insensible (new professions of faith to the contrary) of the feelings of others, so bent as before on confounding the fictions of America with the future of the world? These are some of the questions that circulate through this book and animate its essays. How is one to understand the bases and manifestations of this phenomenon and what are some possible alternatives to it? In an effort to address these issues in a systematic manner, we have arranged this collection to move from chapters theoretical and conceptual to those that deal, first, with religion, next with specific cultural forms and practices, and then, finally, with matters disciplinary and prescriptive.

Ronald Steel sets the stage by rehearsing in "America's Mission" the most recent phases of America's involvement with globalization. A history initiated by the unexpected collapse of the Soviet Union and the end of the Cold War, the United States suddenly found itself living in what seemed like a uni- rather than a bipolar world with the power and the responsibility to give it new direction. An age of prosperity and global, if not regional, peace seemed at hand, supported by the spread of capitalism and democracy and protected by American might. A new world order defined by America's reach had been born whose signature was globalization itself. "Globalization is the United States," as Thomas Friedman boasted; America had become, in the well-known words of former Secretary of State Madeleine Albright "the indispensable nation."

But this narrative overlooked the fact so vividly brought home on 9/11 that globalization is a transformative project that dismantles and destroys as much as it rearranges and develops, leaving the world's most impregnable nation vulnerable to forces whose globally hazardous effects had everything to do with the continued independence of nation-states and the emergence of new global players. The world order that America had first conceived itself able to establish in its triumphant moment immediately following the end of the Cold War—and then able to impose on others after the attacks on the Twin Towers and the Pentagon—would soon begin to unravel as the "crippled giant," in Steel's language, has become more and more "ensnared in its own rhetoric and delusions." A set of processes as neutral to ideologies and technologies as it is to demographics and security, globalization has altered traditional symmetries of power, just as quickly as it has forced nations to recalibrate their vulnerability to each other. Even as it has supported and reinforced discourses of American exceptionalism, it has rendered the political and cultural mission of United States still more problematic in the present era.

However, the two—American exceptionalism and "America's mission"—are often culturally, as Donald Pease explores, mirror images of one another. In "From Virgin Land to Ground Zero," Pease reveals the way the Bush administration has altered the regulatory fictions through which government policy makers exercise normative control over populations. Among the many myths that have underwritten American identity and expansion, none has been more influential than the narrative conception of America as a Virgin Land. Among the various metaphors that have described the United States as it reimagined itself following the events of 9/11, none has been more compelling than the image of America as Ground Zero. Pease provides a genealogy of these two conceptions of the American homeland for the sake of revealing how they have been made to complement their respective interests and associate American identity with the national security state. Pease does not for a moment forget that there have been other mythological tropes for the nation's master narratives—"Redeemer nation," "Nature's Nation," "Chosen Nation," "Millennial Nation"—but he is particularly interested in detailing the way these two in particular have been utilized to reinforce and fortify governance. "The transformation of Virgin Land into Ground Zero brought into visibility an inhuman terrain that the national imaginary had been constructed to conceal. . . . For when it displaced the metaphor of the Virgin Land, the term Homeland rendered the devastation precipitated at Ground Zero at once utterly unexpected yet weirdly familiar." Virgin Land, "American innocence," "Ground Zero" have in effect become "transformative grammars" through which the state now shapes peoples' understandings, values, and beliefs.

In "Pre-Emption, Perpetual War, and the Future of the Imagination," David Palumbo-Liu seeks to illumine how those grammars were produced and why they, and the rhetoric that supported them, could generate such powerful and perverse effects as a result of the massive military counter-response that the United States made to the attacks on 9/11. In an argument that takes us back to Kant, Coleridge, and Clausewitz before moving forward to Robert McNamara's film "Fog of War" and Paul Wolfowitz's proposal to create a "Terrorist Futures Market," Palumbo-Liu shows how the traditional offices of the imagination have been hijacked and subverted, or, as he puts it "recoded," through policies like the Doctrine of Pre-Emption and strategies like "Shock and Awe." What Kant envisioned as a new sense of human community, a "sensus communis" created by the imagination out of the shared experience of affect and empathy, has been banalized and corrupted as the aesthetic realm of the imagination itself has been turned into an instrument of war and war-making. The processes by which this has occurred operate in a discursive realm easily overlooked or disguised, but their consequences for a politics of the future have been dire. Instead of a politics that plays on the possibility of endless war and an insatiable appetite for power, we need a future politics "fueled by an imagination of another kind of world in which affect is not exploited for the sake of terror, and empathy is directed precisely to reaffirm the possibility for being together in the world."

The collaborative essay by Simon Ortiz and Gabriele Schwab seems designed almost as a direct response to Palumbo-Liu's challenge to liberate the imagination in behalf of creating a politics of the future grounded on a new *sensus communis.* In "Imaginary Homeland Security: The Internalization of Terror," however, that *sensus* is not created out of shared forms of understanding but out of shared processes of its painful acquisition, and community must re-found itself on the recovery and re-experience of memories triggered by difference rather than sameness, strangeness not familiarity. Affect, feeling, even mere sensation is created by story, narrative, tale; relationship is achieved by the often troubling and painful renegotiation of boundaries between self and other, between self and its other. The result is a rethinking of ordered worlds and of world re-orderings from the perspective of their remembered deformations and disfigurings. In this new realm, terror is less an event than a history or past of spectacular injury, and the struggle to create a new polis finds its energy in the enablements of dialogical response and recreation.

Mark Juergensmeyer addresses "the internalization of terror" from a more public perspective. Why have secular governments, and not just the United States, been the targets of religious terrorist assaults, he wants to ask, and what has produced these assaults at the present time? The answers to these questions are not easy to come by, but they inevitably compel one to consider cultural as well as political economies. While religious radicalism can define itself most easily in terms of its opposite, its advocates and proponents seem to thrive on the language of cosmic war and performative violence. When worldly struggles are raised "into the high proscenium of sacred battle," believers are ennobled and empowered by the destruction they sow. And by the destruction they sow they also break the state's monopoly on the use of legitimate violence. Yet the religious violence of today would be no different than the sacred slaughter that has often occurred throughout history, Juergensmeyer insists, if it were not for contemporary globalization. Just as globalization weakens many of the institutions of the modern secular nation-state, so it has also created through its technologies and aspirations the fearful possibility of an increasingly multicultural world. Couple this prospect with the sinister image of America's intention to manage and expand global diversity on its own terms and you have a recipe for a religious politics of extreme violence. Ubiquitous images of battle, devastation, and retribution have been, and will continue to be, used to crystallize a universal sense of we/they/us/other. This was one part of the bait Osama bin Laden offered in his public declarations, which President Bush then took when he responded to the attacks of 9/11 as "an act of war."

Wade Clark Roof probes the religious environment surrounding the use of violence and terror from still another direction in "Myths Undergirding War: American Presidential Rhetoric from Ronald Reagan to George W. Bush." His subject is the myths used to justify the war Bush declared on terrorism on September 12, 2001, and then conducted first against the Taliban in Afghanistan and then subsequently against the regime of Saddam Hussein in Iraq. These myths, all of which are oriented around the sacred symbol of freedom or liberty, which provides the chief ideological frame for their continuous support and deployment, were exploited during the presidencies of Ronald Reagan and George H. W. Bush, but they were taken to a new level in the religious rhetoric of the junior Bush. As used in his discourse, one must ask whether their prominence indicates the resurrection of a new civil religion or rather the hardening of a more bellicose religious nationalism? Are the religious myths underpinning the national imaginary being employed to challenge and critique that imaginary in some prophetic sense or to fortify and reify it in some more celebrative priestly sense? The distinction between the priestly and the prophetic recalls the title of Reinhold Niebuhr's *The Irony of American History,* where the great theologian forced his readers to confront the paradox of how virtues can turn into vices when uncritically embraced and arrogantly proclaimed. Following the attack on 9/11, President Bush was amazed to discover that people hated the United States and assumed that the problem simply derived from the way the country had represented itself "because," he added, "I know how good we are." Like Niebuhr before him, Roof thinks otherwise: "Virtues turn into vices when the myths on which they are based are absolutized, when noble intentions and ideals are grossly transformed into self-righteousness, when responsibilities are abandoned in the interest of extending the empire."

Eileen Boris further explores the politics of mythological essentialisms and stereotypes by examining how the tropes of the cowboy and the welfare queen have functioned as images of independence and dependence from the Nixon era to the present. Boris views these icons as "symbols of the nation and the anti-nation." Cowboy ethics and diplomacy informed and reinforced an ideology of white manhood and self-reliance which at a strategic moment was brought to bear on constructing as its opposite the image of the single black woman reliant on welfare. Where the one idealized a figure responsible for creating and maintaining the American system, the other was demonized as a figure devoted wholly to taking advantage of the system. Though certain cowboys like Theodore Roosevelt and Lyndon Baines Johnson cast in the imperialist mode could also be depicted as domestic reformers until 1976, things changed decisively in that year's presidential campaign, when Ronald Reagan turned welfare mothers into an image of female irresponsibility and laziness undermining a culture of male autonomy and responsibility. From here on into the twenty-first century, the new iconography was then further exaggerated to help define a conception of world order in which public welfare and foreign aid would continuously be seen as expressions of weakness and U.S. military power, unilateral presidential action, and the Doctrine of Pre-Emption come to be portrayed as the appropriate answer.

In "Air Raids: Television and the War on Terror," Lisa Parks shows how the extension of empire after 9/11 in the name of a nationalist moral and religious exceptionalism that seemed beyond question led to a literal commandeering of the airwaves. While this process began long before the declaration of the war on terror, it has become radically more intense in the years following it. Her chief exhibits start with the war coverage on CNN's *Military Options* and *Geraldo Rivera Reports,* both of which utilized "technologized military vantage points" and "vengeful warfront reporting." But the attack on the airwaves this programming designed as an extension of the American war effort took still more violent forms in the literal bombing of Al Jazeera and the Palestine hotel where journalists were housed and where three were killed. In addition to targeting a media company and its employees, the attacks on Al Jazeera and other companies demonstrated how closely the War on Terror was—and is—linked with the global media economy, threatens women, and renders still more problematic the relation between the media and democracy. Parks points out that an alternative paradigm of war coverage seemed for a time to be offered by the new women's network called Oxygen, where women were initially given the opportunity to discuss various military options and, at least on live specials, to actively critique militarist policies and promote a feminist demilitarization. But Oxygen soon fell back in its more conventional programming into many of the same sexist patterns exploited by the larger networks, supporting the war by addressing women as mothers and consumers and appealing to them as shoppers rather than as potential sources of dissent. For Parks this leads one to wonder if television in the United States can ever become a medium for serious debate and policy reform. Her answer is that it will depend in part on whether the nation is willing to make a "critical and public investment in the medium" sufficient to bring it back into genuine interaction and dialogue with democracy.

Extending Park's focus on the complicated role of the media, John Carlos Rowe argues that it is only because of the prior work of culture that the militarist and jingoistic policies of the administration of George W. Bush could have so successfully inaugurated a new global order dominated by the United States. What Max Horkheimer and Theodor Adorno first designated as the "culture industry" now so thoroughly dominates the production and management of values that opposing or alternative political positions often reinforce rather than challenge the inflexible system. "Culture, U.S Imperialism, and Globalization" finds evidence for this phenomenon in the news media, television programming, marketing strategies, and the Internet, but focuses the greatest portion of its attention on cultural representations in contemporary U.S. film. Since the Vietnam era, Rowe argues, American imperialism has involved both the internalization and the hypernationalization of transnational issues, and this has created an interesting paradox: antiwar films actually help to re-militarize the United States, and narratives of Western imperialism, which can be told in countless different ways, though with surprisingly few variations, continue to allow "otherness to be internalized, rationalized, historicized, civilized, and nationalized." The problem with all such practices is that they forget or dismiss the fact that viable histories are created or remade only through the appropriation of what is related but different, interdependent but alternative.

Lisa Lowe exhibits genuine doubts about the fate of democracy in a world where sovereignty is more important than information, deliberation, or the kinds of historical processes of concern to Rowe and, in fact, all the other contributors. She is particularly concerned about the way the notion of the "political" in the United States, and specifically within the academic discipline of political science, has been so rigidly framed in terms of the nation-state. This might have been expected from neorealists who are deeply committed to state sovereignty, but it is also characteristic of neoliberals more sensitive to the inter- and transnational dimensions of cooperation and conflict. Both have failed to appreciate the dynamics of globalization even where they give lip service to them, and the result has affected the way developments as seemingly different as the "war on terror" and the immigration crisis are "rationalized." Failing to take the work of culture—and specifically the work of metaphor—more seriously, she argues, political thinkers are unable to appreciate that the global cannot be represented iconically or totalized through a single developmental narrative. Since there is no single history of who or what is global, it can only be grasped in its unevenness in differentially accessed media. But this in turn requires a more critical genealogy of representational paradigms that constitute the way we know its diverse conditions.

Richard Falk has long been sensitive to these matters and closes the volume by bringing the discussion back to a pressing global question: what effect do normative ideals and assumptions have, or should they have, on decisions to intervene in places like Somalia, Rwanda, Bosnia, East Timor, Kosovo, Iraq, and Afghanistan? In what sense, he wants to know in "On Humanitarian Intervention: A New World Order Dilemma," and at what recent historical moments, have humanitarian values prevailed over state interests in determining when the international community should take collective action to prevent blatant cruelty and suffering? Such global questions represent, in his view, a "new world dilemma" because they pit the rights of governments protected by the principle of state sovereignty and self-interest against the rights of individuals and groups protected by covenants like the Universal Declaration of Human Rights whose authority is moral or ethical rather than legal. Yet this conflict is crosscut by a host of ambiguities. To take only one associated with global civil society, how is the rise of "humanitarian diplomacy," as it is sometimes called, to be explained: "as a natural incident of the rising attention given to human rights; more cynically, as a means of sustaining military budgets and national security established in a global setting that lacked strategic threats; as an expression of human solidarity responsive to 'the CNN factor' that conveyed in real time the unfolding of humanitarian disasters; [or] a relatively inexpensive means to divert criticism of neoliberal globalization as a heartless, capital-driven restructuring of global economic relations"?

The answers to such queries are no more apparent than the issue of whether the failure to intervene is the result of the resistant policies of single states, the lack of global, and particularly United Nations', leadership, insufficient pressure from global civil society actors and organizations, or some deficiency in the current structure of world order itself? Falk is persuaded that the ultimate resolution of such inquiries lies with the reform of world order and global governance. Until the Westphalian model has been sufficiently reorganized around the need to honor human rights and guard against their radical infringement, the most we can hope for is a world in which states become less callous in relation to humanitarian concerns and global civil society becomes more effective in advocating in their behalf. This is neither to presume that the representatives of global civil society will always agree with one another on whether humanitarian intervention is called for or how it should be accomplished, any more than it presupposes that states will see it in their own interests or capabilities to undertake it. Neither is it meant to imply that humanitarian intervention will actually succeed in reforming the states where it is required. It merely underscores the fact that globalization is also a moral enterprise and cannot proceed without addressing the dilemma of how to reconcile rights with governance, justice with power, the ameliorating of suffering, and the reduction of cruelty with statecraft.

NOTES

1. Lawrence E. Harrison and Samuel P. Huntington, eds., *Culture Matters: How Values Shape Human Progress* (New York: Basic Books, 2000).

2. James Rosenau, "Imposing Global Orders: A Synthesized Ontology for a Turbulent Era," in *Innovation and Transformation in International Studies,* ed. Stephen Gill and James H. Mittleman (Cambridge: Cambridge University Press, 1997), 221.

3. Mark Twain, New York *Herald,* October 15, 1900; reprinted in James Zwick, ed., *Mark Twain's Weapons of Satire: Anti-Imperialist Writings on the Philippine-American War* (Syracuse, N.Y.: Syracuse University Press, 1992), 5.

4. Quoted in Charles S. Olcott, *The Life of William McKinley,* 2 vols. (Boston and New York: Houghton Mifflin Co., 1916), 2:11.

5. William McKinley, "Speech before the Ohio Society of New York, March 3, 1900," quoted in Olcott, *The Life of William McKinley,* 2:291.

6. Lionel Trilling, *The Liberal Imagination: Essays on Literature and Society* (1950; New York: Doubleday Anchor Books reprint, 1957), 215. Trilling was referring to a general problem with the moral imagination as a whole, but his insight possesses particular relevance to the operations of the political imaginary in America.

7. Thomas E. Ricks, *Fiasco: The American Military Adventure in Iraq* (New York: Penguin, 2006).

8. Quoted in *The Los Angeles Times,* July 6, 2002, A17.

9. Mahmood Mamdani, *Good Muslim, Bad Muslim: America, the Cold War, and the Roots of Terror* (New York: Pantheon, 2004). There are some who have argued with considerable force that this is too simplistic an interpretation of the new kind of terror that gained global attention on 9/11. This mega-terror was not without purpose and point, even if different individuals responsible for it (or influenced by it to dedicating themselves to extend its reach and governance) possessed a great variety of reasons for participating in it. Just as they were responding essentially to political rather than religious factors, so they were motivated by a desire for power. Many of the participants as well as those who admired their actions identified with the emancipatory agenda that portions of radical Islam embraced after the fall of communism in that part of the world. The project was to liberate Islam and the Middle East from the tyranny of the West, and political terrorism offered itself for a variety of reasons as the perfect tactic.

10. See Mamdani, *Good Muslim, Bad Muslim.*

11. In what follows there is no intent to deny that state-sponsored terrorism has been, and remains, a notable feature of political life in the international sphere from the beginning of the nineteenth century to the twenty-first. Nor does the United States' effort to disguise this fact by securing international support for the opposite view that terrorism merely applies to violence directed at legitimate states by nonstate actors alter this situation.

12. The most extensive study of the relationship between global terror in the present and religion is Mark Juergensmeyer, *Terror in the Mind of God: The*

Global Rise of Religious Violence (Berkeley and Los Angeles: University of California Press, 2000).

13. Richard Falk, *The Great Terror War* (Brooklyn, N.Y.: Olive Branch Press, 2003), 7–8.

14. Jacques Derrida, quoted in Giovanna Borradori, *Philosophy in a Time of Terror: Dialogues with Jürgen Habermas and Jacques Derrida* (Chicago: University of Chicago Press, 2003), 98–99.

15. Derrida, quoted in Borradori, *Philosophy in a Time of Terror*, 101.

16. Richard Falk, *The Declining World Order: America's Imperial Geopolitics* (New York: Routledge, 2004).

17. Quoted in Martin E. Marty, *Righteous Empire: The Protestant Experience in America* (New York: The Dial Press, 1970), 5.

18. Martin E. Marty, *Righteous Empire.*

19. Quoted in George Packer, *The Assassin's Gate: America in Iraq* (New York: Farrar, Straus and Giroux, 2005), 38.

20. Quoted in Jonathan Schell, "Too Late for Empire," *The Nation*, August 14/21, 2006, 18.

21. This is the famous memo in which the head of British intelligence reported on a trip to Washington in which he had learned that the Bush administration was adjusting fact and intelligence to support its claims about weapons of mass destruction.

22. See the six-part series "Angler: The Cheney Vice Presidency," by Barton Gellman and Jo Becker, originally published in the *Washington Post* and subsequently reprinted in considerable part in three issues of the *Washington Post National Weekly Edition* 24, no. 38 (July 9–15, 2007): 6–12; 24, no. 39 (July 16–22, 2007): 8–10; 24, no. 40 (July 23–29, 2007): 10–12.

2. America's Mission

Ronald Steel

One of the more inescapable aspects of the phenomenon we call globalization is the pervasive spread of the power and influence of the world's dominant nation: the United States. This transpires on a number of levels: military, economic, political, and cultural. "Globalization is the United States," to cite the proud words of Thomas Friedman, a prominent media celebrant of the process.

But the phenomenon goes beyond the reach, and eludes the grasp, of any single nation. To suggest that the United States can control the course of globalization, or the ways in which it becomes manifest in global power struggles, is to distort the meaning of the process. If globalization *is* the United States, this does not mean that it, or any other nation-state, has the power to dictate its effects.

Globalization is pervasive, but not necessarily a blessing. Indeed it may even, in some of its aspects, be a curse. It turns societies upside down, transforms the relations between ruler and ruled, seeps into the consciousness of men, and destroys even as it creates. Under its impact, in the celebrated words of Karl Marx in a somewhat different, but related, context, "all that is solid melts into the air," and what had seemed eternal becomes transient and even ephemeral.

Human history is a chronicle of great empires swept away in a flash, leaving little but the decaying monuments of their proclaimed glories: Ozymandius in the desert sands. We do not have to travel back very far in history to find examples: the Thousand Year Reich that lasted barely twelve, the Union of Soviet Socialist Republics that endured but a few decades and gently vanished as though it had never been. The story is not over. Even the Cold War, the conflict that hung like an incubus over the lives of several generations of Americans, Russians, Europeans, and even

Asians, has already become ancient history and virtually without meaning to their children. A different and only dimly glimpsed fate awaits them.

But human fates are far more intertwined than in the past. The fall of Troy or the sacking of Constantinople had no discernable effect on the Incas or the Ashanti. Their turn came later, by different means and at other hands. However, today, under the impact of globalization no peoples or nations are immune to the shock waves emanating from afar and reverberating across the globe.

Certainly not the United States. Until 1989 Americans, and their allies, lived in what they considered to be a bipolar world. American power on one side, Soviet power on the other—held in uneasy balance by the unthinkable horror of the atomic bomb. Neither side dared encroach seriously on the domain of the other without unleashing cataclysmic consequences. The world, at least for them, was in relative balance. Conflict was confined to the periphery. At times both states pushed too far in their effort to control: the Russians in Cuba, the Americans in Vietnam. From these adventures each suffered disgrace, but managed to escape intact.

But in 1989 this tenuous balance was destroyed by the collapse of the communist power structure and the implosion of the Soviet state. This astounding event—unanticipated by the vast apparatus of American think tanks, spies, and "intelligence" specialists—was immediately treated as an unqualified victory for the United States. If the Cold War really was a war, then the collapse of one adversary was indeed a victory for the other. The bipolar world suddenly became a unipolar one, with the United States at its center and Washington as its seat of authority.

The victor, perhaps dazed by what had happened, behaved with relative restraint, and the loser was treated with relative dignity—and even with some pity by its rival for its poor performance. Yet the world political structure had been transformed as surely as if there had been a cataclysmic military battle. The balance of power—the presumed staple condition of peace and security—had been destroyed. With its adversary gone, the United States stood alone.

It took some time for the full consequences of this new condition to sink in. If there were no major adversary, there could be no effective counterweight to the reality—and the exercise—of American power. Instead of a tenuous nuclear balance with the clock ominously poised a few minutes before midnight, the American republic now seemed militarily impregnable. Suddenly that seemingly optimal condition that nations yearn for but rarely achieve—absolute security—appeared to be at hand.

This was the moment of American triumphalism. From its position of economic strength and military invulnerability the United States had, so it seemed, the ability to impose the political order it deemed desirable upon the world. It had become, in the proud words of the American secretary of state during the late 1990s, the "indispensible nation."

American officials quickly adjusted to what seemed a new global order and understandably assumed that this enviable condition of American superiority would last for decades. During that time they dabbled in civil and ethnic conflicts in the Balkans and central Africa, but only half-heartedly and without serious commitment. With the Cold War over and the other nuclear power vanquished, the much-vaunted but seemingly unattainable American peace was at hand.

The world, the victors proclaimed, would become capitalistic and democratic, and its people dedicated to the pursuit of prosperity. This was the bright promise of the successor to the deadly stand-off of the Cold War: an era of globalization. The model, proven to be superior, would be American. While there might be some bumps along the way, and a few laggards crushed in the process, the United States would serve not only as the model for a globalized world, but also as its guardian and protector.

But this did not mean that the world would return to "normal," that quests for prestige and dominance would be consigned to the past. To the contrary, the collapse of the communist alternative system meant, its leaders said, the assumption by the United States of an even greater burden: nothing less than the exclusive responsibility for global order. As a Pentagon official explained during the last months of the Soviet empire: "Were the Soviet presence to disappear tomorrow, our role as regional balancer and broker would, if anything, be more important than ever."

Playing that balancing role meant, of course, that other major states would not behave in a way contrary to American desires and interests. They would be deterred from acquiring military forces or pursuing political objectives that might endanger the new post–Cold War power balance. Were they to do so, U.S. officials believed, this would upset the political equilibrium and the flow of trade and capital on which economic growth rests. It is in large part for this reason that the United States continues, twenty years after the end of the Cold War, to police the globe in the name of "international order," and why, even before the ill-fated adventure in Iraq launched in 2003, the U.S. military budget had gone even beyond Cold War levels.

The disappearance of a powerful rival empire has, if anything, only increased the sense of threat. The repression of disorder and a vague, though pervasive, fear of "international terrorism," have replaced containment as the nation's foreign policy doctrine. It has been expressed militarily by the extension of NATO across eastern Europe to the borders of a shrunken Russia, the seemingly permanent maintenance of U.S. military forces in Europe, Korea, and Japan, an army and a ring of air bases in a conquered Iraq, and the creation of mobile brigades for intervention in undetermined "crisis" areas.

Sweeping in its scope, this project is presented as a logical assumption of the nation's international "responsibilities." Under its logic any adverse event in the world is described as a "crisis" and a threat to a "vital interest." By deliberately diffusing priorities it allows maximum freedom of action. However, it also entails maximum entanglement and points of confrontation with other states. A global power with a global conception of its interests has trouble defining either limits or priorities. Rather than strengthening vital interests, such a policy often weakens them, as it weakens the economic base of the imperial state. And it stimulates rivals concerned by what they view as the encroachment on their own interests. The search for absolute global security leads inevitably to a mentality, and even a condition, of absolute insecurity.

Globalization, its more enthusiastic proponents assure us, means greater prosperity, and even common fellowship, for all. But the phenomenon has more than one meaning, as has now become amply apparent. It also means the dispersal of violence, as well as of allegiances, beyond the narrow confines of the nation-state. Neither great wealth nor great armies are needed by those who would challenge the global order, nor do they necessarily serve as protection against them. Americans became traumatically aware of this on September 11, 2001.

Protected by two oceans and weak neighbors, Americans had come to assume that their territory was immune from attack. But an assault by a handful of terrorists on the very symbols of American financial and military power traumatized the entire nation. Though the physical damage was confined, the psychological shock was immense. The illusion of invulnerability that underlay America's approach to the world and sustained scores of military and political interventions, both during and since the Cold War, was shattered. Deterrence—the strategy that had constrained both superpowers for more than four decades—had proven to be useless against those with no homeland to defend. September 11 dramatized the fact that the ability to inflict devastating violence in pursuit of political ends had become both miniaturized and globalized. It had now become the weapon of the weak as well as of the strong.

In the new era of asymmetrical warfare the equations of power had to be rewritten. Nuclear dominance had become irrelevant against those who conducted warfare at a technologically primitive level. The globalization of violence, and the energizing of those willing to commit it without regard to national frontiers and loyalties, dispersed the beatific visions of global communion through the marketplace. The basis of American power—indeed of benign globalization itself—had been challenged and its premises violently tested.

The failure of the American war in Iraq to achieve the objectives of its instigators further demonstrated the new reality. It revealed not only the virtual political irrelevance of nuclear superiority, but also the structural sources of weakness within the American model. It showed that Americans might be willing to tolerate a distant colonial war only so long as their own children were not forced to participate, but that they would not pay for such a war out of their own pockets. The result has been a war financed by credit cards and IOUs held by other governments. This raises serious problems of credibility and commitment. It makes it difficult to maintain that a society dependent on foreign creditors to pay its bill, and unable to persuade its own citizens to fight distant wars of choice, is in any serious way an "indispensable nation." Rather, such a nation more persuasively resembles a crippled giant ensnared in its own rhetoric and delusions.

This reality puts a less optimistic spin on the boast that "globalization is the United States." But its deeper meaning goes beyond American unilateralism and unconstrained interventionism. What the years since the end of the Cold War have demonstrated is that globalization is a threat as well as a promise. While the process may be universal and inexorable, the particular form it takes can be neither predicted nor controlled. Its effects may be deleterious as well as beneficial, and can breed violence and mayhem as well as prosperity and peace. Globalization is no more a blessing to be embraced without qualification and caution than was industrialization in the nineteenth century, or than computerization is today.

The playing field among nations has indeed been leveled as a result of globalization, with the result that brilliant people and new technologies can be found almost everywhere in the developed world. However, it is well to remember that this phenomenon, with variations, goes back at least to the Industrial Revolution. It would be more accurate to observe that while the world is indeed round, in that the circle of production, distribution and consumption is a closed one, this means that no actor can escape the consequences, however unintended, of its actions The metaphor of globalization implies not a flat surface, as many of its enthusiasts claim, but a confined sphere in which actions taken by any single player may ultimately rebound against it.

Globalization is not only about exploiting new ideas and technologies, or finding new sources of labor, or learning new skills. It is an inexorable, and often uncontrollable, process that takes many forms and has sweeping consequences in every realm. For this reason it must be viewed in all its ramifications: social, political, cultural, psychological, environmental. It is refashioning not only how people relate to their work, physical surroundings, and social relations, but also the manner in which states and groups interact with one another.

One crucial aspect of globalization, at least in the minds of its enthusiasts, is that it will knit together divergent cultures into a harmonious whole, and transform them in a way that will make them more receptive to modernization and rationalization. Underlying this is the assumption that such modernization, by breaking down traditional cultural differences and barriers, will lead to greater democratization, and thereby to a more peaceful and harmonious world. In other words, to echo the Wilsonian formulation, globalization can "make the world safe for democracy."

This assumption rests more on faith than on evidence. The past century offers ample proof that there is no clear link between industrialization (or modernization more generically) and democratization. Authoritarian societies are, in fact, generally more efficient than democracies in being "globalized"—that is, in rationalizing production, allocating resources, and stimulating economic and military development. As evidence one need merely to consider the astonishing growth and industrialization of authoritarian China today.

Furthermore, as a system globalization is no more synonymous with peace than it is with conflict. One of its malign side effects is alienation of the sort that is currently manifesting itself in international terrorism. It cuts across cultures, ignores frontiers, molds consciousness, and drives relations among states. Not only does a globalized world provide a terrain which makes it easier for terrorists to operate, but also the social world of globalization—by uprooting traditional cultures through the presumably "liberating" forces of modernization—can intensify the feelings of alienation, impotence, and rage that find an outlet in terrorism.

Rather than alleviating international rivalries, globalization may actually intensify them as newly industrializing nations fight more established ones for markets and for increasingly scarce natural resources. For rising powers, most notably in Asia, globalization offers the means to challenge the dominance of the West. In doing so it both feeds and encourages nationalism as the world's power balance shifts eastward. To imagine that globalization will encourage democratization in historically unsympathetic terrain is to engage in wishful thinking. Indeed its effect is likely to be just the opposite.

While the globalization of industrial innovation and production is one kind of reality, an equally powerful, and perhaps more important, reality is the particularization of culture. The enthusiasts of globalization assume the inexorable rise of a common, modernist, democratic culture linking all the world's disparate peoples, with their particular cultures and religions, into a common civilization. This is a self-deceiving assumption. A McDonalds in Kabul doesn't make Afghans think like—or indeed even like—Americans, any more than a taste for sushi gives Americans the slightest sense of what it means to be Japanese.

Globalization is a value-neutral process. It should not be viewed with unalloyed enthusiasm any more than was industrialization. It brings nations and cultures into closer economic and informational proximity. But in doing so it emphasizes and even creates frictions that produce suspicion, competition, and conflict. It is well to remember that the United States in the mid-nineteenth century was a single nation, a single economy, and a single culture. Yet this did not prevent its component parts from fighting a savage war whose aftershocks are still being felt a century and a half later.

Globalization is as compatible with authoritarianism as it is with democracy. No nation owns it, or can decree the form it takes in any particular culture. Nonetheless, it is not surprising that there are those who would seek to do so. Thus we find President George W. Bush declaring in November 2002 that because the end of the Cold War had been a "decisive victory for the forces of freedom," the world had been transformed in such a way that there was now but a "single sustainable model for national success: freedom, democracy, and free enterprise." This model, epitomized by the United States, was "right and true for every person, in every society."

To ensure the triumph and promulgation of that model against those who might threaten it, Bush unveiled a new strategy by which "America will act against such emerging threats before they are fully formed." In other words, it would use its military forces unilaterally and also pre-emptively, that is, even if not attacked. Its goal was not merely to protect itself, but also in his words, on behalf of others to "promote global security" and "extend the benefits of freedom across the globe." This announcement was not intended as a subject of discussion, but as a declaration of intent.

Although this new strategy was not announced until 2002, a year after the terrorist incidents in New York and Washington, it had been presaged a decade earlier during the administration of the first George Bush. At that time a secret document was circulated in the Pentagon in which highly placed officials outlined a new post–Cold War strategy by which the United States would "discourage the advanced industrial nations from challenging our leadership or even aspiring to a larger regional or global role." When the document was leaked to the press, it was formally disavowed by embarrassed officials. But a decade later, in 2002, it became official policy. And in 2003 it became a plan of action with the American invasion of Iraq: a strategically located, oil-rich land suffering under a tyrant's boot. The mission seemed ideally to combine self-interest with morality.

Although the war was certainly not inevitable, and has had disastrous unanticipated consequences, it was not in its rhetoric or its declared idealism fully alien. Rather, it was a war that had its roots in our national culture, our history, and our political ideology. A belief in the redemptive powers of democracy and the obligation to spread it even by force of arms is deeply embedded in American politics and folklore. Indeed it is epitomized by a president who has become a respected martyr-hero. Woodrow Wilson nearly a century ago took the nation into a distant war in declaring that "the world must be made safe for democracy." He did not achieve this ambitious goal, nor have any of his successors. Sometimes in pursuit of this goal they lost track of their goal. But they never questioned its validity.

Unlike George W. Bush, Woodrow Wilson is viewed as the apostle of internationalism, the rule of law, the self-determination of all peoples, and universal democracy. Nothing about Wilson, or about his foreign policy agenda, would seem to resemble that of Bush. Yet these two wartime presidents have much in common. This can be found in the politics they pursued, the rhetoric they employed, the evangelical religiosity they espoused, their mutual conviction of divine guidance, their willingness to engage the nation in war, and their belief in American righteousness. Both drew up schemes for global democratization through American power and declared that American values were universal and divinely sanctioned.

Many of Wilson's admirers will find this comparison distasteful. But Wilson's inspirational rhetoric carried more than one agenda. That is why this idealist, inspired by utopian visions of global engineering, has been given a new identity as a crusading warrior in the service of a virtuous American empire. When George W. Bush declared that the American invasion of Iraq would "bring the hope of democracy . . . to every corner of the world," he was speaking in the voice of Wilson.

Wilson was not only the prophet of democracy, to which all the world pays at least lip service, but also the champion of American exceptionalism. This rests upon the belief that the United States has not only the power but the right to transform the world into a more perfect place: that is, one more resembling itself.

This is why the American war in Iraq can be called a Wilsonian project. It is a war fought not only over oil and bases and other tangible instruments of wealth and power. It is also a war—both for the Americans who invaded and the Iraqi militants who have resisted—to transform an entire society.

Neither Wilson's war in Europe nor Bush's war in the Middle East was one of self-defense or response to an act of aggression against the United States. Both were wars of choice. Furthermore, both wars were linked to a wider plan to remake world order in ways more congenial to American interests and values. George W. Bush often invoked the ghost of Wilson in defending his policies. "The United States will extend the benefits of freedom around the world," he declared in the wake of the American invasion of Iraq. It would lead the "great mission . . . to further freedom's triumph" over "war and terror . . . the clashing of wills of powerful states . . . the evil designs of tyrants, and disease and poverty."

Lest Americans tremble at the formidable obligation he proposed, Bush assured them that the values he enumerated are truly universal. "And if these values are good enough for our people," he explained, "they ought to be good enough for others . . . because they are God-given values." Bush was not alone in believing that he understood the workings of God. Wilson, when seeking the presidency in 1912, informed voters that "God presided over the inception of this nation [and] that we are chosen to show the way to the nations of the world how they shall walk in the paths of liberty."

Eight years later, following the European war into which he led Americans, Wilson assured Congress that his plan for a world assembly of nations to ensure the peace "has come about by no plan of our own choosing, but by the hand of God who led us in this way." But the plan, despite its divine authorship, was rejected by the U.S. Senate. America turned inward during the 1920s and 1930s. The defeat of the fascist aggressors in 1945 revived Wilson's dream of a more perfect world resting on American power and ideals. But because of Soviet opposition there were now two worlds, and Wilson's vision was put back on the shelf.

The end of the Cold War changed everything. Wilson's formula for democracy, self-determination, and free markets for capital and labor aligned neatly with American interests at a time when the United States gained new freedom to pursue those goals. Thus we find that Wilsonianism, so internationalist in rhetoric, can be a cloak for the pursuit of a dominant nation's strategic and political goals. Its great utility is that it does so not as nationalism or dominance, but in the name of freedom. For this reason Wilson has been resurrected as a prophet of the age: the inspiration for reconstructing the world according to American principles and interests.

Political leaders find in Wilson a good political model because his genius was to find a policy that corresponded perfectly to America's strategic and political interests while packaging it in the language of idealism. Wilsonian rhetoric is a heady elixir. It suits a nation, or at least a political class, eager to remake the world in an image more congenial to American interests and values. The "war on terror" is the functional equivalent of the Cold War without an enemy state, and Bush's declared crusade for the "expansion of freedom in all the world," its version of "making the world safe for democracy."

The debilitating flaw in this ambitious agenda is that most peoples of the world do not want to have "democracy" imposed by force from abroad, or to model their social institutions after those in the West.. As states become more economically developed and "modern" they do not necessarily become more Westernized. More often they emphasize their own particular roots and traditions, seeking to define themselves as different from the alien Western cultures that have often dominated them. Despite television, baseball caps, rap music, and skyscrapers, modernizing cultures seek to establish their own independent identities and to reject what they often view as Western cultural imperialism. Although they may pay lip service to democratic values espoused by the West, they tailor these in ways suited to their traditions and customs.

The West attracts, but it often repels, for it threatens the traditions that are the building blocks of a culture. Insofar as globalization is the instrument for the imposition of alien values and customs, it is viewed with suspicion and even fear. Because no state so exemplifies the power, the allure, and the demands of globalization as does the United States, none is considered so dangerous. Islamic jihadism is one of the responses to this modernizing whirlwind that has trampled on traditions and disrupted cohesive societies.

Americans may look upon themselves as "the particular, chosen people," in the words of Herman Melville more than a century and a half ago, those who "bear the ark of liberties of the world." But those on the receiving end of American power and influence have a different perspective. They see, in the caustic words of the conservative political theorist Samuel Huntington, a nation seeking to "enforce American law extraterritorially in other societies, grade countries according to their adherence to American standards . . . promote American corporate interests under the slogans of free trade and open markets, shape World Bank and International Monetary Fund policies to serve those same corporate interests, intervene in local conflicts in which it has relatively little direct interest, bludgeon other countries to adopt economic policies and social policies that will benefit American economic interests . . . and categorize certain countries as 'rogue states,' excluding them from global institutions because they refuse to kowtow to American wishes."[1]

Insofar as "globalization is the United States," to quote again its most persistent celebrant, it will, in the eyes of many, be as much a threat as a promise. To peoples of the West globalization may mean modernization and the adoption of superior Western social and political values and institutions. But to people in societies emerging from decades of impoverishment and technological backwardness it means using Western technology to liberate themselves from Western domination. Their struggle to do so will be the great drama of the coming decades. This is why the end game of globalization is not likely to be a more harmonious world or one more congenial to Western values.

Globalization is a tidal wave that sweeps all before it. The United States may temporarily ride it, and even claim to epitomize it, but cannot control it. It is a process to be examined with hope but also with suspicion, and pursued cautiously and without illusion. It is a force that can, and will be, utilized for evil as well as good. Americans may come to have reason for disclaiming such a dangerous parentage.

NOTES

Small portions of this text, in somewhat different form, were previously published in "Birth of a Salesman," *The New Republic*, September 5, 2005; "Bush's Wilsonian Agenda," *Berlin Journal*, spring 2005; and "The Missionary," *New York Review of Books*, November 20, 2003.

1. Samuel P. Huntington, "The Lonely Superpower" *Foreign Affairs* 78:2, March/April (1999): 38.

3. From Virgin Land to Ground Zero

The Mythological Foundations of the Homeland Security State

Donald Pease

This essay constitutes an attempt to interpret the master narrative that has emerged in the wake of the events that took place on September 11, 2001, through a discussion of the consensual fictions it has displaced.[1] Each of the keywords in its title—"Virgin Land" and "Ground Zero"—refers to a governing metaphor which has anchored the people to a relationship to the national territory. These terms are freighted with metaphorical significance and performative force. "Virgin Land" refers to a space that coincided with the nation's prerevolutionary origins wherein European settlers' grounding assumptions about America were inscribed; "Ground Zero" designates the site that became visible on September 11, 2001, whereon those grounding assumptions were drastically transformed. Whereas the collective representation "Virgin Land" emerged out of scholarship in the field of American studies, "Ground Zero" was a term of art devised within the realm of statecraft. The narrative organized around the "Virgin Land" metaphor associated U.S. peoples with the national security state, and it entailed their collective wish to disavow the historical fact of the forcible dispossession of indigenous peoples from their homelands. The narrative accompanying "Ground Zero" has linked the people traumatized by the events of 9/11 with a Homeland State which emerged with the loss of the belief in the inviolability of the Virgin Land.

In what follows, I sketch the genealogy of each of these narrative formations and interrogate the political and cultural implications of this master fiction, which has reorganized the U.S. citizenry's relationship with the land. I also speculate briefly on the role that American studies might play in interrogating this reconfiguration.

THE INAUGURATION OF THE BUSH SETTLEMENT

This analysis begins with the assumption that historical and political crises of the magnitude of 9/11 are always accompanied by mythologies that attempt to reconfigure them within frames of reference that would generate imaginary resolutions. The myths that accompany historical crises only become historically real when actors supply the hypotheses they project about contingent events with cultural significance. As the preserve of the discursive spaces wherein the conflicting claims of the imaginary and the historically factual are mediated and resolved, myths gives closure to traumatizing historical events by endowing them with a moral significance.

National cultures conserve images of themselves across time by constructing such larger-than-life myths and transmitting them from one generation to the next. As the structural metaphors containing all the essential elements of a culture's worldview, myths empower writers and policy makers to position historically contingent events within preconstituted frames of reference that would control the public's understanding of their siginificance.[2] Richard Slotkin has explained how national myths accomplish this reconfiguration in terms of their power to assimilate historical contingencies to "archetypal patterns of growth and decay, salvation and damnation, death and rebirth."[3] As the structural metaphors containing the essential elements of a culture's habits of mind, myths take place in the gap between a culture's perception of contingent historical events and their assimilation into the nation's collective memory. In supplying the events they retell with timeless cultural value, myths transform these events into processes of traditionalization that render them central components of the culture that they thereby reproduce. It was through their correlation with processes of traditionalization that core myths like "Virgin Land" acquired their powers of cultural persuasion. Their monopolization of the keys to cultural persuasion enables national myths and symbols to regulate a people's thought and behavior.

As the harbinger of the invariant core beliefs prerequisite to the reordering of reality, the national mythology supplied the master fictions to which George W. Bush appealed to authorize the state's actions after 9/11. These mythological tropes—"Virgin Land," "Redeemer Nation," "American Adam," "Nature's Nation," "Errand into the Wilderness"—sedimented within the nation's master narratives supplied the transformational grammar through which state policy makers have shaped and reshaped the national people's understanding of political and historical events. The state's powers of governance have depended in part upon its recourse to these master fictions that transmit a normative system of values and beliefs from generation to generation. After they subordinated historical events to these mythological themes, the government's policy makers were empowered to fashion imaginary resolutions of actual historical dilemmas.

But the catastrophic events that took place at the World Trade Center and the Pentagon precipitated a "reality" that the national metanarratives could neither comprehend nor master. In his September 20, 2001, address to the nation, President Bush provided a symbolic reply that inaugurated a symbolic drama that was partly autonomous of the events that called it forth. The address to the nation was designed to lessen the events' traumatizing power through the provision of an imaginary response to a disaster that could not otherwise be assimilated to the preexisting order of things:

> On September 11, enemies of freedom committed an act of war against our country. Americans have known wars, but for the past 136 years they have been wars on foreign soil, except for one Sunday in 1941. Americans have known the casualties of war, but not at the center of a great city on a peaceful morning . . . Americans have known surprise attacks, but never before on thousands of civilians . . . All of this was brought upon us in a single day, and night fell on a different world . . . I will not forget the wound to our country and those who inflicted it. . . . Our grief has turned to anger and anger to resolution. Whether we bring our enemies to justice or bring justice to our enemies, justice will be done.

The executive phrases in Bush's address alluded to the foundational myths embedded within the national narrative. These phrases also inaugurated a symbolic drama that would transform the primary integers in the narrative the nation had formerly told itself into terms—"Ground Zero," "Homeland," "Operation Enduring Freedom," "Operation Iraqi Freedom"—that authorized the Bush administration's state of emergency. Specifically, the state's symbolic response to 9/11 replaced "Virgin Land" ("Americans have known wars, but for the past 136 years they have been wars on foreign soil") with "Ground Zero" ("Americans have known the casualties of war, but not at the center of a great city on a peaceful morning") and the "Homeland" ("Americans have known surprise attacks, but never before on thousands of civilians") as the governing metaphors through which to come to terms with the attack. The spectacular military campaigns in Afghanistan and Iraq which followed were in part designed to accomplish the conversion of these metaphors into historical facts.[4]

When Bush cited the historically accurate fact that "with the exception of a Sunday in 1941," the United States had not been subject to foreign invasion, he linked the public's belief in the myth of Virgin Land with the historical record. But when he did so, Bush did not supply the U.S. publics with historical grounds for their collective belief in Virgin Land. The myth that America was a Virgin Land endowed the historical fact that U.S. soil had never before been subjected to foreign violation with a moral rationale: Virgin Land was inviolate because the American people were innocent. In describing the surprise attack as a "wound to our country," Bush interpreted this violation on mythological as well as historical registers.

The wound was directed against the Virgin Land as well as the myth that the people of the United States are radically innocent. The state of emergency Bush erected at Ground Zero was thereafter endowed with the responsibility to defend the Homeland because the foreign violation of Virgin Land had alienated the nation's people from their imaginary way of inhabiting the nation. This substitution anchored the people to a very different state formation. It also drastically altered the foundational fantasy about the relationship between the nation's people and their territory, redefining it in terms of the longing of a dislocated population for a lost homeland.

The myth of Virgin Land enabled the American people to believe in their radical innocence because it permitted them to disavow knowledge of the historical fact that their "native" land was acquired through the forcible dispossession of native peoples. Their belief in their innocence supplied a moral rationale for the fact that the U.S. landscape had not been violated: the land was inviolate because the people were innocent.

Bush's speech possessed narrative and performative dimensions that reinterpreted 9/11 as a wound directed against the core national fantasy of the Virgin Land. The symbolic response to the crisis emptied it of its reality and reorganized the master fiction productive of the national peoples' imaginary relations to actual events. As a symbolic reply to catastrophe, Bush's speech emptied the crisis of its reality and supplanted it with a symbolic drama autonomous of the events that called it forth. After describing how the citizenry had been alienated from the mythology productive of their imaginary relation to the state, Bush linked that alienation with the vulnerability of the Homeland, which became the target of the security apparatus. While the Homeland was collocated with the nation-state, its security required the state to extend its policing authority globally.

The Homeland Security State that Bush erected at Ground Zero was thus endowed with the responsibility to defend the Homeland because the foreign violation of the Virgin Land had alienated the people from their imaginary way of inhabiting their native land. But the violation of the land's "virginity" required that Bush bring the event which the public had formerly disavowed—the forcible dispossession of entire people from their homeland—into spectacular visibility.

9/11: VIRGIN LAND AT GROUND ZERO

The metaphor of Virgin Land condensed a broad range of historically distinct actions—the uprooting, immigration, and resettlement of European exiles on a newly "discovered" territorial landmass—and it regulated the meanings that should and should not be assigned to these actions. At its core, the metaphor was designed to fulfill Europe's wish to start life afresh by relinquishing history on behalf of the secular dream of the construction of a new Eden. The metaphor gratified European emigrants' need to believe that America was an unpopulated space. The belief that the New World was discovered and settled by the Europeans who emigrated there resulted from the coupling of a shared fantasy with historical amnesia.

If the myth of U.S. exceptionalism described the events—the forcible resettlement of indigenous populations, the imperial annexation of Mexican territory—that the state has termed exceptions to its ruling norms, the myth of Virgin Land redescribed these exceptions as lacking a historical foundation. Within the register of the imaginary, "Virgin Land" depopulated the landscape so that it might be perceived in actuality as unoccupied territory. The landscape became a blank page, the ideal surface onto which to inscribe the history of the nation's Manifest Destiny. Virgin Land narratives placed the movement of the national people across the continent in opposition to the savagery of the wilderness as well as the native peoples who figured as indistinguishable from that wilderness; later, they fostered an understanding of the campaign of Indian removal as nature's beneficent choice of the Anglo-American settlers over the native inhabitants for its cultivation.

Overall, the myth of Virgin Land enabled the American people to replace the fact that the land was already settled by a vast native population with the belief that it was unoccupied. And the substitution of national fantasy for historical reality enabled Americans to disavow the resettlement and in some instances the extermination of entire populations. In displacing historical events with the representations through which they became recognizably "American," Virgin Land narratives produced reality as an effect of the imaginary. The fact that this reality could be exposed as unreal did not diminish the control that the national imaginary exerted over the symbolic order; it worked instead to underscore the logic of fetishism as the decisive aspect of its mode of persuasion. U.S. citizens may have known very well that colonists in no way discovered a Virgin Land, but they nevertheless found it expedient to embrace belief over the historical record, for it fostered the complementary belief in the radical innocence of the American people.

The belief as well as the disavowal were linked to the historical fact that U.S. civilian populations had not been subject to foreign attack since the War of 1812.[5] The historical fact of the nation's inviolability associated the belief in a Virgin Land with the desire that U.S. soil would remain forever unviolated by foreign aggression. When this fact was conjoined with the belief that the violation of a native people's homeland took place on foreign soil rather than Virgin Land, the composite determined the United States' uniqueness.

But the catastrophic events that took place at Ground Zero on September 11, 2001, actualized both of the scenarios which the belief in Virgin Land had been designed to ward off. At Ground Zero, U.S. Virgin Land had not merely been violated by foreign invaders—this violation involved the forcible dislocation of a settled population. The buildings erected to symbolize the United States' rise to world dominance were turned into horrific spectacles of violent removal.

The transformation of Virgin Land into Ground Zero brought into visibility an inhuman terrain that the national imaginary had been constructed to conceal. While "Ground Zero" was chosen to describe the unimaginable nature of the events of September 11, 2001, the state's association of them with the demand for the securing of the Homeland invested them with an uncanny effect. For when it displaced the metaphor of the Virgin Land, the term "Homeland" rendered the devastation precipitated at Ground Zero at once utterly unexpected yet weirdly familiar.

After they were figured in relation to the Homeland Security Act, the unprecedented events of 9/11 seemed familiar because they recalled the suppressed historical knowledge of the United States' origins in the devastation of native peoples' homelands. The sites of residence of the Paiutes and the Shoshones had more recently been destroyed as a result of the state's decision to turn their tribal lands into toxic dumps for the disposal of nuclear waste. The events also appeared familiar, as the signifier "Ground Zero" attests, because the unimaginable sight of the crumbling Twin Towers recovered memories of the fire bombings of civilian populations over Dresden and Tokyo, as well as the unspeakable aftereffects of the atomic fallout on the inhabitants of Hiroshima and Nagasaki.

With the destruction of the fantasy that the nation was founded on Virgin Land, the violence it obscured swallowed up the entire field of visibility. Ground Zero evoked the specter of the nation-founding violence out of whose exclusion the fantasy of the Virgin Land had been organized. At Ground Zero the fantasy of radical innocence upon which the nation was founded encountered the violence it had formerly concealed.

But according to what myth-logic were the American peoples constrained either to forget or suspend belief in the Indian removal policies that had effected the violent dispossession of indigenous tribes throughout the preceding two hundred years? And how did the myth of Virgin Land connect the belief in the state's power to secure the people against foreign aggression with belief in their radical innocence?

A BRIEF GENEALOGY OF THE RISE AND FALL OF THE MYTH OF VIRGIN LAND

While the connection between the disavowal of state violence and the construction of the national mythology might seem remote at best, the facilitation of just such a connection was nevertheless a central concern of the founders of the myth-and-symbol school of American studies. With the notable exception of Henry Nash Smith, the founders of the myth-and-symbol school of American literary studies—R. W. B. Lewis, Leslie Fiedler, Leo Marx—were veterans of the Second World War. After the war's conclusion, these soldier-critics produced the patriotic fictions in whose name they could retroactively claim to have fought the war. The national myth they created linked their need for an idealized national heritage with the epic narrative through which that idealization was imagined, symbolized, and supplied with characters and events. The myths about the nation the founders of the myth-and-symbol school invented was at once a narrative about the national heritage in whose name they had fought the war and a screen memory through which they supplanted their recollections of violent military campaigns with the idealized representations of the nation to which they desired to return. But if the myth-and-symbol school originated out of its need to remove representations of violence from the nation's past, it lost its monopoly at the time of the Vietnam War, when the nation, along with its myths and symbols, encountered a historical violence it could neither foreclose from recognition nor deny.

The national tradition that myth-and-symbol scholars invented enabled the symbolic engineers responsible for the forging of the nation's foreign policy to fashion imaginary resolutions for the seemingly intractable political dilemmas that confronted Americans throughout the Cold War. The Virgin Land upon which myth-and-symbol scholars emplotted historical events also supplied a screen onto which they projected the national culture's guilt as well as its fears and desires. Positioned outside the normative control of the social order, this counterworld replaced the vexing facts of the real world with invented characters and events that were compatible with collective social hopes and prejudices.

The idealized representations invented by the founders of the myth-and-symbol school of interpretation came to name, that is entitle, the master texts of the field of American literary studies. These masterworks engaged a prototypical American self (*American Adam*), in an epic quest (*Errand into the Wilderness*), to liberate our native land (*Virgin Land*) from foreign encroachments (*The Machine in the Garden*).[6] While each of these foundational texts provided slightly different accounts of the metanarrative that defined the practices of Americanists, all of them presupposed a utopian space of pure possibility where a whole self internalized this epic myth in a language and a series of actions that corroborated American exceptionalism.

Scholars working within the myth-and-symbol school correlated the scholarly prerogatives of American studies with the formative values of U.S. society. In combining rigorous research with patriotic sentiment, the members of this scholarly community turned nation-centeredness into a professional ideal. As prevalued representations of reality, the myths that they interpreted did not merely codify national metanarrative. The superstructural pressure of national metanarrative transmitted an implied regulating intertext that was present at the level of discourse in the same way that grammar is present at the level of the sentence. This regulatory intertext eliminated any distinction between what the metanarrative meant to say (its rhetoric) and what it was constrained to mean (its grammar).

As coherent structures of belief, these myths and symbols constituted what might be described as objective imperatives that brought historical events into conformity with the nation's pre-existing self-representations. Their myths and symbols measured events against their impact on the cohesion of the national community and created identifiable enemy images against whom to rally. Finally, they suggested a range of moralistic lessons derived from past disasters, about how to act in the present so as to safeguard a future. In so doing they also supplied policy makers and speechwriters with the rhetoric and the grammar through which they forged the addresses that won the people's consent. Following its deployment as the grounding mythos for pedagogy in American studies, the U.S. metanarrative these critics invented thereafter solidified into a relatively autonomous system of meaning production that resulted in a semantic field by which individuals were persuaded to live demonstrably imaginary relations to their real conditions of existence. Each of the foundational signifiers—"Virgin Land," "American Adam," "Errand into the Wilderness"—sedimented within the national metanarrative possessed a performative dimension empowered to bring about belief in the truth of the state of affairs they represented.

Because it involved a universal subject in a transhistorical action, Kenneth Burke has characterized the metanarrative as the "justifying myth" for the material history of the cold war. "An explanatory narrative that achieves the status of perfecting myth serves to reconcile discrepancies and irrationalities while appearing to obviate public or official scrutiny of actual circumstances. Such a narrative becomes effectively monolithic and saturating, demonizing its opposite and canceling or absorbing all mediatory and intermediate terms and kinds of activity."[7] At once a mode of inquiry, an object of knowledge, and an ideological rationale, the myth-and-symbol school of American literary studies facilitated an interdisciplinary formation that empowered Americanist scholars within the disciplines of literature, history, politics, sociology, and government to interpret and regulate the United States' geopolitical order. Through this interdisciplinary approach, the field of American studies collaborated with the press, university system, publishing industry, and other aspects of the cultural apparatus that managed the semantic field and policed the significance of such value-laden terms as the "nation" and the "people."[8]

When Henry Nash Smith published *Virgin Land: The American West as Symbol and Myth,* he analyzed the myths that were generated by the European settlers in their historical encounter with the American West. After comparing these myths with collective representations of the New World that were formulated at the time of the "discovery" of America, Smith explained how this primary metaphor provided a means of spiritual, economic, and masculine renewal for the "sons of Cooper's Leatherstocking" who embraced the myth. In 1950, the year of the book's publication, the United States was engaged in a struggle with Soviet communism over the political disposition of peoples across the globe. Because it was understood to be an expression of the sovereign will of the people that it was also made to represent, the myth of Virgin Land was invoked by policy makers as a representation of the public's approval of the state's policy of rebuilding and developing nations across the planet. After the architects of the Marshall Plan and the New Frontier deployed concepts and themes from this metanarrative to secure spontaneous consent for state policies, the myth of Virgin Land enabled postwar political actors to legitimate the United States' place as the subject and *telos* of universal history.

Throughout the Cold War, U.S. foreign policy was grounded in the credo of American exceptionalism, which required the belief in the United States as a unique political formation. The Cold War state was grounded in a political metaphysics that elevated national security into the foundational national predicate. The metannarrative underpinning the myth of Virgin Land transmitted a national tradition in support of this predication. And during the first three decades of the Cold War, Henry Nash Smith's *Virgin Land* hypothesis supplied the cultural code through which normative Americanist behavior was communicated and regulated. When Smith defined Virgin Land as open national landscape that fostered the construction and realization of self-reliant individualists, he supplied the terrain upon which state policy makers displaced actually existing social and political crises onto a strictly imaginary site where they underwent symbolic resolution. The rugged individualists who populated this transhistorical terrain subjectivized the codes regulating appropriate American behavior, and they thereby legitimated the norms suturing U.S. citizens to the patterns of domination, subjectification, and governmentality that the national security state propagated across the globe.

However, the Vietnam War radically disrupted the historical effectiveness of this metanarrative. Opponents of the war correlated the state's policy of Indian removal in the nineteenth century with the foreign policy that resulted in the massacres at My Lai. In so doing, antiwar activists exposed the myth of Virgin Land as one of the ideological forms through which state historians and policy makers had covered up the nation's shameful history of colonial violence. The war effected what John Hellmann has described as a radical disruption in the nation's self-representations.

> When the story of America in Vietnam turned into something unexpected, the nature of the larger story of America itself became the subject of intense cultural dispute. On the deepest level, the legacy of Vietnam is the disruption of our story of our explanation of the past and vision of the future.[9]

In the wake of the Vietnam War, Americanist scholars desacralized the myths of the United States as a Virgin Land and the myth of the national history as a providential errand into the wilderness. They fostered a new paradigm: communities that replaced essentializing national myths with cultural constructivist models that undermined the aesthetic authority of the national landscape and subverted the literary canon as an instrument of Americanization, and that imagined forms of citizenship that were not subject to the imperatives of the security apparatus.

THE RETURN OF THE NATIONAL MYTHOLOGY AND THE EMERGENCE OF THE GLOBAL HOMELAND STATE

War might be said to begin when a country becomes a patriotic fiction for its population. A nation is not only a piece of land but a narration about the people's relation to the land.[10] And after 9/11, the national myths that had undergone wholesale debunking in the post-Vietnam era underwent remarkable regeneration. Around the time that the U.S. war machine was rolling into the area some biblical scholars have designated as the location of the Garden of Eden, Alan Wolfe published a lengthy review essay in *The New Republic* in which he argued that it was the ethical responsibility of Americanist scholars to rehabilitate the narrative of Virgin Land that had been fostered by the scholars in the myth-and-symbol school. In the opening paragraphs of his article, Wolfe invoked Marx's *The Machine in the Garden* as an authorization for the following characterization of the deleterious consequences of revisionist Americanists' loss of belief in these core narratives: "It does not occur to these revolutionaries that the groups they hope will conquer America cannot do so if there is no America to conquer. Let America die, and all who aspire to its perfection will die with it."[11]

If one of the primary aims of war involves destroying the way an enemy perceives itself, Alan Wolfe represented 9/11 as an act of war in the sense that it brought about the destruction of the national people's foundational fantasy concerning their relation to the land. That foundational fantasy was organized around a traumatic element that could not be symbolized within the terms of the national narrative. In the United States, the fantasy of the Virgin Land covered over the shameful history of internal violence directed against the native populations. But as we have seen, this historical fact was not utterly effaced. It functioned as an occluded supplement to the nation's view of itself as a Redeemer Nation whose Manifest Destiny entailed the commission to undertake a providential errand into the wilderness. The disavowed knowledge of the barbarous violence that accompanied this civilizing mission was the unwritten basis for Wolfe's need to embrace Virgin Land as a representative national metaphor.

But George W. Bush differed from Wolfe in that he turned the enemy's violation of the nation's foundational fantasy into an occasion to fashion exceptions to the rules of law and war, formally inaugurating a state of emergency. In his September 20 address, Bush designated the "enemies of freedom" as the historical agency responsible for this generalized unsettlement of the national people. But neither Osama bin Laden nor Saddam Hussein was the causative agent responsible for the forcible separation of the people from their way of life. Rather, the state of emergency ensuing from the Homeland Security Act required people to depart from the norms and values to which they had become habituated, tearing to the ground the democratic institutions—freedom of speech, religious tolerance, formal equality, uniform juridical procedures, universal suffrage—that had formerly nurtured and sustained them.

With the enemy's violation of the rules of war as a rationale, the state suspended the rules to which it was otherwise subject, violating its own rules in the name of protecting them against a force that operated according to different rules. In order to protect the rule of law as such from this illegality, the state declared itself the occupant of a position not subject to the very rules it must protect. Congress's passage of the USA PATRIOT (Proved Appropriate Tools to Intercept and Obstruct Terrorism) Act effected the most dramatic abridgment of civil liberties in the nation's history. This emergency legislation subordinated all concerns of ethics, of human rights, of due process, of constitutional hierarchies, and of the division of power to the state's monopoly over the exception.

The emergency state is marked by absolute independence from any juridical control and any reference to the normal political order. It is empowered to suspend the articles of the constitution protective of personal liberty, freedom of speech and assembly and the inviolability of home, postal, telephone and internet privacy. In designating Afghanistan and Iraq as endangering the Homeland, Operations Enduring Justice and Iraqi Freedom simply extended the imperatives of the domestic emergency state across the globe.

Following 9/11 the state effected the transition from a normalized political order to a state of emergency by enacting the violence that the Virgin Land myth had normatively covered over. Whereas 9/11 dislocated the national people from the mythology productive of their imaginary relation to the state, Bush linked their generalized dislocation with the vulnerability of the "Homeland," which thereafter became the target of the security apparatus.

Bush endowed the state of emergency which he erected at Ground Zero with the responsibility to defend the Homeland because foreign aggressors had violated the Virgin Land. The violation of the land's inviolability not only disinhibited the state of its need to mask its history of violence; this act of aggression also required the state to bring the event which the public had formerly disavowed—the forcible dispossession of national peoples from their homelands—into spectacular visibility.

But the Homeland that emerged as the justification for the state's exercise of excessive violence was not identical to the land mass of the continental United States. The Homeland Bush invoked to "authorize" these emergency actions did not designate either an enclosed territory or an imaginable home. The Homeland secured by the emergency state instead referred to the unlocatable order that emerged *through and by way of the people's generalized dislocation from the nation as a shared form of life.* The Homeland Security Act put into place a state of exception that positioned the people in a space that was included in the Homeland through its exclusion from the normal political order.

As the relationship between the state and the population that comes into existence when the state declares a state of emergency, the Homeland names a form of governmentality without a recognizable location. As the unlocalizable space the population is ordered to occupy when the state enters the site of the exception to the normative order, the Homeland names the structure through which state of emergency is realized normally.

As we have seen, the national mythology turned the nation into a stage for the enactment of particular forms of life. But if the nation designates the arena in which the national peoples enacted these ways of life, the "Homeland" named the space which emerged when these peoples were dissociated from their ways of life. The introduction of the signifier of the "Homeland" to capture this experience of generalized dislocation recalled themes from the national narrative which it significantly altered. But insofar as these themes were antithetical to the range of connotations sedimented within "Virgin Land," the historical antecedents for the "Homeland" surely must give pause.

The Homeland named the site that the colonial settlers had abandoned in their quest for a newly found land. The Homeland also named the country to which the settlers might one day return. In its reference to an archaic land from which the colonial settlers either voluntarily departed or were forced to abandon, the Homeland represented a prehistoric pastness prior to the founding of the United States. Following 9/11, the Homeland named the space in which the people were included after acts of terrorism had violently dislocated them from their ways of life. The metaphor of the

Homeland thereafter evoked the image of a vulnerable population that had become internally estranged from its "country of origin" and dependent upon the protection of the state.

When it was figured within the Homeland Security Act, the Homeland engendered an imaginary scenario wherein the national people were encouraged to consider themselves dislocated from their country of origin by foreign aggressors so that they might experience their return from exile in the displaced from of the spectacular unsettling of homelands elsewhere. This imaginary scenario and the spectacles through which it was communicated sustained the dissociation of the people from recognizably "American" ways of life. Insofar as the Homeland named what emerged when the population became dislocated from the conditions of belonging to a territorialized nation, its security required the domestic emergency state to extend its policing authority to the dimension of the globe.

VIRGIN LAND AS GROUND ZERO

The Homeland Security Act regressed the population to the condition of a minority dependent upon the state for its biopolitical welfare. But the state thereafter correlated this political regression with the reenactment of a formerly suppressed historical event. After the people were regressed to minority status, the state produced a series of spectacles that returned the population to the historical moment in which colonial settlers had deployed the illicit use of force against native populations. With the invasions of Afghanistan and Iraq, the figurative meanings associated with Virgin Land were demetaphorized into the actuality of state violence. The state's spectacular violation of the rights of the "enemies of freedom" was thereby made to coincide with the emergency state's radical abridgment of domestic civil rights.

The putative insecurity of the Homeland's civilian population and the threat of terrorist attack were co-constituting aspects of the Homeland Security State. The state's representation of a vulnerable civilian population in need of state protection was fashioned in opposition to the captured Taliban, and Iraqis who were subjected to the power of the state yet lacked the protection of their rights or liberties.

This new settlement required the public to sacrifice their civil liberties in exchange for the enjoyment of the state's spectacular violations of the rights of other sovereign states. For the Bush administration did not exactly represent the military operations in Afghanistan and Iraq as wars conducted between civilized states that respected one another's sovereignty. Rather, it constructed them as confrontations between the emergency state apparatus and terrorizing powers that posed a threat to the Homeland. If the modern state is construed as the embodiment of Enlightenment reason, and the neoliberal principles of market democracy comprise the means whereby this rationality becomes universalized, then neither the Taliban regime in Afghanistan nor the Ba'athist regime in Iraq could be construed as either modern states or rational actors in the global economy. In its military operations in Afghanistan and Iraq, the U.S. emergency state apparatus imposed this modern state formation and that market logic on the Afghan and Iraqi peoples. As a result of these acts of "defensive aggression," Iraq and Afghanistan were relocated within the global order of the Homeland Security State.

The spectators' enjoyment derived from the spectacles' violation of the normative assumptions—that the United States was a redeemer nation rather than an aggressor state, whose manifest errand was civilizing rather than brutalizing, etc., etc.—sedimented within the national imaginary. Because the spectators could not enjoy the state's spectacles without disassociating from the assumptions that would have rendered them unimaginable as *American* spectacles, these spectacles enforced the separation of the state's spectatorial publics from their national forms of life. After these spectacles intermediated between the people and their forms of life, they substituted the lateral linkages with the emergency state apparatus for the people's vertical integration with a democratic way of life.

In Iraq and Afghanistan the emergency forces of the state openly re-performed the acts of violence that the myth of Virgin Land had formerly covered up. "Operation Infinite Justice" quite literally intended to depopulate the Afghan landscape so that it might be perceived as a blank page onto which to inscribe a different political order. "Operation Iraqi Freedom" fostered an understanding of "regime change" as the Iraqi people's beneficent choice of the political exemplar of its Anglo-American occupiers for the institutions of its new political order. As witnesses to the state's colonization of Afghanistan and Iraq, the United States' spectatorial publics were returned to the prehistoric time of the colonial settlers who had formerly spoliated Indian homelands. By way of "Operation Infinite Justice" and "Operation Iraqi Freedom" the Homeland Security State restaged the colonial settlers' conquest of Indians and the acquisition of their homelands. The terror and killing became the Homeland State's means of accomplishing anew the already known *telos* of U.S. history as the inaugural event of America's global rule in the twenty-first century.

These spectacles redescribed imperial conquest as a form of domestic defense in a manner that reversed the relationship between the aggressor and the victim. The Homeland Security State constructed the pre-emptive strikes against others' homelands as a spectacular form of domestic defense against foreign aggression. Both spectacles invited their audiences to take scopic pleasure in the return of the traumatic memory of the unprovoked aggression that the colonial settlers had previously exerted against native populations. These massacres, which could not be authorized or legitimated by the Virgin Land narrative, became the foundational acts which inaugurated the global Homeland as a realm outside the law.

Whereas the myth of Virgin Land produced historical continuity by suppressing the traumatic memory of lawless violence, the events of 9/11 demanded the recovery of this traumatic memory so as to reverse the national people's relation to violence, and to inaugurate a new global order. The spectacles which unfolded in the deserts of Afghanistan and Iraq transformed the U.S. spectatorial population into the perpetrators rather than the victims of foreign aggression. The state's literal recovery of the traumatic memory of barbarous aggression against native peoples thereby overcame the traumatizing experience of aggression at the hands of "foreign" terrorists.

These spectacles of violence encouraged the public's belief that it participated in the state's power because it shared in the spectacle through which the state gave expression to its power. But the people were also the potential targets of the shows of force they witnessed. In transforming citizens into spectators, the state created a disjunction between the people and the ways of life that the state protected through its exercises of retributive violence. After this new settlement induced the people to suspend their civil liberties in exchange for the enjoyment of the state's spectacular violations of the rights of its enemies, the emergency state transposed the nation and the citizen into dispensable predicates of global rule.

HOMELAND SECURITY AS A GLOBAL BIOPOLITICAL SETTLEMENT

As we have seen, the Homeland enacted into law by the Homeland Security Act did not have reference to an enclosed territory. And it was not exactly a political order. The Homeland Security Act was the political instrument on whose authority the state transformed a temporary suspension of order erected on the basis of factual danger into a quasipermanent biopolitical arrangement which as such remained outside the normal order. After the passage of the Homeland Security Act, the state of exception no longer referred to an external state of factual danger and was instead identified with the juridico-political order itself. This juridical political apparatus thereafter authorized a biopolitical settlement which inscribed the body of the people into an order of state power which endowed the state with power over the life and death of the population.[12]

This biopolitical sphere emerged with the state's decision to construe the populations it governed as indistinguishable from unprotected biological life. The body of the people as a free and equal citizenry, endowed with the capacity to reconstitute itself through recourse to historically venerated social significations, was thereby replaced by a biologized population that the state protected from biological terrorism. The biopolitical sphere constructed by the provisions of the Homeland Security Act first subtracted the population from the forms of civic and political life through which they recognized themselves as a national people and then positioned these life forms—the people, their way of life—into nonsynchronous zones of protection with the promise that their future synchronization would resuscitate the nation-state.

After undergoing a generalized dislocation from the national imaginary through which their everyday practices were lived as recognizably "American" forms of life, the national peoples were reconstituted as a biological life forms. Their dislocation from the national imaginary resulted in their mass denationalization. As naked biological life under the state's protection, the biopoliticized population also could play no active political role in the Homeland State's re-ordering of things. The Homeland State thereafter represented the population as an unprotected biological formation whose collective vitality must be administered and safeguarded against weapons of biological terrorism. But insofar as the Homeland state's biopolitical imperative to regulate the life and death of the population it governed was irreducible to the denizens of the nation-state, the Homeland State's biopolitical regime became potentially global in its extensibility.

It was the state's description of the weapons which endanger the aggregated population as "biological" that in part authorized the state's biopolitical settlement. In representing its biopolitical imperatives in terms of a defense against weapons of biological destruction, the state also produced an indistinction between politics and the war against terrorism. This redescription produced two interrelated effects: it transformed the population's political and civil liberties into life forms that were to be safeguarded rather than acted upon. More important, it turned political opponents of this biopolitical settlement into potential enemies of the ways of life that the state safeguards.[13]

AFTERWORD: THE PART OF NO PART

Overall, 9/11 brought to the light of day the Other to the normative representation of the United States. It positioned *unheimlich* dislocates within the Homeland in place of the citizens who exercised rights and liberties on the basis of these normalizations. When the signifier of the Homeland substituted for the Virgin Land, the national security state was supplanted by the emergency state. Whereas Virgin Land enforced the disavowal of the state's destruction of indigenous population's homelands, Ground Zero demanded that spectacle of the destruction of a homeland as compensation for the loss of the land's "virginity."

In tracking the radical shift in the governing frames of reference, I have indicated the ways in which the state coordinated the signifiers "9/11," "Ground Zero," and "Homeland" into a relay of significations undergirding the biopolitical settlement of the global Homeland state. But in recollecting the radical shift in the nation's relationship to its master fictions that took place during the Vietnam War, I have also alluded to the inherent instability of the nodal points that have been constructed to coordinate these newly invented governing representations.

When he inaugurated the prerogatives of the emergency state at Ground Zero, Bush conscripted the traumatic power of the events that took place there to offer pre-emptive strikes as compensation for the loss. But the events that took place on September 11, 2001, fractured the nation-state's continuist time. As the locus for events lacking a preexisting signification in the social order, 9/11 exists as a sign of what cannot take place within the order of signification. But if it marks the rupture of the time kept by the nation-state, 9/11 is no less discordant with the mode of historical eventuation the Bush administration has inaugurated in its name. Inherently nonsynchronous, 9/11 calls for a time to come.

The Bush administration attempted to supplant the loss of the belief in Virgin Land that underwrote the myth of U.S. exceptionalism with the arrogation of the power to occupy the position of the exception to the laws of the world of nations. But insofar as the Homeland state's exceptions to the rules of law and war are themselves instantiations of force that lack the grounding support of norms or rules, they resemble the traumatic events upon which they depend for their power to rule. As such, these exceptions will maintain their power to rule only as long as U.S. publics remain captivated by the spectacles of violence the state has erected at the site of Ground Zero.

If the global Homeland has erected an order in which the people have no part, that order has positioned the people in a place that lacks a part in the global order. As the surplus element in the global Homeland, the people also occupy the place of an empty universal. This place may currently lack any part to play in the Homeland's global order. But the very emptiness of this space, the fact that it demarcates the peoples of the global Homeland, included but with no part to play in the existing order, simultaneously empowers the people to play the part of articulating an alternative to the existing order. Because the people are without a part in the order in which the people are nevertheless included, they also constitute a part in an alternative to that order. The part without a part in the given global order constitutes an empty universal in an order to come that the global peoples can particularize differently.[14]

That order to come will not begin until the global state of emergency state is itself exposed as the cause of the traumas it purports to oppose.

NOTES

1. This essay builds upon but also significantly revises my afterword to Stanley Hauerwas and Frank Lentricchia, eds., *Dissent from the Homeland: Essays after September 11* (Durham, N.C.: Duke University Press, 2003).

2. Henry Nash Smith supplied an insight into the mobilizing effects of these collective representations on the U.S. population throughout history when he observed: "These illustrations point to the conclusion that history cannot happen—that is, men cannot engage in purposive group behavior—without images which simultaneously express collective desires and impulses and impose coherence on the infinitely varied data of experience. These images are never, of course, exact reproductions of the physical and social environment. They cannot motivate and direct action unless they are drastic simplifications." Henry Nash Smith, *Virgin Land: The American West in Symbols and Myth* (Cambridge, Mass.: Harvard University Press, 1950, ix). But the historian William H. McNeill provided the most cogent description of the role myths played in the articulation of state governance policies in a 1981 article entitled "The Care and Repair of Public Myth." In that article, McNeill argued the indispensable role that myths and symbols played in the manufacturing of the public's consent for domestic and foreign policy. And he admonished revisionist scholars for the propagation of their demythologizing proclivities: "A people without a full quiver of relevant agreed upon statements, accepted in advance through education or less formalized acculturation finds itself in deep trouble, for, in the absence of believable myths, coherent public action becomes difficult to improvise or sustain." *Foreign Affairs* 61 (1981):1–13.

3. Richard Slotkin, "Myth and the Production of History," in *Ideology and Classic American Literature,* ed. Sacvan Bercovitch and Myra Jehlen (New York: Cambridge University Press, 1986), 70.

4. I first began to think of the biopolitical settlement that the Bush administration had constructed out of the relay of signifiers it installed in between 9/11 and the Homeland Security State while I listened to Amy Kaplan deliver a talk at the Dartmouth American Studies Institute in June 2002 in which she ruminated over the connotations of the terms "Ground Zero," "Homeland," and "Guantánamo Bay." Kaplan has since published those remarks in "Homeland Insecurities:

Reflections on Language and Space," *Radical History Review* 85 (winter 2003): 82–93. I am indebted to her meditation even as I diverge from it.

5. When Bush observed that "Americans have known wars, but for the past 136 years they have been wars on foreign soil," the conclusion of the Civil War in 1865 was his historical benchmark. But the last occasion on which the mainland was subject to "foreign attack" was the War of 1812, which had taken place 189 years earlier. In recalling the Civil War rather than the War of 1812 as the historical precedent for 9/11, Bush also wanted to invoke the South as the symbolic geography for his "crusade" against world evil.

6. R.W.B. Lewis, *The American Adam: Innocence, Tragedy and Tradition in the Nineteenth Century* (Chicago: The University of Chicago Press, 1959); Perry Miller, *Errand into the Wilderness* (Cambridge, Mass: Belknap Press of Harvard University Press, 1956); Henry Nash Smith, *Virgin Land;* Leo Marx, *The Machine in the Garden: Technology and the Pastoral Ideal in America* (London and New York: Oxford University Press, 1964).

7. In *Framing History: The Rosenberg Story and the Cold War,* Virginia Carmichael describes Kenneth Burke's notion of a justifying myth as "[a]n explanatory narrative that achieves the status of perfecting myth serves to reconcile discrepancies and irrationalities while appearing to obviate public or official scrutiny of actual circumstances. Such a narrative becomes effectively monolithic and saturating, demonizing its opposite and canceling or absorbing all mediatory and intermediate terms and kinds of activity." *Framing History: The Rosenberg Story and the Cold War* (Minneapolis: University of Minnesota Press, 1993), 7.

8. Robyn Wiegman and I have elaborated upon the myth-and-symbol school as an aesthetic ideology of the centralizing postwar state in the introduction to our edited volume *The Futures of American Studies* (Durham, N.C.: Duke University Press, 2002); see especially 16–21 for a more nuanced discussion of this dynamic.

9. John Hellmann, *American Myth and the Legacy of Vietnam* (New York: Columbia University Press, 1986), x.

10. My understanding of the fantasy structure of war draws upon Renata Salecl's discussion of this topic in *Spoils of Freedom: Psychoanalysis and Feminism after the Fall of Socialism* (New York: Routledge, 1994), especially 15–19.

11. Alan Wolfe, "Anti-American Studies," *The New Republic,* February 10 2003, 25.

12. My discussion of the biopolitical settlement as well as my understanding of the state of emergency and the space of the exception is indebted to Giorgio Agamen's remarkable discussion of the relationship between forms of life and biopolitics in *Means without End: Notes on Politics* (Minneapolis: University of Minnesota Press, 2000).

13. Agamben examines the transformation of politics into biopolitics through a reconsideration of Foucault's account of this mutation in "Form-of-life," in *Means without End,* 3–14.

14. My understanding of the empty or singular universal draws upon Slavoj Žižek's discussion of this concept in his *The Ticklish Subject: The Absent Center of Political Ontology* (New York: Routledge, 1999), 187–239. Jacques Rancière elaborates upon the importance of the phrase "the part of no part" to political contestations in his *Disagreement: Politics and Philosophy* (Minneapolis: University of Minnesota Press, 1999) , 1–60.

4. Pre-Emption, the Future, and the Imagination

David Palumbo-Liu

This collection of essays makes a bold move—it argues the centrality of the idea of "culture" for understanding the policy decisions of the George W. Bush administration, decisions that have had a profound effect on staking out the role of the United States in the global political community.[1] By any account this role has been seen by most of the world community as belligerent, unilateral, narrow-minded, and informed by a particular sense of the future. In mapping the future, the hard and realistic nature of most political science (and social science in general) would seem to have little use, and perhaps much disdain, for such a fuzzy concept as "culture." One would expect rather that solid statistics and regression modeling would be the foundation for any serious discussions in the present. And yet here I will argue that in envisioning the future, relatively fuzzy notions of culture and more precisely the imagination (as opposed to the faculty of precise calculation) play a critical role. Indeed, I argue that the relatively unconstrained aspect of the imagination can make it a particularly potent and dangerous generator of visions of the future when placed in the context of terror.

Not only does the imagining of the future then generate specific exercises of the imagination, it can also provide, weirdly, a hypothetical alibi for present-day and past miscalculations, if, again, imagined in a particular manner with a specific logic and effect in mind. When asked in a BBC interview to reflect upon decisions made by her president, Secretary of State Condoleezza Rice confessed: "we've made tactical errors—thousands of them, I'm sure." However, she maintained that "one of the things that's very difficult to tell in the midst of big historic change is what was actually a good decision and what was a bad decision. And I will tell you that decisions, when you look at them in historical perspective, that were thought at the time to be brilliant, turn out to have been really rather bad, and vice versa."[2] No one can really argue with that as an historical point, but it certainly does not seem to be the kind of thinking that can much help inform our decision making in the present. Furthermore, and most germane for this essay, this manner of conjuring up an imaginary future view to neatly (or maybe not so neatly) exculpate present-day errors means that only the future can finally adjudicate our acts on earth. The problem is that once this notion is set in motion it creates an endlessly deferrable day of judgment—assessments made in *which* future, when? In short, so much depends on the future, it seems. And yet of course we have no access to the future, only to an imagined future. This essay thus looks at how conjuring up a particular, culturally linked *imaginative* sense of the future can indeed inform a rational decision; this imagination is not secured or constrained by any empirical data. There *may* be weapons of mass destruction; Saddam Hussein may or may *not* be linked to the bombing of the World Trade Center, et cetera. In these and other instances, the "fuzzy" or "foggy" can be enabling, not paralyzing, forces that drive a perpetual attempt to pre-empt a future they invent. And to understand how this might be true we need to go onto the cultural realm, not avoid it.

At an October 2003 Washington conference on alternate national security strategies, former National Security Advisor Sandy Berger noted several alarming features of the "Bush Doctrine." One was the abandonment of deterrence in favor of pre-emption, in which uncertainty becomes a reason for action.[3] The "fog of war," rather than leading to caution, became now an imperative for action, the abandonment of the commitment to act on hard empirical evidence is the fueling point for a particular kind of imagination. Pre-emption had for its goal the maintenance of hegemony. Bruce Cumings concisely articulates the interdependency of force and hegemony: "Hegemonic power is ultimately conditioned by technological and industrial power, which helps us understand its beginnings; that advantage is locked in by military power, which helps us understand the long middle years of a hegemonic cycle; and the requirements of military supremacy and a (probable) later tendency toward financial speculation and resultant capitalist torpor helps us grasp its decline."[4] If Cumings is correct, then in the latest manifestations of required military supremacy we can postulate a subtext of weakness and vulnerability. Yet in the case of pre-emption another sort of speculation also fuels the compulsion to display power and exercise it emphatically and even hyperbolically.

As Richard Falk notes, "Pre-emption . . . validates striking first—not in a crisis . . . , but on the basis of shadowy intentions, alleged potential links to terrorist groups, supposed plans and projects to acquire weapons of mass destruction, and anticipation so future dangers. It is a doctrine without limits, without accountability to the UN or international law, without any dependence on a collective judgment of responsible governments and, what is worse, without any convincing demonstration of practical necessity."[5] Nevertheless, an inescapable contradiction abides—as a doctrine, pre-emptive force in the service of hegemony must always seek out threat in order to reanimate itself. It must imagine always a potential state of (its own) weakness as a pretext to reassert its strength. It lives therefore in the gray zone between the empirical and the possible, shuttling between reaffirmations of both strength and weakness, of both invincibility and vulnerability. The main point of this essay is that in the tortuous playing-out of these contradictions, recent United States foreign and domestic policies have appropriated and instrumentalized the basic humanistic and ethical character of the imagination as found in Kant. Indeed, it would not be an exaggeration to say that what we find in today's U.S. program of pre-emption and perpetual war is no less than a perverse, pathological recoding of the entire sphere of the imagination.

Now certainly, the notion of pre-emption in U.S. policy is not new. John Gaddis has pointed out that the twentieth-century precedent for Bush's policy is Pearl Harbor:

> The basis for Bush's grand strategy, like Roosevelt's, comes from the shock of surprise attack and will not change. None of F.D.R.'s successors, Democrat or Republican, could escape the lesson he drew from the events of December 7, 1941: that distance alone no longer protected Americans from assaults at the hands of hostile states. Neither Bush nor his successors, whatever their party, can ignore what the events of September 11, 2001, made clear: that deterrence against states affords insufficient protection from attacks by gangs, which can now inflict the kind of damage only states fighting wars used to be able to achieve. In that sense, the course for Bush's second term remains that of his first one: the restoration of security in a suddenly more dangerous world.[6]

To make the world safer required "that shocks be administered in return, not just to the part of the world from which the attack came, but to the international system as a whole . . . Shock therapy would produce a safer, saner world."[7]

What we find now is a perpetual production of "shock" to the world body, a conjoining of active and reactive violence that is at once philosophically, psychically, and politically/militarily manifested. In this machinery, the very capacity to imagine, to feel, to empathize, indeed to register the world is instrumentalized and "security" founded upon a belief that the therapeutic effects of shock are guaranteed in the long run. And yet this "shock and awe" therapy requires moving from an assumption of universal humanity to a static and deadly balance between two halves of a world—of power and of weakness, of dominance and submission, of life and death.

There are three parts to my essay: first, I briefly note how two key eighteenth-century documents—one literary and one military—each diagnose a particular pathology of the imagination. Next, I will show how this pathology can be linked to the perversion of the Kantian notion of the aesthetic imagination. I will be specifically interested in explaining how this perversion decimates the Kantian notion of the aesthetic as that which postulates a transcendental human community founded upon an assumption of common affect and empathy, what Kant calls *sensus communis*. Instead, today we find the deployment of imagination for particular, antihumanistic purposes that channel the imagination into specifically strategic and destructive modes of thinking, even while appropriating the rhetoric of the aesthetic. The essential point to bear in mind is that this strategic thinking would be far less lethal and much more contained without the compelling force of the humanistic imagination behind it. Finally, I give two examples of this phenomenon in contemporary U.S. political and strategic discourse.

To make this clearer, think of the term "Shock and Awe." The subtitle of the document that first proposed a U.S. tactic of "Shock and Awe" is especially germane, for it forms the link between the aesthetic and the strategic that is at the core of my thesis. The subtitle to the pamphlet that proposes "Shock and Awe" is "achieving rapid dominance." The violent aesthetic of shock and awe, the terrifying appropriation of the Sublime, is thus materialized in emphatically pragmatic and lethal ways and put to a specific strategic purpose: it enlists a particular brand of imagining the shared effect of terror on civilian populations, transforming civilians into weapons of psychological and political warfare.[8] It counts at once on an aesthetic *affect* of horror and demoralization, which in turn forms its corresponding strategic *effect*. In this regard, Edmund Burke's conceptualization of the Sublime, which links the effects of the Sublime specifically to the production of terror and "astonishment," adds an important element to our discussion of affect. According to Samuel H. Monk, "The keystone of Burke's aesthetic is emotion, and the foundation of his theory of sublimity is the emotion of terror."[9] For Burke, sublime ideas include "obscurity, where darkness and uncertainty arouse dread and terror; power, where the mind is impelled to fear because of superior force; privations, such as darkness, vacuity, and silence; vastness, whether in length, height or depth; infinity, or any object that because of its size seems infinite" (34). In producing terror, sublime objects produce as well the emotion of astonishment. "that state of the soul in which all its motions are suspended with some degree of horror . . . The mind is so entirely filled with its object, that it cannot entertain any other, nor by consequence reason on that object that employs it . . . [the Sublime] hurries us on by an irresistible force."[10] It is precisely this invasion and overwhelming of the mind itself by the terrible object of contemplation, and this compulsion past reason that characterize the effects and affect of shock and awe, the immediate effect of overwhelming force compounded by uncertainty, the power of a superior force, an infinite dimensionality. I develop the relation between shock and awe and the Sublime later in this essay; at present I wish to isolate the element of terror and the absorption of the mind by the object of contemplation that we find in Burke and relate it to the eighteenth-century diagnosis of pathology of the imagination and link that pathology to the perversion of Kant's aesthetic and its ethical ramifications.

In the late eighteenth century, we find the imagination evoked in two very different texts. Despite their differences, each text not only articulates a similar sense of the power of the imagination, but also acknowledges and analyzes its pathology. The two contemporaries I refer to are Coleridge and Clausewitz. Coleridge's conceptualization of the imagination is inward turning . In its healthy form, the imagination is "that Sublime faculty, by which a great mind becomes that which it meditates on" (ch. 4, p. 85n3).[11] This description of the imagination echoes Coleridge's characterization of the transcendental philosopher's "dual capacities": one "tends to expand infinitely, while the other strives to apprehend or find itself in this infinity" (ch. 13, p. 297).[12]

But what happens when it goes too far? What happens when its remove from the empirical world and its inward scope become excessive? One recalls that Coleridge uses Fancy as a countermeasure to the imagination. Fancy is the lesser form, an activity best characterized by the haphazard yoking together of random elements. In contradistinction, the imagination is creative, vital, shaping, rather than merely inventing. But if the Fancy is less creative, it is also correspondingly less dangerous: "The excess of fancy is delirium, of imagination, mania. Fancy is the arbitrary bringing together of things that lie remote, and forming them into a unity. The materials lie ready for the fancy, which acts by a sort of juxtaposition. *On the other hand, the imagination under excitement generates and pro-*

duces a form of its own" (ch. 4, p. 84n2).[13] In terms of today's perpetual war, this "form" is intimately connected to a corresponding term: "terror." It is real, it is imaginary, and its uncanny duality fuels the perpetuation of uncertainty and fuels an excessive expansion *and* interiorizing of the imagination. And the response to uncertainty has been to try to achieve, by any means necessary, the end of terror.

But once one embarks on this flight of the imagination, there can be no end. Coleridge notes the almost facile manner in which a poet can produce fear by tapping into the "invisible world":

> The fear of the invisible world is the most dazzling. Its influence is abundantly provided by the one circumstance, that it can bribe us into a voluntary submission of our better knowledge, into suspension of all our judgment derived from constant experience, and enable us to peruse with the liveliest interest the wildest tales. . . . On this propensity, so deeply rooted in our nature, a specific *dramatic* probability may be raised by a true poet, if the whole of his work be in harmony: a *dramatic* probability, sufficient for dramatic pleasure, even when the component characters and incidents border on impossibility. The poet does not require us to be awake and believe; he solicits us only to yield ourselves to a dream. (ch. 23, p. 218)

This critical and timely note on improbability and obsession also fascinates von Clausewitz. One of the central innovations of von Clausewitz's theory is the notion that modern wars are increasingly beyond the reach of the mathematical exercises in symmetry and logic that informed prior war strategizing. Instead, for von Clausewitz modern wars were a matter of chance, fear, and mere probability. (The term "fog of war" is attributed to him, though he actually never used those precise words. I will argue that what he actually said is much more specific and interesting.) Modern war could thus most properly be situated within the realm of the imagination, which then opens the door for obsession.

First, von Clausewitz removes War from the realm of animate, moral forces, and places it not only into the realm of the uncertain, but also into a broad spectrum of scale, signaling its amorphous and hence eminently imaginative character: "The art of war has nothing to do with living, moral forces. It therefore follows that it can nowhere attain the absolute and certain; there remains always a margin for the accidental, in great things and small."[14] Again, in a passage that strongly echoes Coleridge's remarks on the imaginative power of fear, and the one to which the "fog of war" is attributed, von Clausewitz takes us into the spectral environment of "mere twilight": "The great uncertainty of all data in war is a characteristic difficulty, because all action must be directed, to a certain extent, in a mere twilight, which in addition not infrequently—like the effect of fog or moonlight—gives to things an exaggerated size and grotesque form" (155).

Nevertheless, not only do we not back away from such uncertain chasing of phantoms, we become obsessed with fixing the unfixable, drawn away from the search for clarity and instead toward deeper and deeper uncertainty, taking pleasure in the excesses of imagination, echoing again Coleridge's statements on the pathologies of the excessively inward-turning, self-productive manic imagination: "Although our intellect always feels itself urged toward clarity and certainty, our mind still often feels itself attracted to uncertainty. Instead of threading its way with the intellect along the narrow path of philosophical investigation and logical deduction, in order, almost unconsciously, to arrive in strange and unfamiliar territory, it prefers to linger with the imagination in the realm of chance and luck. Instead of being confined, as in the first instance, to meager necessity, it revels here in the wealth of possibilities" (80). Finally, this mania takes us well beyond logic, the empirical world, and reality altogether: "What this feeble light leaves indistinct to the vision, talent must discover, or it must be left to chance. It is therefore again talent, or the favor of fortune, on which we must depend, for lack of objective knowledge . . . talent and genius would act *beyond the law,* and theory would be the opposite of reality" (155–56).

To sum up, then, what we find in these writers is a critical questioning of the points of transit between the empirical world and the interiorizing movements of the subjective imagination. The inward movement, which then articulates a vision of the imagination, can linger too long in the terms of its own making.[15] Strikingly, in a similar movement, for both Coleridge and von Clausewitz the particular effects of a fearsome work of art can result as well in carrying "talent and genius" "beyond the law" of nature. It is now clear how the pathology of the imagination mentioned in Coleridge and von Clausewitz may be linked to the removal of the imagination far away from the empirical world—in its self-generating frenzy, unchecked by the otherness of the external world, the imagination becomes "manic." Add to that the specific element of fear or terror, and we have an unlimited force, a perpetual machine of imagination. It should be obvious how this would link up with the notion of pre-emption, which adds the distinct feature of motivatedness—we wish to imagine terror, for it is a matter of survival, on one hand, and, more importantly and immediately, hegemony. These pathologies may be read psychically and subjectively, but they should be read socially and politically, as well, and it is here that Kant's notion of the aesthetic imagination is crucial.

If for Coleridge and von Clausewitz the countervailing force to the free flight of the imagination is the empirical and rational world, in Kant's treatment of the aesthetic imagination we find the imagination grounded by two elements. First, by a force called "understanding," that is, the conceptual and rational operations of the mind. More important for this essay is the second, which involves an assumed universal common sense, an assumed shared *affect* upon being stimulated by the aesthetic. Not only is the beautiful assumed to register similarly across a universal human category, but this universal affect is best assumed if one stands outside one's subjective position and assumes that of the Other. We would call that "empathy." I will argue that the George W. Bush administration's "Shock and Awe" and the deployment of "empathy" by Robert McNamara (the former U.S. secretary of defense) provide two exemplary instances of the hijacking of the sphere of the imagination. Let me first briefly go through the significance of affect and empathy in Kant's aesthetic.[16]

First, as stated before, the imagination stands in a particular relation to nature: "The imagination (as a productive faculty of cognition) is a powerful agent for creating, as it were, a second nature out of the material supplied to it by nature . . . the material can be borrowed by us from nature in accordance with the law, but be worked up by us into something else—namely, what surpasses nature."[17] In this surpassing of nature, the imagination "spread[s] over a multitude of kindred presentations that arouse more thought than can be expressed in a concept determined by words" (177). "In a word," Kant summarizes, "the aesthetic idea is a representation of the imagination, annexed to a given concept, with which, in the free employment of the imagination, such a multiplicity of partial representations are bound up, that no expression indicating a definite concept can be found in it" (316).

The key question in the *Critique of Judgment* is, however, how would we recognize, how would we know, if what we were experiencing as a beautiful or pleasurable representation of the imagination were shared, verifiable, given the necessary absence of a definite and defining concept? In answering, Kant evokes the second maxim of common human understanding: "to think from the standpoint of every one else"—a man of "enlarged mind" "detaches himself from the subjective personal conditions of his judgment and reflects upon his own judgment from a *universal standpoint* (which he can only determine by shifting his ground to the standpoint of others)" (153).

In turn, Kant resorts to the notion of a *sensus communis,* which is difficult to translate fully but might be called a common sense (*not* "common sense"): "For the principle [of *sensus communis*] while it is only subjective, being yet assumed as a subjectively universal (a necessary idea for every one), could, in what concerns the consensus of differing judging Subjects, demand universal assent like an objective principle, provided we were assure of our subsumption under it being correct. This indeterminate norm of a common sense is as a matter of fact, presupposed by us" (85). As Antoon Van Den Braembussche argues: "Kant tries to construct sensus communis as an operation of reflection which enables us to free ourselves from our own prejudices by comparing 'our own judgment with human reason in general' . . . We compare our judgments not with the actual but rather with the merely possible ones of others in order to put ourselves in the position of everyone else."[18] It is, in short, a particular form of empathy that tries to intuit the universally shared affect of a work of art: "we introduce this fundamental feeling not as a private feeling, but as a public sense." One's disinterested free play of imagination is thus an image of the morally good; the sensus communis is connected to acting in such a way that one's actions can be the basis for a universal order. In short, the private is thus connected to the intersubjective and the public.[19] Taking up these key elements of the aesthetic imagination and its social aspects of community, affect and empathy, the very core of being together via the imagination, we find their perverse appropriation in today's political discourse, and this, I will argue, accounts in no small way for the effectiveness of the propaganda machinery of the state.

How has the security state construed the public? How have policy makers and pundits such as McNamara instrumentalized affect and empathy, and put the imagination to deadly use? In pre-emption, the imagination is retooled to serve a pathological purposefulness that exploits the fearsome elements of an obsessive use of imagination.

Now certainly it might well be said that every war deploys the imagination in just these ways—harnessing the human capacity to envision various future scenarios, and to neutralize potential dangers.[20] In politics in general, affect and empathy have been evoked to sway public opinion. Indeed, in his seminal work of 1922 entitled *Public Opinion,* Walter Lippmann noted in his chapter "The Enlisting of Interest" that "the idea conveyed [by pictures and words] is not fully our own until we have identified ourselves with some aspect of the picture. The identification, or what Vernon Lee has called empathy, may be the most subtle and symbolic."[21] And as for affect, Lippmann writes, "If among a number of people, possessing various tendencies to respond, you can find a stimulus which will arouse the same emotion in many of them, you can substitute it for the original stimuli. If, for example, one man dislikes the League [of Nations], another hates Mr. Wilson, and a third fears labor, you may be able to unite them of you can find some symbol which is the antithesis of all they hate" (132). Thus, in what Lippmann calls "transfer of interest," the shaper of public opinion can find ways to consolidate opinion from diverse populations if he can find a universally affective symbol. Dewey makes similar points in his book *The Public and Its Problems.*[22]

Nevertheless, the recent situation exhibits three rather new characteristics: first, the interpenetration of formerly separate (or more distinct, in any case) spheres, or Habermasian "worlds." If modernity is marked by increased bureaucratization, specialization, and rationalization, and human action parceled out accordingly into these differentiated spheres, then in the United States today, these borders have become extremely porous under the imperatives of our current foreign and domestic antiterrorist policies. This means that the realm of the aesthetic and the imagination is appropriated to the service of the new security state on a scale unheard of previously. Not only does it seem that every facet of human life is touched upon by the imagination, but by a particularly instrumentalized imagination.

Second, this instrumentalized form of the imagination is not only found in texts and documents and policy papers, but now widely dispersed and disseminated extensively by multiple media, including the Internet, and that lends it a particular reality effect. Third, I argue that this brand of the imagination has a particularly distinct feature—its ahistoricity. If before we were used to the rhetorical appeals to the past and traditional values, in today's imagination we have a very singular point of historical reference—September 11—and not much else. That means that the empirical counterweight to the imagination is even more fully absented. That also means that "terror" has but one point of historical reference, and a seemingly unlimited horizon before it.

Consider how this positive capacity of the human imagination is commandeered to the service of efficiently waging war. In Errol Morris's 2003 documentary about Robert McNamara, *The Fog of War,* McNamara's first "lesson" is that we have to empathize: "We must try to put ourselves inside their skin and look at us through their eyes. Just to understand the thoughts that lie behind their decisions and their actions."[23] More specifically, this is geared to waging war in a more efficient manner: "In the Cuban missile crisis, at the end, I think we did put ourselves in the skin of the Soviets. In the case of the Vietnamese, we didn't know them well enough to empathize. And there was total misunderstanding as a result. They believed that we had simply replaced the French as a colonial power, and we were seeking to subject South and North to our colonial interests. And we, we saw Vietnam as an element of the Cold War. Not what they saw it as: a civil war." While several people have commended McNamara's "lesson," arguing that empathy here is meant as a deterrent to war (if we had only understood the Vietnamese as well as we did the Soviets, if we could only have put ourselves in their place), I think that is an overly generous reading. I find in his remarks rather the disingenuous transcoding of the aesthetic imaginary, its deployment in a particularly narrow set of applications in the political imaginary of the modern United States, and a consequent rescripting of the terms of a global community.

Now what does empathy actually mean? The *OED* has it as such: "The power of projecting one's personality into (and so fully comprehending) the object of contemplation."[24] But for McNamara and James G. Blight in their book, *Wilson's Ghost: Reducing the Risk of Conflict, Killing, and Catastrophe in the Twenty-First Century,* this "power" is only useful if strategically deployed to certain ends. They set forth what they call "the empathy imperative": "The West, led by the United States, must seek by all possible means to increase its understanding of the history, culture, religion, motives, and attitudes of those who have declared themselves to be its adversaries. This effort should begin by developing empathy toward the Islamic fundamentalists, specifically those groups allied with, or sympathetic to, the international terrorist network known as al-Qaeda. Empathy does *not* imply sympathy or agreement; it *does* imply curiosity, leading to deeper understanding of an adversary's mindset, as a prerequisite to resolving differences and eliminating threats to peace and security" (234).[25] The slippages here are both obvious and telling, and the imperative to "secure" the nation carries with it the imperative and license to deploy shocking and awful force.

McNamara and Blight then pose and answer the question: "Why empathy? And why now? Because the 9/11 attacks were unanticipated, even *unimaginable,* to Americans before they occurred" (ibid.). In the face of the manifestation of the unimaginable, empathy is marshaled as not only "realistic understanding" (236), but also a "*preemptive* strategy" (237). Importantly,

> we believe it is urgent that the connection be made between the deployment of empathy toward the Great Powers, and toward the Islamic fundamentalists: whereas empathy can and should be deployed pre-

> emptively with the Great Powers to prevent dangerous crises from arising we are, in fact, already in a deep crisis with committed, organized, well-subsidized adversaries whom we do not understand, who appear to be convinced that the United States and the West are responsible for their long and dire list of grievances, and who are actively seeking to acquire weapons of mass destruction, including nuclear weapons—not for deterrence, but for *use* against targets in the United States and the West generally . . . In this case, empathy must be deployed urgently and massively, but not to prevent a crisis. It is too late for that. (237)[26]

The interpenetration of the "applied imagination" and the public sphere is nothing new, nor is the particular enlistment of fields like psychology and anthropology. But, again, what is noteworthy is the appropriation of the aesthetic to both reinforce and mask. This is a more obvious and limited example of the strategic instrumentalization of the aesthetic, empathy, and affect. A more dramatic, massive, and violent case is the one I alluded to at the beginning of this essay, that of "Shock and Awe."

As a doctrine of warfare, this "Shock and Awe" was introduced in a 1996 book by military strategists Harlan K. Ullman and James P. Wade and published by the Command and Control Research Program (CCRP) within the Office of the Assistant Secretary of Defense of the United States. Here is the most germane passage from this text—we can sense the weird and certainly unpremeditated appeal to the aesthetic embedded in it:

> The basis for Rapid Dominance rests in the ability to affect the will, perception, and understanding of the adversary through imposing sufficient Shock and Awe to achieve the necessary political, strategic, and operational goals of the conflict or crisis that led to the use of force. War, of course, in the broadest sense has been characterized by Clausewitz to include substantial elements of "fog, friction, and fear." In the Clausewitzian view, "shock and awe" were necessary effects arising from application of military power and were aimed at destroying the will of an adversary to resist. . . . In Rapid Dominance, the aim of affecting the adversary's will, understanding, and perception through achieving Shock and Awe is multifaceted. To identify and present these facets, we need first to examine the different aspects of and mechanisms by which Shock and Awe affect an adversary.[27]

Now we come to the most explicit appropriation and perversion of Kant's notion of a universal *sensus communis:* "One recalls from old photographs and movie or television screens the comatose and glazed expressions of survivors of the great bombardments of World War I and the attendant horrors and death of trench warfare. These images and expressions of shock transcend race, culture, and history. Indeed, TV coverage of Desert Storm vividly portrayed Iraqi soldiers registering these effects of battlefield Shock and Awe."[28]

According to Gaddis, the deployment of Shock and Awe was multivalent and not limited to enemy soldiers. Indeed, his broad and multiple uses of the terms comes to a point of confusion. After the initial instantiation of shock and awe, there were secondary instances, perpetrated indeed by the enemy itself, but the effect was to be the same—democratization. "The shock and awe that accompanies the invasions of Afghanistan and Iraq were meant to begin the process [of democratization], but Bush and his advisors did not rely solely on military means to sustain its momentum. They expected that September 11 and other terrorist excesses would cause a majority of Muslims to recoil from the extremists among them." But even beyond that, "the president and his advisors seem to have concluded that the shock the United States suffered on September 11 required that shocks be administered in return, not just to the part of the world from which the attack came, but to the international system as a whole . . . Shock therapy would produce a safer, saner world."[29]

At the beginning of this essay, I remarked upon how Shock and Awe instrumentalized the Sublime. Let me return to that concept to comment on Gaddis's seemingly circular descriptions of the phenomena of shock and awe. The Sublime has two facets—first, the encounter with an unrepresentable, unabsorbable force that exceeds one's capacity to master it perceptually or conceptually. Second, and crucially in Kant, there is the reassertion of the ego (individual or national) after its dissolution in the face of power or magnitude. Kant notes, "the feeling of the sublime is a pleasure that only arises indirectly, being brought about by the feeling of a momentary check to the vital forces followed at once by a discharge all the more powerful, and so it is an emotion that seems to be no sport, but dead earnest in the affairs of the imagination" (91).[30] In this regard, what we have historically, then, is the encounter with shock, belittling and humbling force, only to produce the resurgence of force. What is interesting in this last instance is the added combination of psychic and political therapy for an unbalanced world, made possible by this aesthetic and material assault.

What I have been interested in here is not only the retaliatory strategies and tactics of shock and awe which have commandeered the Sublime, but moreover the enlistment of the Beautiful, with its deep connection between private experiences and the acting of the individual toward collective moral good via *sensus communis* and empathy. It is the dynamic between the terrible and legitimized application of material force and broad, often fatal affect that is at work in shock and awe. The very receptivity toward sensation and the capacity to empathize with others is cynically and brutally exploited, and legimitized in the interests of hegemony, that legitmitation of course taking the logic of national security, noblesse obligée, and the imperative to spread democracy. The logic of the immediate post-9/11 United States and the United States' going to war in Iraq is of the same strategic trajectory as the current applications of democratization. And let us not lose sight of the actual material forces needed to achieve such a massive effect: "Late in 2002, the Pentagon built four maintenance hangars at a cost of $2.5 million designed to house as many as sixteen out of the total fleet of twenty-one B-2 Stealth bombers. Along with the B-52s and B-1s, Diego Garcia's [naval communications facility] B-2s led the 'shock and awe' bombing attacks on Baghdad on March 22, 2003, dropping 4,200 pound 'bunker busters' on the essentially undefended city. It was the first time in history that all three types of American long-range strategic bombers targeted the same place at the same time."[31]

We attribute this strategy to the Bush regime, but its specific articulation goes at least as far back as 1937, and it is worth both excavating that history and marking a particularly weird case of instrumental historical amnesia. It was in Spain, in 1937, that we find the first modern instance wherein civilians were deemed proper targets of war—they were given the status of enemy combatants because, in this theorist's mind, their fear would be an effective weapon against their own troops. On April 26, 1937, 100 aircraft of the German Luftwaffe's Legion Condor, under the command of Major General Hugo Sperrle with Lieutenant Colonel Wolfram von Richthofen serving as his chief of staff, conducted a three-hour bombing attack on the city of Guernica, then held by the Loyalist Republican Army. Participating units included Bomber Group K/88, Fighter Group J/88, Experimental Squadron VB/88, and two Italian fighter squadrons.

What does this have to do with the current enactments of "Shock and Awe"? On February 5, 2003, the day that Colin Powell was to appear before the UN Security Council to make the case for a war with Iraq, UN officials had the tapestry reproduction of Picasso's depiction of the bombing in his famous painting, *Guernica,* covered in a blue shroud. UN officials claimed that the (literal) cover-up was simply a matter of creating a more effective backdrop for the television cameras. "When we do have large crowds we put the flags up and the UN logo in front of the tapestry," asserted Stephane Dujarric. *New York Newsday,* however, reported that "Diplomats at the United Nations, speaking on condition they not be named, have been quoted in recent days telling journalists that they believe the United States leaned on UN officials to cover the tapestry, rather than have it in the background while Powell or other U.S. diplomats argued for war on Iraq" (February 6, 2003).

This account is corroborated by Chalmers Johnson, who points out that "[i]n autumn of 2001, Defense Secretary Donald Rumsfeld created within the Pentagon an 'Office of Strategic Influence' with the function of carrying out what defense planners call 'information warfare'—disinformation and propaganda against foreign enemies as well as domestic critics who do not support presidential policies. Only when it became clear that the new office's operations would include funneling false stories to the American news media did Rumsfeld say that it was all a mistake and officially shut the operation down."[32] Johnson continues: "Nonetheless, the idea did not go away . . . on January 27, 2003, the government arranged to have a large blue curtain placed over a tapestry reproduction of Pablo Picasso's *Guernica* hanging near the entrance to the UN Security Council. . . . The government decided that the carnage wrought by aerial bombings was an inappropriate backdrop" (299). Thus, this particular, concrete act of the imagination was not appropriated, but ex-appropriated, erased entirely. What possibilities exist, therefore, to restore or re-invent the imagination outside these circuits of domination and revisionism?[33]

CODA: BACK TO THE FUTURES

John Gaddis ends his assessment of the first Bush II administration with a critical caution: "Some such therapy [shock and awe] was probably necessary in the aftermath of September 11, but the assumption that things would fall neatly into place after the shock was administered was the single greatest misjudgment of the first Bush administration." What the Bush administration should have done, according to Gaddis, was to ask one basic question of the dead—more precisely, of the first practitioner of shock and awe: "What would Bismarck do?" That is, what follows shock and awe? Gaddis then uses Bismarck as an example of someone who, after applying shock and awe, properly embarked on "the careful, patient construction of a new European order."

The move toward patient rationality after furious applications of shock is reflected bizarrely in the Terrorist Futures episode. During his tenure as Under Secretary of Defense, Paul Wolfowitz referred to an act of the imagination that seems to bring this all together—the infamous "terrorist futures market" or, as it was more benignly named, the "Policy Analysis

Market" invented by DARPA (Defense Advanced Research Project Agency). Its premise was that multiple knowledges, manifested in market investments, could best predict the likelihood of acts of terrorism. It was initially heralded by Wolfowitz as "brilliantly *imaginative*." Later, upon public outcry, Wolfowitz conceded that DARPA "got *too* imaginative." We should not be complacent or self-congratulatory about the withdrawal of the program; we would do well to recognize not only just how deep-seated the logic of pre-emption has become, but also how it relies on a self-generating manic imagination that seems to—and I would optimistically underscore "seems to"—it *seems to* have hijacked our notions of the future.

To end on a less depressing note, I want to recall that almost immediately after the news of the Terrorist Futures Market was leaked, both politicians and other public figures responded with such intuitive disgust and horror that the plan was scuttled immediately. Does this mean that some political and social facet of the Kantian *sensus communis* still exists? Despite the hurried rationalizations by both military, administration, Defense Department spokespeople and economists, the "public" had such an automatic and vocal response that the plan was defeated. A small victory, indeed, but one from which we should learn and develop into a politics of the future, fueled by an imagination of another kind of world in which affect is not exploited for the sake of terror, and empathy is directed precisely to reaffirm the possibility for being together in the world.

A second example. After the horrifying photographs of prisoner abuse at Abu Ghraib were made public, the response of some was that the photos were taken "out of context." The images, it was said, were isolated and then compiled in a manner that created the worst possible impression. The most infamous and iconic one was of course the hooded figure standing atop a crate with electrical wires taped to his finger tips. Rationalists said that they were dead wires, and that the guards had simply *suggested* that they might be live and *might* electrocute the prisoner if he moved his arms down. "In reality" it was a harmless set-up. Yet the imagining of the imaging that was set into motion by that suggestion made many viewers ignore "the facts" and see the instance and the image as an index to a larger, systemic, horror, and these rationalizations as beside the point. [34] In this case we have the inverse of the violence-generating deployment of the imagination—we have a positive response to it. We need to discover what, if any, possibilities exist of tapping into this still extant (or residual) form of human community, and ways to nurture other modes of imagining the future.

NOTES

1. This chapter is based on an essay originally written for the 2004 conference "America and the Reshaping of a New World Order" at the University of California, Santa Barbara. Much of that essay was later published as "Pre-emption, Perpetual War, and the Future of the Imagination," *boundary 2* 33, no. 1 (2006). I have added some new thoughts for the current text.

2. Secretary of State Condoleezza Rice, remarks at BBC Today–Chatham House lecture, Ewood Park Blackburn, United Kingdom, March 31, 2006. http://www.state.gov/secretary/rm/2006/63969.htm.

3. In a speech delivered on October 9, 2002, Senator Edward Kennedy drew the distinction between pre-emptive war and preventive war, noting that the Bush administration was deliberately confusing the two: "Traditionally, 'pre-emptive' action refers to times when states react to an imminent threat of attack. For example, when Egyptian and Syrian forces mobilized on Israel's borders in 1967, the threat was obvious and immediate, and Israel felt justified in pre-emptively attacking those forces. The global community is generally tolerant of such actions, since no nation should have to suffer a certain first strike before it has the legitimacy to respond. By contrast, 'preventive' military action refers to strikes that target a country before it has developed a capability that could someday become threatening. Preventive attacks have generally been condemned. For example, the 1941 sneak attack on Pearl Harbor was regarded as a preventive strike by Japan, because the Japanese were seeking to block a planned military buildup by the United States in the Pacific." http://www.antiwar.com/orig/kennedy1.html.

4. Bruce Cumings, *Parallax Visions: Making Sense of American–East Asian Relations at the End of the Century* (Durham, N.C.: Duke University Press, 1999), 205–6.

5. Richard Falk, "The New Bush Doctrine," *The Nation*, July 15, 2002.

6. John Lewis Gaddis, "Grand Strategy in the Second Term," *Foreign Affairs*, January/February 2005. Available at http://www.foreignaffairs.org. In his book *Surprise, Security, and the American Experience* (Cambridge, Mass.: Harvard University Press, 2004), Gaddis traces pre-emptive strategies back to the Monroe Doctrine, and even before that to the pre-emptive invasion of Spanish Florida in 1818 by General Andrew Jackson.

7. Gaddis, "Grand Strategy in the Second Term."

8. For an interesting set of meditations on "shock and awe" during the Iraq war, see Breggie van Eekelen, Jennifer Gonzalez, Bettina Stozer, and Anna Tsing, eds., *Shock and Awe: War on Words.* (Santa Cruz, Calif.: New Pacific Press, 2004).

9. Samuel H. Monk, "The Sublime: Burke's *Enquiry*," in *Romanticism and Consciousness: Essays in Criticism*, ed. Harold Bloom (New York: Norton, 1970), 27.

10. Monk, "The Sublime," 33, quoting Edmund Burke, *A Philosophical Enquiry into the Origin of Our Ideas of the Sublime and the Beautiful* (London, 1759), 2:1.

11. All references to Coleridge come from his *Biographia Literaria*, ed. James Engell and W. Jackson Bate. (Princeton, N.J.: Princeton University Press, 1983). On this subject his most famous comments include the following: "The Imagination . . . I consider either as primary, or secondary. The primary Imagination I hold to be the living Power and prime Agent of all human Perception, and as a repetition in the finite mind of the eternal act of creation in the infinite I AM. The secondary I consider as an echo of the former, co-existing with the conscious will, yet still as identical with the primary in the *kind* of its agency, and differing only in *degree*, and in the *mode* of its operation. It dissolves, diffuses, dissipates,

in order to re-create; or where this process is rendered impossible, yet still at all events it struggles to idealize and unify" (ch. 13, p. 305).

12. In the thirteenth chapter of Coleridge's *Biographia,* Kant is a conspicuous presence, evoked and praised for his application of the "intuitive" art of geometry to philosophy. Coleridge refers to the "Sage of Koenigsberg," his "enlargement" of "the discoveries of geometry to the philosophical subjects" (ch. 13, p. 298). This is "intuitive" rather than "discursive" (i.e., empirical). "Geometry is always and essentially Intuitive" (ch. 10, p. 174, note to epigraph).

13. Coleridge continues, "You may conceive the difference in kind between the Fancy and the Imagination in this way,—that if the check of the senses and the reason were withdrawn, the first would become delirium, and the last mania. The Fancy brings together images which have no connection natural or moral, but are yoked together by the poet by means of some accidental coincidence. . . . The Imagination modified images, and gives unity to variety; it sees all things in one." By a "sort of fusion" it forces "many into one" (ibid.).

14. Karl von Clausewitz, *War, Politics and Power,* trans. Edward Collins. (Chicago: Gateway, 1962), 82.

15. In his essay "The Internalization of Quest-Romance," Harold Bloom remarks on the double-bind of the Romantic poet, compelled away from the social and yet finding himself compelled equally toward a nihilistic inwardness. "The Romantic movement is from nature to the imagination's freedom (sometimes a reluctant freedom), and the imagination's freedom is frequently purgatorial, redemptive in direction but destructive of the social self." The individual ego must thus "search for an anti-self consciousness, a way out of the morass of inwardness." In Bloom, *Romanticism and Consciousness,* 6.

16. One of the chief advocates of American empire today is of course Robert Kagan, whose use of Kant is well known; in arguing for the essentially different positions and worldviews of Europe and the United States, Kagan claims that Europe is "entering a post-historical paradise of peace and relative prosperity, the realization of Kant's 'Perpetual Peace.' The United States, meanwhile, remains mired in history, exercising its power in the anarchic Hobbesian world where international laws and rules are unreliable and where true security and the defense and promotion of a liberal order still depend on the possession and use of military might." Americans "tend toward unilaterialisms" and Europeans "insist they approach problems with greater nuance and sophistication. They try to influence others through subtlety and indirection." America therefore lives in a chaotic Hobbesian world where the raw exercise of power is the only modus operandi (but nonetheless a "behemoth with a conscience"); Europeans are enjoying the peace brought about by U.S. might: "What this means is that although the United States has played the critical role in bringing Europe into this Kantian paradise, and still plays a key role in making that paradise possible, it cannot enter this paradise itself. It mans the walls but cannot walk through the gate. The United States, with all its vast power, remains stuck in history, left to deal with the Saddams and the ayatollahs, the Kim Jong Ils and the Jiang Zemins, leaving the happy benefits to others." Robert Kagan, "Power and Weakness," *Policy Review* 113 (June/July 2002). Kagan later elaborated on these ideas in *Of Paradise and Power: America and Europe in the New World Order* (New York: Knopf, 2003). Yet Etienne Balibar and many others have pointed out how selective and imprecise Kagan's use of Kant is. This fact only goes to support my general claim here—that the neoconservative regime has instrumentalized and colonized all manner of ethical and aesthetic discourse. See Etienne Balibar, "Whose Power? Whose Weakness? On Robert Kagan's Cri-

tique of European Ideology," *Theory and Event* 6, no.4 (2003). http://muse.jhu.edu/journals/theory_and_event/v006/6.4balibar.html.

17. Kant, *The Critique of Judgment,* trans. James Creed Meredith (Oxford: Oxford University Press, 1978), 176. Page numbers in the text refer to this edition.

18. Antoon Van Den Braembussche, "*Sensus communis:* Clarifications of a Kantian Concept." http://home.concepts-ict.nl/~kimmerle/framebraemb.htm.

19. I thank Regenia Gagnier for discussions on the Sublime and Beautiful.

20. There is of course a huge literature on this subject. What is especially fascinating is counterintuitive game strategizing, Nixon's "madman strategy" for instance, or the argument proffered by the military *against* developing a civil defense system (I thank Kenneth Arrow for informing me of the second example).

21. Walter Lippmann, *Public Opinion* (1922; New York: Free Press reprint, 1997), 105.

22. John Dewey, *The Public and Its Problems* (New York: Swallow Press, 1954), 153.

23. *The Fog of War* (2003), dir. Errol Morris.

24. For the aesthetic application of the term, see Rebecca West, *The Strange Necessity* (Garden City, N.Y.: Doubleday, 1928), 102, who remarks on "[t]he active power of empathy which makes the creative artist, or the passive power of empathy which makes the appreciator of art."

25. Robert S. McNamara and James G. Blight, *Wilson's Ghost: Reducing the Risk of Conflict, Killing, and Catastrophe in the 21st Century* (New York: Public Affairs, 2001). Page numbers will be given in the text.

26. The authors also have something to say how this might affect our own universities and colleges: "How does a society close an 'empathy gap' with another, alien, and (at the moment) hostile society—or possibly a cluster of societies? A successful strategy must emphasize the critical significance of an intensified focus on the language, culture, history, religion, and psychology of those who pose the threat. These areas were left to languish in the years following the Cold War era, as such programs were cut in colleges and universities and in the U.S. State Department and Foreign Service as well" (*Wilson's Ghost,* 239). "This time, cultural 'ju-jitsu' [a kind of asymmetrical applied cultural knowledge] and its prerequisite, empathy, must be practiced even by the conventionally powerful if disaster is to be avoided" (239).

27. Harlan K. Ullman and James P. Wade Jr., *Shock and Awe: Achieving Rapid Dominance* (Washington, DC: National Defense University, 1996), 19–20. http://www.dodccrp.org/files/Ullman_Shock.pdf.

28. Ibid., 20. One should note that in 2003, upon the Bush regime's attempt at enacting this doctrine, Ullman wrote an opinion piece in the *Baltimore Sun* (April 1, 2003) chastising the poor performance of the war, calling it "Shock and Awe Lite." It simply did not go as planned: "The aim was to win decisively, rapidly, with little loss of life and limited damage. To achieve that, shock and awe were employed to influence and control an adversary's will and perception and, therefore, behavior. Using all elements of psychological and physical power, the adversary was to be rendered so vulnerable and intimidated by our capabilities that resistance would be regarded as futile. From the outset, military leadership and forces as well as the political levers of power such as Baath Party headquarters were to be hit hard. But there are no guarantees in war."

29. Gaddis, "Grand Strategy in the Second Term," 14.

30. For excellent applications of the Sublime to American nationalist ideology, see Donald Pease, "Sublime Politics," *boundary 2* 3 (spring/fall 1984), and Rob

Wilson, *American Sublime: The Genealogy of a Poetic Genre* (Madison: University of Wisconsin Press, 1991).

31. Chalmers Johnson, Blowback: The Costs and Consequences of American Empire, 2nd ed. (New York: Holt, 2004), 222.

32. Johnson, *Blowback*, 298–99.

33. Indeed, on his Web site the comic book artist and political satirist Tom Tomorrow posted a "restored" image of the event that never took place. Unfortunately, according to the artist that image was made for the occasion; he has since removed it from his site. Readers interested in viewing it may download it from www.stanford.edu/~palboliu/ttomorrow.jpg.

34. See, for example, the documentary *Standard Operating Procedure*, directed by Errol Morris (2008), along with Morris's article, co-written with Philip Gourevitch, "Exposure: The Woman behind the Camera at Abu Ghraib," *The New Yorker*, March 24, 2008. There are of course countless other narratives and reports on the subject.

5. Imaginary Homeland Security

The Internalization of Terror

Simon Ortiz and Gabriele Schwab

It is in the dictator's sensing of people's inner worlds that terror makes nature its ally . . .

MICHAEL TAUSSIG

FRAME

Our piece, "Imaginary Homeland Security" is part of a collaborative book project titled *Children of Fire, Children of Water.* It is composed of a dialogical encounter of memory pieces that speak to each other across our different cultures. These pieces also speak to the present moment from the distance of historical experiences that color what and how we live now, often without conscious awareness. In a sense we are looking at the *New World Order* through the lens of what children call "making strange." Taking the historical event of September 11 out of its context and scripted half-life in the media, we trace aspects of its idiosyncratic, diffuse, and emotionally charged experience. We call our mode of presentation creative non-fiction. Rather than offering a political analysis, we are putting into words a sequence of personal responses that try to retain, even emphasize, the messiness, ambiguity, and, at times, contradictory nature of remembered immediacy. In sending pieces back and forth to each other, we tried to stay open to what they triggered in us and how we impacted each other through shared memories and writings. Weaving a quilt of words and memories, we rely on what happens not only in our individual pieces but also in the space between them. Writing together, we position ourselves differently in a transitional space between cultures and between self and other. We use each other as evocative objects that trigger a memory we could not have recalled in the same way just from within ourselves. In this space, boundaries become fluid, contested, and renegotiated. Affected by each other's stories, our individual memories transform themselves into a new synthetic memory born from crossings between different cultures and communities. We hope our collaboration will evoke our readers' own memory leaps across historical and cultural distance.

I stood very still in the ten o'clock Manhattan night. I had to. I had no choice. Yes, there was traffic and there were people on Broadway; there was city noise. And there was a terrible, terrible anger. O my, what shall we do now? What can we do? They were silenced screams, silenced hollering, silenced keening. They were not the mutants. Can you hear them? They were us. Can you hear us?

September 11, 2001. We buried my mother in a small cemetery in Tiengen, my German hometown, at the exact time of the attacks on the World Trade Center and the Pentagon. On my way to the funeral from Australia to Germany via the U.S., I had contracted such a bad case of food poisoning that I needed to go from the cemetery right into emergency care. When I finally joined my family in a restaurant people broke the news of the attacks on the Twin Towers. Under the strain of converging states of emergency and the fever delirium, my mind drifted into a quiet space far away. I only remember my older son's pale face and eyes of terror as he put his arms around me. In deadly calm I stared at the surreal pictures on the screen, an airplane crashing into the tower, a crumbling building in flames, a body diving from a window, still in mid air when the camera turned.

I didn't feel a thing. While I stood there in serene indifference, the Germans from my hometown already shared memories about the allied bombing of German cities during WWII. I didn't feel a thing until late at night when my son was sitting at my bedside, thinking aloud, agitated, jaws clenched. "What are we gonna do now? This is fuel on Bush's militarism! It will make the whole world change so much for the worse."

That's when my feelings returned, a wave of panic first followed by a familiar sense of terror from a long, long time ago. The images that continued to flicker before us as we talked seemed to come from an imaginary no-man's land. In my dazed mind they merged with other images familiar from my mother's war stories, recounting over and over again the same scenes of the air raids on Freiburg, my family's hometown. I remember as a child almost literally seeing my mother escaping from the cellar of her demolished house, carrying her infant son in a backpack through a city imploding in flames. The story goes that from a few blocks' distance, she watched in disbelief as the house crumbled into ruins before her eyes.

I know that's what my mother would have remembered had she lived but a few days longer to watch the Twin Towers crumble. What a perfect final image it would have been to condense two historical eras in her mind that, as it let go of the world, gradually merged everything, freely dissolving time, mixing together generations, husband and son, children and grandchildren, places and their memories.

Talking to my son through most of the night, I saw myself suspended between two eras, two countries. I belong to neither one, I thought. The one I have disowned, in the other I am a foreigner. When I was born, after World War II, into a family, indeed a people crazed with terror and hunger, and when I finally learned about the Holocaust in my early teens, the sense or illusion of not belonging provided a strategy of psychic survival. Of course, I was not aware of this as a child. But I can detect the mood today and trace where it comes from: this almost instant panic followed by dissociation in the face of terror. "I do not belong here," I think, "it's not my country, not my people, not my family, I'm not part of this war." I felt it as a child; I feel it now.

Then, during the night of September 11, I suddenly awake with a flash of recognition: this mood of mourning, despair, fear, and horror in the wake of the attacks on America's emblems of hegemony, was the closest I have ever come to the mood that pervaded my childhood. It resonated with uncanny familiarity, a deadly logic. I, who always felt uprooted, was after all overcome by a paradoxical sense of belonging, at home in that visceral sense of uprooted disorientation, at home in the very lack of belonging.

Too Late. That's what I felt. It's too late for the USA. The USA lost its chance years ago. In the last century. No, even before that. When it established itself as the United States of America. And even before that when it stole, lied, cheated, and killed so that it could become the USA. It was too late for the liars, thieves, and killers. That's what I felt, and no one could blame me.

That's what a lot of Indigenous people felt, I believe. Too late for forgiveness. Even if the United States of America had asked to be forgiven—which it never really has anyway—no one would have listened.

When the World Trade Center came tumbling down September 11, 2001, because of the jet airliners flown into it, the first thing I thought was "Aakuuh, druutyuyuuh tchuuwaatyuu!" This is an invective remark-expression that loosely but stridently means "Hooray"—spoken vindictively—"now it's your turn to find out what happens!"

What else would you expect me to say? What else could you expect Indigenous people to say? For years, no for generations, the USA and its liars, thieves, and killers have lied, stolen, and killed. What else could any Indian have said? I thought and said what I said spontaneously. And I repeated vengefully, "Aakuuh, druutyuyuuh tchuuwaatyuu." I said it slowly, savoring it in my mind and in my mouth.

And I thought of my late father Joe. Insane with wine and beer, maybe a pint or two of cheap whiskey or vodka in him, my father would rant and rave drunkenly about the hard week he'd just spent with some AT&SFRY railroad section crew replacing iron rails or heavy wooden ties, his hands all torn and his muscles aching so badly only the most rancid terrible tasting and sour gut-churning wine could soothe scorching pain. Hot, hard desert work in Arizona or California keeping the railroads repaired so freight could be shipped efficiently across the country. Everyday that was always the order of the day. Move the automobiles, grains, oil, chemicals, steel, lumber, beef and hogs on the hoof, all kinds of countless merchandise and goods for the department stores and supermarkets across the country. Vast stores of the USA moved through the Acoma Pueblo Reservation! All the merchandise—plunder!—shipped by railroad freight from East to West Coast and vice versa daily through the reservation in freight carload after freight carload. Daily, daily, daily. Freight car after freight car after freight car. And the men of the Pueblo, men like my father, worked to maintain the railroad tracks so that the USA could move its merchandise plunder across the country from one coast to the other. And all the cities, towns, villages in between.

I remember our family going on Sundays to the railroad station in Grants, the nearby border town, when my father returned to the railroad section crew. He would be gone for another week or perhaps two weeks or more. Or for who knew how long. Things always felt indefinite and undetermined. I always felt fearful because it was uncertain if he would return. And because he was an alcoholic, he was prone to erratic and unpredictable behavior that was not only dysfunctional but also made his family dysfunctional.

Generations and years sweeping upon us suddenly like flood tide, that's what life felt like at times.

When my father spoke about hard labor work for the railroad, you had to believe him. There was no way you could think of the railroad and trains that went through the Acoma Pueblo Indian reservation without thinking how much the Mericano railroads had changed our lives! You could not help but know the World Trade Center was a force in that change!

There is no way I can know what it's like. I've never lived through any of it. Yet my whole life has been shaped by the War, its aftermath, its psychic fallout. Secondhand emotions placed into me by a mother who, insane with terror and grief, needed to expel her own feelings. Yet the terror was real, the grief was real, and so was the trauma, secondhand or not. And today, again, there is no way I can know what it's like. Again, I receive terror through secondhand images or emotions. We tend to de-realize the images of war before they can hijack our feelings. We return to our lives, never mind that they will never be the same.

I had such difficulties writing these pieces and think it was because it is hard to access the wide range of confused and overdetermined feelings. In the face of terror or terrorism our feelings never seem quite adequate. We let our unconscious surprise us with raw emotions. Dissociation. Paralyzing fear or blind rage.

When Simon first shared his vengeful reaction to September 11, I was startled. I tried to argue with his feelings. Simon suggested we integrate my reaction. Here is what I wrote: "Reading *Too Late,* I felt startled, our responses being so radically different. I remember my sinking feeling back in Germany that now the U.S. government has the perfect excuse to use September 11 to take away the inroads we have made over the last decades in fighting for civil rights and social justice." I thought of the people who died in the Twin Towers or planes, many of them just simple workers. I felt the attack would be a disaster for immigrants and indigenous people alike, that it would increase racism, xenophobia, and paranoia in the U.S. and strengthen the right wing fundamentalists. While I could see that for the first time the U.S. had to face the kind of violence it never had any qualms about dealing out to other peoples, I nonetheless was convinced that September 11 would only increase the violence and lead to the killing of more and more people. After all, it was my mother's war stories that turned me into a radical pacifist before I even knew what that could mean.

So my reaction was despair. We are in this together, whether we like it or not. Forgiveness and revenge seem too narrow to grasp the magnitude of the event. Of course, it was an act of revenge or what Chalmers Johnson calls "blowback," the unintended consequence of empire. But the attack on the World Trade Center did not help the people in Afghanistan or Iraq, nor did it help the indigenous people in the Americas or anybody else but militaristic governments, war profiteering corporations and power elites.

Looking back at my response in light of my feelings about my own country of origin, I realize, however, that I would never have challenged anybody who felt vengeful about a similar attack on an icon of Nazi Germany. And yet, at the same time I count the air raids by the Allied Forces on German cities and civilian populations and the bombing of

Hiroshima among the terrifying atrocities of war. Our feelings in the face of terror never seem quite adequate or conflict-free or simply tall enough.

The mind is stunned stark.

At night,
Africa is the horizon.

The cots of the hospital
are not part of the dream.

Lie awake, afraid.
Thinned breath.

Was it a scream again?
  Far
below, far below,
the basement speaks
for Africa, Saigon, Sand Creek.

Souls gather
around campfires.
Hills protect them.

Mercenaries gamble
for odds.
  They'll never know.
Indians stalk beyond the dike,
Carefully measure the distance,
count their bullets.

Stark, I said,
stunned night in the VAH.[1]

So this is what it comes to. So this is where you end up. Maybe not the end of the line but close to it. Yeah. Not even ten years after the military. That's why you're here. Because you're qualified. Because you're eligible!

1966 to 1974. Eight years, not ten years. So fucking what? So who's counting? A fucking sick drunk all shaky wobbly and blue, hoo man, just look at you. You can't even think.

Yeah, all I could do was keep notes mentally. Remember. Remember, I tell myself. Waiting to be processed into the hospital. I didn't know what was going to happen. I was just there. Fort Lyons Veterans Hospital. Fuck. Oh fuck. Fort Fucking Lyons VAH. Processing into the rehab ward.

Yeah, Big Joe and Fabian had taken me up there and now they were leav-

ing me fucking there. Fort Fucking Lyons Veterans Administration Hospital! Man o man. What was I doing there? I didn't belong there. Shit, I didn't even have any money for cigarettes. There was nobody else around but us Indians in that little cement room with ugly gray-green painted walls and little windows way high up on one wall. No cigarettes, no money, no shit, no chance, no nothing.

You'll be okay, bud, Fabian says.

Yeah? I say, nodding my head. Yeah, he says.

I look at Big Joe. They said they'd bring you a tray of food, he says.

That's okay, I say, I'm not hungry.

I am feeling sick, fucking sick, my stomach, head, eyes, my thighs shaking, oh shit, shit, shit, damn, even my toes shaking! And aching!

We better get going, Joe says to Fabian.

And Fabian nods, Yeah.

And Puts his hand on my shoulder.

He says, I know how it feels, pal, I know how it feels.

I look at him, then look away at the ugly gray-green wall.

I feel like shit, I say, that's how I feel, like I'm in hell. Shit! You must feel like shit then.

And Fabian laughs. And Big Joe smiles and stands before me. He says, Hahtruudzaimeh, Dyuumu. Be a man.

And Big Joe shakes my hand.

I can barely lift my hand. Why the hell were they leaving me here? Why the hell they bring me all the way up here? Geesuz, I wished I had a drink. I haven't had a drink since sometime yesterday. Or the day before. Or when was it I last had a drink? Vodka or whatever the shit I was drinking. One last drink before you leave me, please! I'll be okay then.

My stomach is turning and my intestines are strangling me and I'm gonna die and you don't give a shit. That's what I'm thinking as Big Joe and Fabian walk out the door, out of that ugly gray-green painted room. O shit, I might as well die, I say to them but they're gone already. So I say to the door, Just tell the folks back home I went to hell.

After her life was shaped by two World Wars, my mother couldn't have chosen a more dramatic time for its ending. Born in 1918, the year World War I ended that took her father's life, she was barely twenty-one when Hitler started World War II. Her older brother was killed on the front lines during the first weeks of the war. A few years later, my mother gave birth to her first son during an air raid in the basement of a hospital. She had just been released from the hospital when another air raid destroyed her family home. My mother escaped, carrying her baby through the town's smoldering ruins. Yet after inhaling the toxic smoke of burning houses, he slowly died of smoke poisoning, alone and in excruciating pain in a hospital filled with wounded and dying soldiers. On special leave from the armament factory where he oversaw French prisoners of war, my father returned to bury his son. During curfew, he rode with my mother though the city's blackout, transporting his child's coffin on a bike to a small village where they had found refuge. The funeral took place during another air raid. My mother had never wanted a war baby.

THEY STARTED YET ANOTHER WAR[2]

Today they bombed Iraq again.
I had a vision of you, mother
running through war-torn streets
with your infant son
choking on smoke and fear.

You had barely survived
his birth in a musty cellar
below the eye of an air raid,
his first scream drowning
in howling sirens,
and the exploding thuds
of bombs.

I thought of you,
dying slowly,
dying lonely,
brother I never knew
but was meant to replace
in a world all crazed,
pushing back
against the war.

Welcome to this brutal world,
this baptism of fire
killing you silently,
lungs black,
body in pain,
poisoned by smoke,
the fallout of war.

As they lowered your coffin
Bombs ripped up the earth
Again.
Our mother buried her grief.
Our mother buried her soul

I thought of you,
dying slowly,
dying lonely,
mother I knew too well
yet never knew at all
in a world all crazed,
pushing back
against the war.

When I was born after the war, my family was in the throws of starvation. While diffuse and evanescent, my memories of the first years of my life are intensely sensuous. I recall our house filled with extended grief, terror, and—as I understood only much later—barely acknowledged shame and guilt. Belonging to a perpetrator nation made it hard to mourn one's losses . . . as if one had deserved them after all. For years, my parents and grandmother would spend their evenings going through rituals of telling and retelling the same war stories. I heard them over and over again until the day I last saw my mother. Emerging from these stories rather than a visceral first-hand experience, the horrors of war began to form my imaginary worlds. My inner life is built on war stories. I knew about German children whose bodies had been torn apart by bombs and Japanese children whose eyeballs had melted before I was old enough to go to school. Yet until my teens I didn't hear a word about the Jewish children who died in the camps and gas chambers. I used to have recurring nightmares about bomb attacks or an invasion of Russian soldiers. The images were always the same: I am running through thick smoke, our town on fire, my eyes burning, flames catching up behind me. We grew up with the fear that a new world war with another nuclear bomb could materialize any day. I was determined to hide out in the nearby forest until the war was over. I thought I could survive living on berries and leaves. My first paintings show burning houses and people fleeing the city.

So that's what I told myself because I didn't have any paper or pencil or anything to keep notes with. Keep notes mentally. Remember everything.

Nineteen seventy four AD. 1974 AD. That's what I put down in my memory. I even pictured myself jotting it down with my shaky hand. November 1974.

I had just got fired from IAIA in Santa Fe. Yeah. For drinking and acting crazy and messing around with pretty girls and organizing students against the IAIA school administration and talking and teaching Indian power in class. And drinking some more. And consorting with students. Yeah. One of the faculty administrators even said, You're the teacher. You can't drink with students. Okay, I said, and had a party that night. Incorrigible? No, I was mad. The Bureau of Indian Affairs had fucked up Indian people's lives! And it deserved to be organized against by Indian people. And I was smoking too although dope made me sleepy and slow and slurry. I made it back home somehow. To the reservation, I mean. Hell if I know how, I just did. So Now?

So now I lie down on hard cement floor because I can't stand sitting on the hard plastic chair anymore. I just lie flat out on my back staring at the ceiling. But not for long because a guy walks into the ugly gray-green room. Big, husky, white guy wearing a black leather jacket and motorcycle gear. He stands just inside the door looking down at me laid out flat on the floor. I looked into his hard white and scruffy bearded face. And I waved with my right hand without raising my arm. He nodded and said something with a grunt. And I said, Yeah, with a grunt too although I don't know what the hell he said. He sat down on one of the plastic chairs and took a cigarette from a pack in his pocket. Dh shit, a cigarette, I thought, maybe he's got an extra one. And I rolled over and struggled to get on my feet and nearly fell trying to stand up. Dh shit, mother fucking, I can't even stand, I muttered. Take it easy, Chief, the motorcycle guy said. Be happy. We're in the bosom of the beast.

September 11, 1973. The day the Chilean military orchestrated a CIA supported *coup d'état* in Chile, killing President Allende and replacing him with Pinochet who would soon become one of the century's worst dictators. I still lived in Germany then. We went back into the streets to protest. Two of my best friends, the indigenous Chilean artist Catalina Parra and her husband, the poet and literary critic Ronald Kay, had recently moved back to Chile. I was afraid they were in danger. A group of students-and faculty mobilized to bring political refugees from Chile to the university of Constance. Catalina and Ronald, however, decided to stay in Santiago. There, Catalina began to document Chile's brutal political upheaval and state terrorism in her art, mainly collages that included news photographs of street violence. Catalina stitched the photos into her paintings, stitched up torn bodies, stitched silenced history back into the picture with thin white thread.

As soon as I began working with Chilean refugees, I was put under surveillance. Each time I used the phone I could hear the familiar click indicating that my phone was tapped. Angrily I used to interrupt my conversation to address the invisible spy directly. The infamous lustration laws *(Berufsverbot)*, designed to establish Germany's own homeland security after the sixties revolution, were firmly in place by then. Prohibiting the employment of left activists in state institutions, these laws forced many of the movement's active people out of schools and universities. But they were also responsible for the firing of postal officers or gravediggers—all state employees—because they had once joined a leftist organization or signed a petition in support of the revolutionary struggle. When I received an offer as an assistant professor at the university of Constance, I was screened intensely but cleared after several months of investigation. The paranoid system of state control and surveillance with its inflammatory rhetoric of good and evil and its public legislation of patriotic feelings radicalized the scene. Four years later Germany witnessed the rise of its own wave of homegrown terrorism.

September 11, 1977. My first son was born during the so-called German Autumn. In 1977, members of the RAF, Germany's Legendary Red Army Faction, kidnapped the chief executive of Daimler Benz, Hans Martin Schleyer. A child's pram with hidden weapons was pushed into the street to block Schleyer's car. During the subsequent terrorist search, a veritable hysteria ensued that turned all mothers with babies as well as pregnant women into potential suspects. Konstanz became a heavily patrolled border town, and I was not only visibly pregnant but also still looking like a sixties student, often wearing colorful headscarves that the German police falsely associated with the ones worn by Muslim women. To make matters worse, my husband at the time wore long dark hair and drove a Citroen DS, the large French model favored by terrorists. For a while I was stopped, searched, and interrogated on an almost-weekly basis. A few months before my son's birth, a policeman stopped us on campus, made us get out of the car and ordered us to put our hands up. As I stood spread-eagled, he came from behind, touching my belly. "What do you have here, a little terrorist?" he asked. I felt violated and helpless, hiding under my calm an unfathomable fear for my unborn baby and his father. Seeing the rage in my husband's eyes, I silently repeated a mantra: "Oh please, let him not lose his temper, let him keep quiet." It was not my first encounter with police brutality.

Events escalated when four hijackers forced a Lufthansa Jet to land in Mogadishu. On October 18, a week before my son was born, German commandos stormed the plane and, in response, the RAF executed Schleyer. The scandal at Stammheim followed with the alleged collective suicide of the imprisoned RAF members. This mood of the time colors the memories of my son's birth. It came back to my mind when, nearly a quarter of a century later, he was released from jail after being arrested during the IMF/World Bank demonstrations in Washington. This is where he had his own encounter with police brutality. Upon his arrest, the police sprayed pepper spray directly into his eyes. They also severely bruised his wrists by deliberately narrowing the grip of plastic handcuffs. For months afterwards, his hands were still getting numb occasionally. He had complained to the police that the handcuffs cut off his circulation, but they had waited until his hands were blue and he nearly fainted from excruciating pain. After about thirty hours of detention without food or water, and without having been granted his legal phone call or access to a lawyer, he was released, yet left with a sense of defeat. The worst thing, he said, was to see how easy it is to break your spirit of resilience when you are in pain, under threat, in isolation, and tortured by hunger and thirst. All he wanted was for it to be over.

My son was thirteen years old when he took part in another demonstration, his first. It was to oppose the United States declaration of war against Iraq, the Persian Gulf War. When he came home he wrote this poem:

YELLOW BLISS[3]

Looking out at the world through rain-speckled sunglasses
feeling a rush of blue as a yellow ribbon
zooms past a deadening message on a street corner war sign.
A dry-cleaned American flag
waves in the exhaust of a Porsche.
This war may be over

But who knows when you're neurotic.
When the desert screams
when voices that care clean out your head
when over the denseness of a city
a relentless storm pounds the troops
who are victoriously fading into yellow bliss,
then heatrock eyes can look at the world
and say
it's over.

I wonder how Lori Piestewa's two young kids are? Are they at one of the Hopi mesas in Arizona? Or at Tuba City, a Navajo-Hopi town nearby? Where are they? Who's taking care of them since their mother is gone, since she was killed last year during the U.S. invasion of Iraq? She was one of the U.S. Army troops of the invading and colonizing force. The occupying force, the "liberating" force, whatever name you want to call U.S. imperialism. Lori was only twenty-three years old, I think. She had joined the U.S. Army for training she hoped to receive which would make it possible to support herself, her children, and to help her Hopi people.

Growing up in an Indian family and community, you're always told you are "to help." You are always one of us. You are always one of our people. You are nothing but one of us. Your mother, grandma, your father, and sisters and brothers. Your aunties and their children, all your relatives, you are one with them. They love you, they want you to be safe, they want you to come home safely. I know that's what her folks said to her. All your relations care for you. Probably even the Army recruiter who talked Lori into joining up used words like that. Over the years, especially since the Vietnam war, recruiters have become slick, cagey, persuasive types, trying to get you into their clutches. Using the tactic of "learning military skills you can use to your benefit in civilian life." After the Vietnam war, there has been no military draft so military recruiters have resorted to selling military training as good for you. I wonder what they said about the fact Lori Piestewa was a young Hopi mother of two very young children? They probably said nothing. They probably didn't even care. She was just a body.

When I was in the U.S. Army in the early 1960s I knew a Hopi man who was a U.S. Army chaplain. True, that's true. Even though it may sound incongruous—or ironic?—that Native people are in the U.S. military. What? The same U.S. military that fought the Apaches, Cheyennes, Navajos, Lakota Sioux, Seminoles? The same military that massacred Indigenous people at Wounded Knee, Washita, Sand Creek? Yeah, the very same one. I was in the U.S. Army from 1963 to 1966, yep, right during the Vietnam War. But I lucked out and didn't get sent to Vietnam since it was just starting to get heavy when I was discharged. And how about the Hopi chaplain, how long was he in the military. As a chaplain for a U.S. Army Air Defense (Hawk) Battalion at Fort Bliss, Texas, he was a major when I knew him; later I heard he became a colonel, so that means he served some years. And I heard he was sent to Vietnam. I remember him vividly though because he was a clog in the works at Fort Bliss. I mean he used to piss off the conservative soldiers, mostly white guys, because he spoke about peace, justice, and racial equality. The air defense soldiers used to grumble that he was a commie. While the Hopi major didn't outright preach against the U.S. military presence in Vietnam, he was close enough to make some guys notice. Some of them were more than a bit nervous about this Indian talking like that. I remember that.

So how does this work out? How does such a thing come about? Is it an incongruity or what? Here we have three Indigenous soldiers, Indian soldiers. Me, Lori Piestewa, and the Hopi chaplain. We were all in the U.S. Army. And this is all within the historical context of the USA where Indian people have been faced by the USA as a colonial and imperial power. Not only since 1776, not only in the nineteenth century, not only in the twentieth century, but right now! Indian people have been part of the fray since the beginning of European invasion and occupation of the Americas. And they have "served" in the national wars since then, especially since the beginning of the twentieth century. World War I, World War II, the Korean War, the Vietnam War, and countless little wars, military actions, too many to keep track of. How does that correlate with the fact that the USA and its military might have been the enemy of Indians and yet Indians have served it as regular and conscripted soldiers? And how does that work out with the federal legislation and edicts facilitated-implemented by Homeland Security and PATRIOT Act laws. Does an explanation of how it works out make Lori Piestewa's children feel any better about losing their mother violently because she was part of an invading United States military force in Iraq? Does that explain the Hopi chaplain wearing the uniform of the U.S. Army that was also occupying Vietnam while he spoke about peace, justice, and equality. Does an explanation of "how it works out" make me feel any better about my own service in the U.S. military?

When I was fourteen, I had a crush on a seventeen-year-old boy whom I had known since childhood. During long walks through the Black Forest with my dog, we used to raise all the existential questions we could think of, exploring mortality and the likelihood of an afterlife, the reasons for human cruelty and war, the impossibility to imagine eternity, or life on other planets. Once, when I was eleven, he dared me to walk though the old cemetery at night, telling me that those buried *with* crimes in their souls hovered as ghosts above their graves. He also claimed the devil appeared in the flesh to get the living who dared to walk the cemetery. I had to prove not only my courage but also the fact that I didn't believe in the devil anymore.

Our friendship changed abruptly when we saw *Hiroshima mon amour* together and he revealed that he wanted to join the air force in order to become a pilot. We got into a terrible argument. Didn't he see what war did to people? How could he ever think of being part of it? During those hours my feelings for him vanished. I fell out of teenage love and there was nothing I could do about it. I sometimes wonder what happened then.

All I remember is a sense of panic listening to him while he argued for the necessity to defend one's country in case of an attack. I tried to convince him it was screwed logic. Neither of us gave an inch. It scared the hell out of me to see feelings disappear irrevocably in a flash.

Later, for the politicized sixties generation in Germany, it was almost unthinkable to serve in the military. The Nazi legacy weighed too heavily. There was a mandatory draft for men, but many became conscientious objectors. It was not easy. My brother's case was denied with the argument that his plea was too well thought through to be believable. He appealed and I had to appear in court as his character witness. I was so furious I angrily blasted the system that—in a country whose military had been involved in a genocide but two decades earlier—even dared to question a well-thought-through stance against participation *in* warfare. The case went through and my brother was ordered to do two years of civil service in a drug rehab center. That's where he became a drug addict. It ruined his life. He didn't go to the military but to prison for two years for selling dope to his friends.

When I hear today's arguments for reinstating the draft in the U.S., I think in horror of my two sons. I would do anything to prevent them from going into the military, let alone a war. But I also fear the militarization on home ground in the name of homeland security. A chilling memory emerges of Germany's own movement for "homeland security" by the Buergerwehr, a volunteer Civil Guard. The setting is Konstanz again, this old historical town at the border of Switzerland. In the seventies, it hosted one of the first open-air concerts in Germany, a small-town Woodstock of sorts. Young hippies with long hair, sleeping bags, guitars and hash pipes came from all over Germany. The local movie-theater still played *Easy Rider.* The next day, in the early morning sun, everybody lingered on park and city benches, playing music, talking and smoking. The city looked colorful and came alive with youthful energy. This is when a member of the *Buergerwehr,* the voluntary Civil Guard, emerged with a rifle proclaiming he was going to shoot himself a hippie. His four-year-old son came running after him, crying "Don't do it, Daddy, don't do it!" The father proceeded in cold blood and shot one of the young men through the heart. The eighteen-year-old died on the spot.

In court, the unrepentant man described the murder as an act of self-defense. Character witnesses testified to his integrity and service to the city. Among those testifying were the parents of the murdered child. They said they couldn't blame the murderer. Their son had it coming; they had told him all along to cut his hair and stop hanging out with the hippies.

The murderer was put on probation on account of acting in self-defense. He felt that the city was endangered by a horde of hippies that were, after all, no better than the gypsies. Homeland security was restored.

Probably,
they didn't know
that walls would be constructed,
that wars were to make
these men possible.
That there
would be a time
when eyes would grow shallow,
when bones were to be broken
when eardrums would be shattered,
and the final atomic waste swept
into piles and used
to estimate futures.
But then, they did not think,
they would have survived
if they did not know arrogance
and would have to share reports
of history which now rise
before us as mutant generations.

We are mutants already. It's too late. There was this tall, muscular staff sergeant in basic training. Lean, white, narrow-hipped, a loud growly voice. Mean, deadly face, flinty eyes. And he was always yelling at this German-American draftee from Chicago. Joaquim was his name I think. Heavy German accent when he talked English. Little thin guy. "You can't talk English, you damm mother fucking kraut!" the sergeant would holler. "You talk American English, goddamm you, not that German Deutsch shit!" Joaquim was always beside me and I could feel him cringe and tremble. I trembled and cringed too. Sometimes I could barely help myself from lunging at the sadistic sergeant but he, at six foot four, would have easily killed both me and Joaquim. So we would just cringe.

We have barely buried our dead. Over three thousand who died was it? The dust barely settled and the smoke not even cleared away.

Just over two years later, I walked south on lower Broadway. Past the empty space fenced off a block and half away. I was just going to walk past grimly. On the way back to my hotel. I had just done a poetry reading from my new book Out There Somewhere at the American Indian Community

House at 708 Broadway. My chin held level, my face immobile, aware that my body was insignificant and tired. But I couldn't stand it. I had to stop. Earlier that day I had come through airport security. Airport security in Toronto and La Guardia, and I would have to go through it again going the other way. Coming and going, coming and going. You have no goddamn chance or choice anymore. If you ever did. I hate the nervous tension, the anxiety, the wordless fear confusing the travelers. The random searches, the wary calculating eyes trained on you. I'm dark, I'm Indian, I'm one of them! Oh shit. Watch out for those savages! I couldn't help it; I couldn't help myself; I couldn't help but hear them. I had to stop and listen. They were silent screams. And angry hollering. And a keening, keening. Oh my, is it me or is it them? Sorrow? Sorrow, was it? I stood very still in the ten o'clock Manhattan night. I had to. I had no choice. Yes, there was traffic and there were people on Broadway; there was city noise. And there was a terrible, terrible anger. Oh my, what shall we do now? What can we do? They were silenced screams, silenced hollering, silenced keening. They were not the mutants. Can you hear them? They were us. Can you hear us?

NOTES

EPIGRAPH: Michael Taussig, *Shamanism, Colonialism, and the Wild Man: A Study in Terror and Healing* (Chicago: University of Chicago Press, 1987), 6.

1. Simon J. Ortiz, *From Sand Creek* (Tucson: University of Arizona Press, 2000).
2. Written on my birthday, March 20, 2003.
3. Manuel Schwab, "Yellow Bliss," in *Journal of the Gulf War: Poetry from Home*, ed. Michael Logue, John Penner, Meg Reed, and Tina Rinaldi (Fullerton, Calif.: Poets Reading Inc., 1991) p. 58. Reprinted with permission of the author.

6. From Ronald Reagan to George W. Bush

What Happened to American Civil Religion?

Wade Clark Roof

The Reagan presidency marked the beginning of a resurgence of national religious rhetoric, quite distinctive in style and content. It carried over into the presidency of George Herbert Walker Bush and later resurfaced after the Clinton years even more stridently during George W. Bush's terms in office. Invoking biblical symbols and myths, this "religion of the nation" was noisy and combative, and in this latter period was voiced by figures in the highest echelons of the American government as well as by religious leaders; indeed, the period was characterized by a close alignment of conservative evangelical Christian faith and politics, and manifest both domestically and internationally. If, as Benedict Anderson says, a country can be thought of as an "imagined community," then during this period the United States reimagined itself and its role within the world.[1] And critical to this process of reimagining was a fused religio-political rhetoric reflective of the times.

If we think of religio-political rhetoric as a cultural repertoire of myths, symbols, rituals, stories, and texts that can be selectively drawn upon, then this period offers an opportunity for examining significant shifts in national religious language emanating from the White House. As is widely known, Robert N. Bellah's classic essay "Civil Religion in America" described how critical moments in the nation's history combined with the pivotal role of presidents had shaped its mythological content.[2] Soon thereafter, during the Vietnam War and the Watergate crisis, he came to view such rhetoric as having become little more than an "empty and broken shell."[3] And now, looking back over this entire period of more than forty years, we gain perspective on the broader course of rhetorical development. Against the backdrop of the civil religion Bellah had so elegantly described and saw arising out of the nation's struggles over a period of two hundred years drawing upon biblical narrative and symbol, what are we to make of the quality of religio-political rhetoric of the post-1980s period? In effect, what happened to civil religion as it had once been understood?

In approaching this question, I focus in this chapter particularly on the national myths invoked during this period—from the time of the Cold War with the Soviet Union to the post-9/11 mobilization against Islamic terrorists and the Iraq war. Myths are the means by which a nation affirms its deepest identities and frames its rationale for political action; they are the elementary, yet profound stories giving meaning and purpose to the collective life of a people; they evoke the imagination, so crucial to national self-understanding. Functioning largely at the unconscious level in the minds of citizens, they are activated though ritual, and particularly during times of national threat—indeed, as historian Richard T. Hughes points out, in such moments myths are easily absolutized, or turned into hardened, reified realities taken to be literally true.[4] In this essay I argue that some grasp of America's national myths and their reification is essential to understanding not just the resurgence of nationalistic religious rhetoric but also the country's domestic and foreign policy during this recent period. Because myths give direction and legitimacy to social identity and action, they are the powerful constructs around which national ideologies are formed.

My analysis draws upon yet differs in its scope and emphasis from that put forth by Roberta L. Coles in her excellent essay on American presidential rhetoric.[5] Rather than focus upon Manifest Destiny as the central theme as she does, I examine the particular myths resurfacing in this rhetoric and what they reveal about American identity, themes quite discernible in statements by all four presidents during this period but most especially by the three Republicans. As such, the doctrine of Manifest Destiny is not one of the foundational myths of the United States but is instead a composite drawing upon several myths—in particular, the myths of Chosen Nation, Nature's Nation, and Millennial Nation. The myth of a Chosen Nation arises out of the Hebrew Bible and suggests that Americans are exceptional in having a covenant with God: they are the New Israel in the language of the early Puritans. A second myth of origin—Nature's Nation—emerging out of the Enlightenment and Deism gave rise to the notion that the United States was an extension of the natural order, and that the country reflects the way God had intended things to be from the beginning of time. Building upon both of these foundational myths, the Millennial Nation implies that God chose America to bless the nations of the world with the unfolding of a golden age. The latter two are obviously complementary: one looking to the beginning of time, the other looking to the end of time. Focusing upon these particular myths, how they are used, by whom, and in what circumstances, we gain insight into the shifting styles of religio-political rhetoric and their meanings. Hence the task in this essay is twofold: first, to sort out these mythic themes relating especially to war and the role of the United States globally; and second, to offer commentary on how this rhetoric resonates with the broader religious and political shifts within the United States over the past quarter-century, and what all this might imply for conceptualizing civil religion.

RONALD REAGAN AND RELIGIOUS RHETORIC

Ronald Reagan stepped onto the national stage at a propitious moment. The country was mired in an energy crisis, with Americans facing long gas lines and double-digit mortgage rates. President Jimmy Carter was an easy target for blame. Carter's presidency had also raised expectations among religious conservatives that the country would become more aligned with traditional religious and moral values. These expectations were fueled by a growing fundamentalist and evangelical wing of American religion at the time—a backlash in religious mood in response to the youth culture of the 1960s and early 1970s, and more specifically the 1962 decision banning organized prayer in public schools and the 1973 Supreme Court *Roe v Wade* decision that guaranteed the right to an abortion. Despite Carter's being a "born-again" Southern Baptist, his moderate religious views and failure to endorse positions of the Reverend Jerry Falwell, and after 1979 those of Falwell's newly organized Moral Majority and other conservative organizations such as Christian Voice and Religious Roundtable, led many to become disenchanted with him. Reagan emerged as the leader who would ride the crest of dissatisfaction on the part of a growing majority of white evangelical Protestants especially, one who could truly advance a social conservative agenda. His leadership meshed well, too, with worries about the country's diminished power abroad and fear that the Soviet Union had achieved military superiority over the United States. More than just the Vietnam debacle, there was the Arab oil boycott, the Iran hostage crisis, and other international setbacks all having deeply eroded American national pride and reputation. Thus both domestic and global concerns sparked a new level of aggressive political involvement on the part of the Religious Right, bringing together many evangelical Protestants, traditional Catholics, and Orthodox Jews.

Given this religio-political context, Reagan's use of sacred symbols and mythic themes was reassuring and hopeful for the future: "America was weak and freedom everywhere was under siege," he would later say in 1988, speaking as a national hero describing the situation when he took office and indicating who turned the country around.[6] Without calling it as such, he made use of the myth of the Chosen Nation, thereby restoring pride and a sense of superiority to people who felt that something had gone wrong with the country. Time and time again in his speeches Reagan defined the nation's identity by making use of this mythic framework. For example: "If you take away the belief in a greater future, you cannot explain America—that we're a people who believed in a promised land; we were a people who believed we were chosen by God to create a greater world."[7] In reaching out to religious conservatives often he juxtaposed highly charged national symbols. In his well-known 1983 speech to the National Association of Evangelicals, he cited a long list of ills facing the country—abortion, illegitimate births, the possible loss of parental rights, the banning of prayer in public schools, modern-day secularism—and then appealed to his audience to join him in the "struggle between right and wrong, and good and evil" and in believing that "freedom prospers only when the blessings of God are avidly sought and humbly accepted."[8] Phrases like these galvanized public support by effectively conflating notions of God, country, freedom, and goodness. In asking Americans to "join him" in these crusades, he created close, if fictive, bonds with his audiences, inspiring them to align themselves with a moral vision of God-fearing individuals who lived in a very special and blessed country. Blurring distinctions between public and private faith, his rhetoric had the effect of tapping deeply-felt sentiments that religion had lost its presence within the public arena and should be restored.

He made effective use as well of the other two primal myths—Nature's Nation and Millennial Nation—and again, did so with words and symbols meaningful to ordinary people. According to the myth of Nature's Nation, because the country and its way of life, including democracy and capitalism, is rooted in the design of nature, then it is unique among countries by being above the plane of ordinary history; and if removed from the vicissitudes of history, then America is good and innocent in a manner unmatched by other nations. Closely aligned with this myth was the notion that America is ever evolving, unlimited in its possibilities as long as freedom is maintained. "The calendar can't measure America because we were meant to be an endless experiment in freedom, with no limit to our reaches, no boundaries to what we can do, no end point to our hopes," Reagan said in 1987, which captures well what lies at the heart of the myth of Nature's Nation.[9] Implicit was the assumption that the American people and their social and political institutions are ordained by Divine Providence by virtue of their special creation as God's people, unlike others in the world but who may yearn for freedom.

Similarly, the myth of the Millennial Nation locates the nation outside of ordinary time, but at the end of history rather than at its beginning. It envisions America in a leadership role within the world, and which in time will usher in the final golden age giving the entire world what the United States uniquely has to offer—"freedom, democracy and human dignity for all mankind," as he said in 1984.[10] Reagan was most passionate and articulate—some would say eloquent—when projecting a millennial vision of America within the world. In that same address to the National Association of Evangelicals in 1983, which perhaps more than any other speech outlined a comprehensive moral agenda for his presidency, he spoke of keeping "alight the torch of freedom" around the world, of preserving "peace through strength," and of defending the nation against the "aggressive impulses of an evil empire."[11] Though he spoke of an evil empire on other occasions, nowhere was this phrase used more effectively than with this audience, who, hearing him would immediately couch its meaning in theological terms. He was skillful with generic symbols—such as the "shining city upon a hill" adapted from the early Puritan John Winthrop, who, in Reagan's words was "an early freedom man"—capturing in the same sentence the attention of *both* religious audiences and those who were less religious, even secular-minded but deeply patriotic and freedom-loving. His public oratory in fact often blurred perceptions of his own personal faith and practice; although perceived as deeply religious, he was not a churchgoing man. In 1985, the sociologists N. J. Demerath III and Rhys H. Williams commented as follows:

> In many ways, Reagan is a prototype of the secularizing although not fully secularized person. With only vague denominational ties, his own religious practices are unclear and unintimidating. . . . Some on the Religious Right are unsure if he is born again. According to others, he may be the least personally religious president in recent memory, and one for whom religion could be almost entirely a matter of form without function. . . . In a secularizing America, a vote for Reagan may have become the political equivalent of attending church only on Christmas and Easter.[12]

Reagan brought Americans together less because of his visible religiosity than through his appeal to generalized mythic realities, and particularly when he described the United States as a God-fearing nation locked in a struggle with atheistic Communism. As the sociologist Neil J.

Smelser has convincingly argued, fear of an external threat in a setting where God and country were closely aligned reinforced a Manichean-type morality, or tendency to frame conflicts with other nations as essentially a struggle of "good" versus "evil."[13] In this instance it evoked a deep sense of "nationalism-patriotism," or pride in and defense of what was understood to be genuinely American, as opposed to anything that might appear "un-American." Such language was not new in American history, but Reagan as an actor and orator especially understood the power of words and symbols and used them effectively for political purposes.

"FREEDOM"—A PIVOTAL THEME

Freedom, or liberty, is the most cited sacred symbol in all the presidential speeches surveyed in this essay. It is the keystone around which political and religious visions come together. Not surprisingly, the Berkeley linguist George Lakoff singles it out in his analysis of ideological "framing" in the book *Whose Freedom? The Battle over America's Most Important Idea.*[14] By "framing" he means mental structures that shape how we view and understand the world, a picture of how things are, or should be, that we construct. In 1988, for example, Reagan spoke of "the love of freedom that God places in each of us and whose defense He has entrusted in a special way to this nation."[15] The frame connects God to freedom, and defending the latter to the nation, thus pulling all four into a composite picture. Or cast in the terms of this present essay, framing is the means by which the three myths we are examining—Chosen People, Nature's Nation, and Millennial Nation—come together describing, more or less, what America is about, at home and abroad. For political conservatives in particular, no other word evokes as much patriotic emotion as does the notion of freedom today precisely because its meaning is linked to these mythic realities.

Preserving and extending freedom is the rationale often put forward for why America must be militarily strong and maintain a powerful role in a world threatened by tyranny. In 1991, President George Herbert Walker Bush announced the National Day of Prayer for Operation Desert Storm as follows: "As one nation under God, we Americans are deeply mindful of both our dependence on the Almighty and our obligation as a people. . . . Entrusted with the holy gift of freedom and allowed to prosper in its great light, we have a responsibility . . . to use our strength and resources to help those suffering in the darkness of tyranny and repression."[16]

Here the customary "one nation under God" phrase, added to the Pledge of Allegiance during the Cold War years of the 1950s, is set forth as the fundamental premise of civil religious faith. Because Americans are chosen by God, in the spirit of a covenant they must uphold its obligations. What they must respect above all else is the "holy gift of freedom." Because freedom arose out of the natural order, it is the state of being that was originally intended by the Creator, an entitlement owing to the laws of nature and of nature's God. For Bush, as was the case for Reagan before him, freedom is prized not just for its own sake but because it yields valuable rewards—most notably, economic prosperity. Hence the free-enterprise system is not an arbitrarily constructed economic system, but instead one that springs out of freedom as the natural condition of mankind. Not surprisingly, then, there would be a "timeless yearning to be free" as President Bush asserted when speaking to the troops in Saudi Arabia in 1990.[17] In the late nineteenth and early twentieth centuries it had been the immigrant masses entering the United States that had yearned to be free, according to popular myth, but with the collapse of the Soviet Union such yearning now extended to those in the world who were suffering from the "darkness of tyranny and repression," and presumably wanted to be liberated. America's experience of being free and making freedom possible for others thus was a plan for the entire world.

This extension in rhetoric about people generally yearning to be free reflected both the changing world conditions at the end of the Cold War and American renewed hopes. Unhampered by dictators and state-dominated economics, people were now free to pursue their dreams, so the American myth would have it. Commentators and politicians alike predicted the embrace of democracy and capitalism on the part of countries that had once been in the Soviet orbit. This expectation was intensified by a millennial mentality: atheistic ideology was collapsing, belief in God and the embrace of freedom would naturally follow. Reagan had envisioned this restoration of democracy, but President George Herbert Walker Bush could now point more concretely to its realization. "Today," he proclaimed in 1991, "a transformed Europe stands closer than ever before to its free and democratic destiny." The new world order was not only emerging, it had America's strong stamp upon it. He elaborated:

> This order gains its mission and shape not just from shared interests, but from shared ideals. And the ideals that have spawned new freedoms throughout the world have received their boldest and clearest expression in our great country the United States. Never before has the world looked more to the American example. Never before have so many millions drawn hope from the American idea.[18]

Given that freedom and prosperity are rooted in the natural order and should be yearned for by all mankind, it is but a short leap to the millennial vision in its strongest expression: America had a divine mission to lead in bringing these ideals to quick fruition. At times the rationale expressed was that the United States had a role to help those suffering in the darkness of tyranny and repression, the assumption being that people would naturally respond favorably to a more democratic order; other times the argument was that freedom and prosperity would inevitably follow because people elsewhere greatly admired, or would soon come to admire, America as an example of democracy.

Clinton made less use of freedom rhetoric, and when he did his focus was more on the domestic scene. In his first inaugural address in 1993 he spoke of "our democracy" as "the engine of our own renewal," emphasizing that "we need each other" and that we "build that America, a nation ever moving forward realizing the full potential of all its citizens."[19] His millennial vision was that of the United States addressing inequality among its citizens and building social institutions to meet all their needs. Earlier, when giving his acceptance speech at the Democratic National Convention in July 1992, he had called upon the nation to enter into a "New Covenant," drawing on a major civil religious symbol, which he defined as "a solemn agreement between the people and the government, based not simply on what each of us can take, but on what all of us must give to the nation."[20] Greatly influenced by President John F. Kennedy, he sought to rekindle a style of patriotism that would orient energies and commitments toward building a better country. Clinton identified the United States with people "building" democracy and freedom elsewhere in the world, saying it was this nation's cause as well, but rather vaguely and implying more the importance of solidarity among peoples in a common cause of humanity than as a reason for American intervention.

Clinton's style stands in marked contrast, of course, to George W. Bush, who has spoken most fervently about America's mission to carry freedom to the world, especially so after September 11, 2001. Extending freedom to Iraq would become the cause on which he would stake his legacy; in his second inaugural address in 2005, for example, he invoked the words "freedom," "free," and "liberty" forty-nine times.[21] Exactly how or when freedom is sufficiently established was left somewhat open-ended. The logic generally was that American effort is necessary for initiating a process of political change, but that freedom would only come when people in Iraq themselves championed this noble cause. No president in the past half-century has become so deeply enmeshed in a global mission resting on so precarious a set of assumptions, rooted as the Iraq invasion was on some presumed affinity between America's millennial role and optimistic belief in a predestined political outcome. As the president said in 2003: "The advance of freedom is the calling of our time; it is the calling of our country . . . we believe that liberty is in the design of nature; we believe that liberty is the direction of history."[22]

In this speech to the National Endowment for Democracy, President Bush buttressed his confidence in a triumphant outcome by calling attention to the number of democratic countries in the world that had increased in the years since the Reagan presidency. But it is not exactly clear how this count was made or what criteria were used in defining a democratic country. What he seemed sure of was that the United States was at the forefront of this march toward freedom, and that its drumbeats were being heard around the world. He went further to clarify why he thought American-style democracy had and should continue to have great global influence: "It is no accident that the rise of so many democracies took place in a time when the world's most influential nation was itself a democracy. . . . Freedom honors and unleashes human creativity and creativity determines the strength and wealth of nations. Liberty is both the Plan of Heaven for humanity and the best hope for progress here on Earth."

Nations of the world differ but "people everywhere, from all walks of life, from all religions," the president said, "prefer freedom to violence and terror." People at times may be unable to act on this preference at present because the world is temporarily locked in a conflict between the "enemies of freedom" and the inevitable "force of freedom," but freedom would inevitably occur, especially he emphasized if the United States stood firm in its appointed role as "the heirs of the tradition of liberty." Despite much struggle, suffering, and setbacks in the moment, ultimate success was assured for two reasons, each voiced at differing times. First, "freedom and fear, justice and cruelty, have always been at war, and we know that God is not neutral between them," he stated in 2001, implying that the divine plan will necessarily work out.[23] Second, "because of who we are—because even when it is hard," he later said in 2004, "Americans always do what is right."[24] God's plan for global freedom and the nation's righteousness are explicitly conflated, perhaps the most staggering of all his claims arising out of American mythology. President Bush sometimes referred to God, sometimes to the somewhat more inclusive conception of the Almighty when describing this struggle for freedom, but most often to such related mythic realities as "the force of freedom," "liberty," "progress," hope," "Americans' righteous causes," "prosperity," "the Plan of Heaven," all intended to make the point that the nation's mission is indeed God's mission.

PRIESTLY AND PROPHETIC ROLES

A distinction is often drawn between priestly and prophetic uses of civil religious rhetoric, to which we now turn. Priestly rhetoric blesses America as a chosen nation with a special mission to fulfill and legitimates its actions. It is the dominant chord in the civil religious chorus historically within the United States. Prophetic rhetoric, in contrast, deemphasizes notions of chosenness and uniqueness and, at its best, calls the country into question when it fails to live up to its own ethical ideals.

Clearly, both the forty-first and forty-third presidents—the two Bushes—operated more in the priestly style, speaking of the nation's duties to carry freedom and democracy abroad, stressing the leadership qualities of the United States, and frequently invoking the banner of the Almighty in support of these causes. President George H. W. Bush acted priestly in 1990 during the Gulf War when he requested "that in churches . . . prayers be said for those who are committed to protect American interests." His candid acknowledgement of protecting American interests as a reason for prayer was unusually explicit; more typically, presidents have used their office to invoke blessings generally upon the country and its military forces in times of war.

President Clinton also drew upon the "chosen nation" and "promised land" myths during the Kosovo years. But as Roberta L. Coles points out, he often connected these myths with the task of building a nation "where our children can grow up safe from the shadows of intolerance and oppression."[25] Compared with President Bush before him, he offered a more balanced perspective on the role of the United States in the world, often pointing to its responsibilities as a superpower in relation to other countries. In 1999, Clinton said, "Because of the dramatic increase in our own prosperity and confidence in this, the longest peacetime economic expansion in our history, the United States has the opportunity and, I would argue, the solemn responsibility to shape a more peaceful, prosperous, democratic world in the 21st century."[26] He looked upon the United States' as that of being a good model of democracy and responsibility, linking this to the country's fortunate economic prosperity. On occasion he engaged more directly in national self-critique and reflection: he called attention to the United States, for example, as having fallen short of its promise to work toward being more perfect, and in one of his most pointed statements, urged that "if we want to be a force for good abroad, we must be good at home."[27] Comparing Clinton and the first Bush, Coles quite correctly observes that "while Bush presents America as a shining example, Clinton, in his more humble style, presents a slightly tarnished example that nevertheless elicits the admiration of others."[28]

Clinton advanced the idea that the nation was bound by a compact, and in so doing sought to diffuse social and ideological cleavages, both within the country and those separating the United States from other nations. In this respect he drew upon a political theology that envisioned opportunity and responsibility as integrally related. Civil religion's symbols and values provided a basis for prodding the country, not just blessing it or presuming God's favoritism.[29] Consequently, he tended not to make claims about the country's innocence and exceptional righteousness, choosing instead to emphasize that the United States could lead in modeling democracy only if it embodied the ideals for which it stood. While his was not a prophetic vision in any strong sense, he did make Americans think about who they "were" as a nation as compared to what they "could be." And consequently, Clinton's appeal was primarily to moderate-minded, socially responsible Americans open to reason and who would embrace a political theology merging, as commentator Steven Waldman says, "the stern rhetoric of conservatism with the generosity of liberalism."[30]

In comparison, George W. Bush envisioned much more clearly an "us" versus "them" world in which good and righteous Americans struggled against evil-doers who hate the freedom, democracy, and values for which the United States stands. His Manichean rhetoric was enhanced after the attacks on the World Trade Center and the Pentagon. Fears intensified about the likelihood of continued globally organized terrorism within the United States at the hands of radical Muslims and possibly other non-Western religious groups (such as Sikhs and Hindus), as well. With this stronger identification of an enemy there was a resurfacing of the nation's myths of innocence and goodness, not all that surprising in a moment of "cultural trauma," as Smelser has described it.[31] The attacks aroused a righteous defensiveness reinforced, as he says, by a strong sense of religious "chosenness." Given the nation's identity, so deeply rooted in Judeo-Christian myths, any attack on American soil from the outside would likely be seen as an attack not just upon the nation's fundamental political, economic, moral, and religious values and institutions, but upon divine purpose itself. The attacks therefore resulted in calls for immediate and strong action, unilateral if necessary, to assert both the nation's military superiority and, in a broader sense, its alignment with divine purpose.

Thus the stage was set for Bush's fervent and continued invoking of mythic rhetoric in support of military intervention in Iraq during his last six years in office. Beginning with his State of the Union address in 2003 he proclaimed that "free people will set the course of history," and that the United States and its freedom-loving allies would inevitably define the world's future. He acknowledged that this course of history might not seem obvious in the short term and that some people would envision other outcomes, but in the long run its direction was assured. Later, in 2003, and speaking very much in a priestly mode about the suffering and sacrifice the country had endured, he declared that "since America put out the fires of September the 11th, and mourned our dead, and went to war, history has taken a different turn."[32] By doing what was right and taking swift political and military action in a cause sanctioned by God, history was put back on its proper course. Much the same logic lay behind the decision for a pre-emptive war against Iraq: the idea that short-lived suffering and tragedy were unavoidable but success would follow. Advancing freedom abroad, the president also argued, required that Americans maintain "security at home." At times the emphasis in his speeches was upon the inevitable triumph of divine purpose, other times it was about the necessity of Americans showing responsibility to the world and to God by maintaining national security. Belief in the innocence and goodness of the United States over against the "axis of evil"—Iraq, North Korea, and Iran—justified a strong defense while at the same time meshed well with a millennial vision. These themes are obviously similar to those of President Reagan two decades earlier, with radical Islamic terrorists having replaced the Communists as the evil-doers.

Bush's perspective broke significantly with Clinton's on the nature of American destiny as well, as Coles makes clear.[33] If Bush saw the United States at the helm of history and destined to prevail ultimately in its mission, Bill Clinton offered a much more cautious, less arrogant perspective. Speaking in 1999, he had the following to say with regard to America's dominance in the world: "Destiny . . . is what people make for themselves, with a decent respect for the legitimate interests and rights of others. . . . [We] have to act responsibly, recognizing this unique and, if history is any guide, fleeting position the United States now enjoys of remarkable military, political, and economic influence."[34] Clinton interpreted "destiny" as a product of a nation's own actions as just or unjust, and therefore offered a prophetic commentary whereas Bush saw himself as the high priest presiding over a divine design.

REFLECTIONS

So what are we to make of all this? For Robert Bellah, American civil religion affirmed a transcendent order expressed through myth, symbol, story, and practice that was capable, at least potentially, of holding the nation to a higher moral principle. That is, it could critique the nation functioning in a prophetic, and not just a priestly manner, the most cited example being Abraham Lincoln's creative use of religious language during the Civil War when he spoke of "an almost chosen people."[35] But the line between prophetic critique and the idolatrous worship of the nation itself is easily blurred. Bellah noted that the dangers of distortion are particularly acute and threaten to undermine American civil religion's power of critique particularly when its myths, beliefs, and symbols are marshaled to legitimate actions against other countries for selfish political and economic interests. He worried about "fundamentalist ossification," or religious language interpreted literally, and the likelihood of civil religious beliefs and myths becoming little more than a "cloak for petty interests and ugly passions."[36] The description fits much of the presidential rhetoric described here, especially the absolutizing of American myths, or the tendency to turn these powerfully evocative and evaluative ideals into self-righteous justifications for the country's actions within the world. In this respect the country's religio-political rhetoric in the post–September 11 period took on the appearance more of a flaunted religious nationalism than of a civil religion of the sort that Bellah portrayed.

But the issue is complex and questions have long been raised about the very concept of an American civil religion itself. Several matters arising out of the analysis of myth and rhetoric examined here bear upon this larger debate.

To begin with, we should keep in mind, as Phillip E. Hammond points out, that civil religion is "a construct, not an objective thing."[37] From a Durkheimian perspective, the constituent elements of a sacred symbolic system are present within society, but how to describe it is disputed. Various constructions are placed upon the same or similar realities within the United States—religion-in-general, civic piety, religion of the republic, the American Way of Life, political religion, civil religion, and religious nationalism, to cite only the most prominent. These all capture some aspect of a historically complex religio-political culture, each more or less appropriate to a particular historical situation and on occasion more prophetic than in other times. Moreover, like the ever-changing configurations of a kaleidoscope, the narration of the country's myths, beliefs, symbols, stories, and rituals varies over time in tone and style. We can go further and say that the social functions of this narration have differed as well: on occasion, a particular interpretation has fulfilled the collective function of locating the country in a broadly defined transcendent order, combining both prophetic and priestly roles; yet on other occasions, and the immediate past is certainly one of these occasions, the breadth of civil religious interpretation, even the grasp of what constitutes the "civil" aspects of such a belief system, is sacrificed in the interest of more narrowly defined national goals. If the Vietnam War was a "time of trial" for American civil religion, as Bellah argued in 1967, major developments since that time—the nation's enhanced religious pluralism, conservative religious and political upsurge, the collapse of Communism, globalization and a changing world order, and most recently, confrontations with Islamic terrorism—have all helped to shatter anything approaching a cohesive and widely accepted set of civil religious beliefs, symbols, narratives, and rituals within the country.

Related, too, is whether Bellah's conception of civil religion itself reflected a "consensus" perspective emphasizing a particular style of Judeo-Christian normative culture that emerged in the mid-twentieth century. His vision was shaped by biblical symbols and mythic themes resonating with an earlier Protestant establishment, but interpreted broadly to accommodate Catholics and Jews and in keeping with the reigning religio-political beliefs and values at the time. The sociologist Rhys H. Williams quite correctly observes that "many versions of civil religion are forms of, or at least remnants of, Protestant—specifically Puritan—religious hegemony."[38] Today's more conservative evangelical Christian, hegemonic-aspiring religious culture shares some of the same themes but gives them a more narrow, absolutist interpretation. But neither Bellah's culturally assimilated model nor the more fragmented constructions are politically or ideologically free. Nor does his formulation adequately take into consideration the extent to which civil-religious prophetic versus priestly elements in any historical period are contested. American national faith might be thought of as a cultural resource which at any given time is forged through contested appropriations of particular myths, beliefs, symbols, stories, and ritual practices. Its discursive elements are amorphous and multivalent, subject to the motives and manipulations of the interpreters vying with one another. Thus approaching the construction of national religious meaning in this more open, competitive manner, we avoid the assumption of a singular, widely accepted and historically normative version, and call attention instead, and quite appropriately to its fluid qualities.

We should also distinguish between "public religion" and "civil religion." Whereas this latter conveys an image of a watered-down religious unity, the former signals the fact that various religious constituencies seek to advance a collective story for the nation, that in a diverse society groups compete with one another trying to establish a hegemonic interpretation of God and country. The sociologist Robert Wuthnow, for example, argues that the United States is deeply polarized ideologically in visions of public faith, conservative and liberal, each trying to make a persuasive case for its views.[39] Since the 1970s especially, conservatives have succeeded in gaining sufficient influence and political power to implement their vision (not without internal struggles, of course, within that constituency); not surprisingly, they present their vision as a civil religion for the nation when in fact it is but one, though strong, religio-political ideology. Popular religious movements historically have sought to mobilize the public with hegemonic goals in mind, and today's special-purpose organizations representing a wide range of religious and political ideologies engage in such efforts, often with much success. The role of such groups today in mobilizing public constituencies drawing upon mythic conceptions of the country should not be underestimated. Mounting broadly based appeals by means of mass mailings, media advertising, the Internet, and political action committees, conservatives select biblical texts and beliefs as claims for support of particular national myths. This allows them, for example, to reimagine the nation's Founding Fathers as faithful Christians, or to create a "chain of memory" essential to ordering what is actually a far more diverse American religious history.[40] They are superbly skilled in forging legitimating myths for the nation-privileging themes of freedom, democracy, and free enterprise. A sectarian religious perspective framed as "faith" over against "non-faith," it might be said, has achieved majority status; that is, evangelicalism as a "public faith," variously defined around one or another social issue, now exercises considerable influence over views about national identity and purpose.

Other considerations, too, help to account for the success of these grassroots movements. Over the past quarter-century, and owing in no small part to the skilled leadership of special purpose and para-church groups, symbolic resources have come to be recognized as highly significant, manipulative weapons in the culture wars. Public religious movements often play down differences separating Protestants, Catholics, Jews, and even Buddhists, Hindus, and Muslims, emphasizing instead highly charged, unifying symbols such as "family values" and "common values." Religious conservatives in a more diverse religious era have learned how to expand their sphere of influence by gaining support from those sharing a common ideology *across* old-style religious divisions. Computerized profiles on hundred of thousands of Americans allow groups to target potential similar-minded audiences on a scale that is unprecedented. Unlike reliance upon coalitions among groups for extending social and political influence as was often the case in earlier times, this new technology allows for widespread, popular appeal to what are now openly called "values voters." In effect, in an age of organizational innovation and of course cyberspace, new symbolically charged constituencies are easily created in support of causes.

Presidential personalities, values, and scripted rhetoric too are critically important in a media age. The Clinton presidency intervening between the two Bush administrations makes the point. Clinton's softer and more compassionate style demonstrated that much depends on the "interpretive frame" a president brings to the office and how religious faith is envisioned and projected into the political process. Overall, with the succession of presidents covered in this essay we witnessed recognizable shifts in national vision and narrative, illustrating the larger point of this discussion: the discursive elements of the civil religious heritage are selectively drawn upon to tell the story of the nation. In a country where, as the political scientist Alan Wolfe says, people "cannot make up their minds whether religion is primarily private, public, or some uneasy combination of the two," such ambiguity opens the way for presidents and other political and religious leaders with affable personalities and good oratory skills—Reagan and Clinton, and more recently Obama, as very prominent examples—to galvanize considerable public support around their own mythic visions of the country and its values and purpose.[41]

ABSOLUTIZED MYTHS

George W. Bush's connection with the public rested neither upon his exceptional personality nor his oratory skills. Rather, the president and his neoconservative advisers were skillful in responding to and legitimating a grassroots movement of "public faith" blending religious and political goals. They capitalized upon an evolving realignment of religion and politics that began with Reagan: in the early 1980s evangelical Christians were just beginning to switch party loyalties from Democrat to Republican; years later they would identify as Republican in much larger numbers (56 to 27 percent, according to a Pew Research Center survey conducted in July 2003). For this and other reasons described above, Bush was able to position himself publicly as an evangelical Christian president in a way that neither

Reagan nor Carter could. A triumphal tone was evident in his inauguration in January 2001, when Americans across the country heard the new president's Methodist pastor from Texas close the benediction by saying his was a "humble prayer in the name that's above all names, Jesus the Christ. Let all who agree say, Amen." The second inaugural, in 2005, was more respectful of other faiths, though it still privileged the president's evangelical faith. On this occasion the same pastor closed the benediction saying, "respecting persons of all faiths, I humbly submit this prayer in the name of Jesus Christ. Amen." Such careful orchestration of rhetoric and symbols for the purpose of infusing sectarian faith into a national ritual signals just how politicized American presidential inaugurations had become.

No occupant in the White House in memory has so publicly meshed national political ideals with a personal, highly particularistic religious conviction as has George W. Bush. Even before announcing his candidacy for the presidency, he supposedly confided to fellow believers he thought God wanted him to be president.[42] After becoming president, it is claimed that he viewed himself as "owing" God his service and looked upon his reelection in 2004 as a sign that he was divinely appointed to carry on an aggressive foreign policy against radical Islamic terrorists.[43] "His rhetoric has come close to justifying United States policy in explicitly religious terms," writes former Secretary of State Madeleine Albright.[44] So close an affinity of the beliefs and actions of an American president with the presumed will of God—in effect, claims of a divine plot of war played out on the global stage—is at best unsettling to imagine, and at worst an arrogant instance of an absolutized millennial myth with potential cataclysmic consequences. Commenting on the impact of Bush's faith on foreign policy, John B. Judis writes:

> What sets this president off from some of his more illustrious predecessors is that in making foreign policy—a task that requires an empirical assessment of means and ends—he has been guided both by the objectives of Protestant millennialism and by the mentality it has spawned. That has made for some stirring oratory, but it has detracted from a clear understanding of the challenges facing the United States.[45]

When myths are absolutized, people are blinded to social realities and lose their power to critique that which they are caught up in believing. As Reinhold Niebuhr once observed, there is "the ironic tendency of virtues to turn into vices when too complacently relied upon."[46] Civil religious symbolism takes on the colors of its national environment, but should the latter overtake the former the potency of the prophetic component is undermined and what emerges looks more like religious nationalism. Critical in all its varied historic expressions is how the nation's defining myths are used: if these evoke national ideals in a manner unfettered by selfish interests, that most fundamental of American civil religious visions—unity amidst the plurality of faiths—is honored. But it was this very vision of course that was threatened, and which calls us as social scientists and citizens to reimagine national faith in its more balanced, priestly-versus-prophetic expression.

NOTES

I wish to thank Nathalie Caron at the University of Paris 12 for helpful comments on an earlier version of this chapter. This chapter expands upon original remarks presented at the conference "America and the Reshaping of a New World Order" at the University of California, Santa Barbara, in April 2004. Portions were published as "American Presidential Rhetoric from Ronald Reagan to George W. Bush: Another Look at Civil Religion," *Social Compass* 56 (2009): 286–301.

1. Benedict Anderson, *Imagined Communities: Reflections on the Origin and Spread of Nationalism* (London: Verso, 1983).
2. Robert N. Bellah, "Civil Religion in America," *Daedalus* 96, no.1 (1967): 1–21.
3. Robert N. Bellah, *The Broken Covenant* (New York: Seabury Press, 1975).
4. Richard T. Hughes, *Myths Americans Live By* (Urbana: University of Illinois Press, 2003).
5. Roberta L. Coles, "Manifest Destiny Adapted for 1990's War Discourse: Mission and Destiny," *Sociology of Religion* 63, no. 4 (2002): 403–26.
6. Ronald Reagan, "Annual Message to the Congress on the State of the Union, January 25, 1988."
7. Reagan, "Our Noble Vision," speech, March 2, 1984.
8. Reagan, speech, March 8, 1983.
9. Reagan, speech, July 3, 1987.
10. Reagan, speech, March 2, 1984.
11. Reagan, speech, March 8, 1983.
12. N.J. Demerath III and Rhys H. Williams, "Civil Religion in an Uncivil Society," *Annals of the Academy of Political and Social Science* 480 (July 1985): 162–63.
13. Neil J. Smelser, "September 11, 2001, as Cultural Trauma," in *Cultural Trauma and Collective Identity*, ed. Jeffrey C. Alexander, Ron Eyerman, Bernard Giesen, Neil J. Smelser, and Piotr Sztompka (Berkeley and Los Angeles: University of California Press, 2004), 276.
14. George Lakoff, *Whose Freedom? The Battle over America's Most Important Idea* (New York: Farrar, Straus and Giroux, 2006).
15. Reagan, State of the Union speech, 1988.
16. George H.W. Bush, *Weekly Compilation of Presidential Documents* 27, nos. 1–9 (1991):1–2.
17. George H.W. Bush, quoted in *The New York Times*, August 9, 1990.
18. George H.W. Bush, *Vital Speeches of the Day* 57, May 15, 1991.

19. William J. Clinton, First Inaugural Address, January 21, 1993.
20. William J. Clinton, "A Vision for America: A New Covenant," speech, July 16, 1992.
21. George W. Bush, Second Inaugural Address, January 20, 2005.
22. George W. Bush, speech at the National Endowment for Democracy, November 18, 2003.
23. George W. Bush, speech, September 20, 2001.
24. George W. Bush, speech, February 4, 2004.
25. Coles, "Manifest Destiny," 414.
26. William J. Clinton, *Weekly Compilation of Presidential Documents* 35, nos. 1–22 (1999): 1–1188.
27. Clinton, *Weekly Compilation of Presidential Documents* 35 (1999): 353.
28. Coles, "Manifest Destiny," 414.
29. Jonathan A. Sarna, "Forum: American Civil Religion Revisited," *Religion and American Culture* (winter 1994): 19–23.
30. Steven Waldman, *The Bill: Legislation Rally Becomes Law in a Case Study of the National Service Bill* (New York: Viking Press, 1996), 5.
31. Smelser, "September 11, 2001, as Cultural Trauma," 276.
32. Bush, National Endowment for Democracy Speech, 2003.
33. Coles, "Manifest Destiny," 419.
34. Clinton, *Weekly Compilation of Presidential Documents* 35 (1999): 1–1188.
35. Bellah, "Civil Religion in America," 19.
36. Ibid., 18–19.
37. Phillip E. Hammond, "Civil Religion," in *Contemporary American Religion,* vol. 1, ed. Wade Clark Roof (New York: Macmillan, 2000), 133.
38. Rhys H. Williams, "Public Religion and Hegemony: Contesting the Language of the Common Good", in *The Power of Religious Publics: Staking Claims in American Society,* ed. William H. Swatos and James K. Wellman. Jr. (Westport, Conn.: Praeger, 1999), 175.
39. Robert Wuthnow, *The Restructuring of American Religion: Society and Faith since World War II* (Princeton, N.U.: Princeton University Press, 1988), 241–67.
40. Danièle Hervieu-Léger, *La Religion pour Mémoire* (Paris: Editions du Cerf., 1993).
41. Alan Wolfe, "Judging the President," in *What's God Got to Do with the American Experiment?* ed. E. J. Dionne and John J. Dilulio Jr. (Washington, D.C.: Brookings Institution Press, 2000), 90.
42. Richard Land, comment on NBC's *Meet the Press,* March 27, 2005.
43. Seymour M. Hersh, "Up in the Air," *The New Yorker,* December 5, 2005.
44. Madeleine Albright, *The Mighty and the Almighty* (New York: HarperCollins, 2006), 160.
45. John B. Judis, "The Authority of Liberty," *Dissent* (fall 2005): 61.
46. Reinhold Niebuhr, *The Irony of American History* (New York: Scribner's, 1962), 133; see also Hughes, *Myths Americans Live By,* 5.

7. Why America Has Been the Target for Religious Terror

Mark Juergensmeyer

The global post–Cold War encounter between religious and secular politics was characterized by a strident anti-Americanism that developed in the last decades of the twentieth century and continued into the twenty first. The political and economic might of the United States became regarded as the source of problems both local and large. In this essay I want to explore some of the reasons why this was the case—in addition to the obvious explanation, that American foreign policy had become arrogant and provocative, especially after September 11, 2001.[1] But even before then the United States was regarded as the source of an oppressive secular political ideology that elicited religious as well as political responses.

In some instances European powers were also targets of animosity, indicating that a revived anticolonialism was part of the picture. In Algeria, for instance, France became the focus of religious violence soon after the Algerian elections were abandoned in 1991. Though supporters of the country's Islamic Salvation Front were angry about the military coup that terminated the election process just when it seemed that the militant Muslim parties were on the brink of success, the wrath of many of the activists turned to their old colonial regime. The French government had supported the military coup, but more to the point, it was regarded as responsible for setting up the Western-style secular government in Algeria in the first place. Hence a series of terrorist acts rocked the streets and subway system of Paris in protest. The Algerian activists regarded the French rejection of Islamic politics as resistance to what they regarded as the "march of history" away from Western-dominated society to ones based on indigenous cultures.[2] In their eyes, history was advancing toward a world filled with religiously oriented nations.

The 1990s constituted a decade of social dissent linked with religions of various kinds: Christianity, Judaism, Sikhism, and Buddhism, as well as Islam of both Sunni and Shi'ite varieties. America was regarded as the fount of secularism and hence often was the target of disaffection with secular politics. Many who attacked it were incensed by what they regarded as economic, cultural, and political oppression under the "new world order" of a secular, America-dominated, post–Cold War world.

Some of the most fierce opponents of the United States' secular power were themselves Americans. The venom of the Christian militia and other extremist Christian groups in the United States led to a series of terrorist acts on abortion clinics, gay and lesbian bars, and individuals perceived as being Jewish or immigrant. These attacks culminated in the 1995 bombing of the Oklahoma City Federal Building by Timothy McVeigh, a follower of William Pierce's racist Christian ideology that he called "Cosmotheism."

In the same year, in Japan, members of a Buddhist religious movement, the Aum Shinrikyo, imagined an apocalyptic and catastrophic world war in which American global military power would once again be focused on Japan. The group unleashed nerve gas in the Tokyo subways as a way of demonstrating the validity of their prophecies, dire predictions that condemned America's superpower status as sinister and manipulative.

Many radical Muslim groups saw American military and economic power the same way, but with a more realistic basis for their critique. The United States' economic interests in the oil reserves of the Middle East, and its unchallenged cultural and political influence in a post–Cold War world led many Muslim activists to see America as a global bully, a worthy target of their religious and political anger. It appealed especially to those whose resistance methods had been honed through the anti-Soviet struggle in Afghanistan, which also was seen as a fight against enemies of Islam. In 1993, a group of Muslim activists in the New York City area, many of them Egyptians who had been implicated in President Anwar Sadat's assassination and had weathered the Afghan resistance struggle, attempted to blow up the World Trade Center towers. Though the attempt was unsuccessful, it was an impressive display of their abilities to coordinate a complicated event involving a wide collaboration of activists. Some of the conspirators—such as Ramzi Yousef—were linked to a new network of activism associated with the former Saudi businessman and engineer, Osama bin Laden. The global jihadi network seemed fixated on symbols of U.S. military and economic power, and a series of terrorist attacks on American outposts were linked to bin Laden. In 1998, a simultaneous series of explosions were aimed at American embassies in Kenya and Tanzania, and in 2000 a daring ship-based bomb attacked the *USS Cole* in a Yemeni harbor.

Because this new spate of anti-Americanism arose in the 1990s, the decade that followed the collapse of the Berlin wall, it is legitimate to ask whether there is any connection between the end of the old Cold War and the rise of this new global encounter. There was certainly a direct relationship in the areas of the former Soviet Union, where indigenous new religious movements were reactions against the homogenous secular ideology enforced during the Soviet era. A whole new outburst of Christian cultural nationalism occurred in Eastern Europe and the former Soviet Union in the 1990s. In the early 1990s, Buddhist nationalism emerged in Mongolia, and Muslim nationalism gained strength in areas far from the Middle East: in Afghanistan, in Tajikistan, and in other Central Asian countries of the Commonwealth of Independent States. New leaders rode the crests of power provided by these movements, and found in religion a useful support.

There was also an indirect relationship between the end of the old Cold War and the rise of the new religious rebellions. The collapse of the global polarity between communism and capitalism meant that the West was the sole remaining superpower, but it also left the perception that superpowers were flawed bastions, and could crumble and fall. At the same time America's and Europe's economic superiority was being challenged by the rise of the East Asian economies, and America's moral authority was under question after Vietnam and the Watergate scandal. This perception that the old order was weak and could be destroyed was the occasion for new religious challenges against the pretensions of old secular European and American powers. Times of social turbulence and political confusion—which the collapse of the Soviet Union and the decline of American economic power and cultural influence created around the world—are often occasions for new ideological solutions to surface. It was inevitable that many of these would involve religion, sometimes perceived as the only stable point in a swirl of economic and political indirection.

Moreover, as nations rejected the Soviet and American models of nationhood, they turned to their own pasts and to their own cultural resources. Secular ideologies often lead to frustration because their material promises usually cannot be fulfilled in one's own lifetime; the expectations of religious ideologies do not disappoint in the same way because they are not fulfilled on the worldly plane. Religious nationalism raised new hopes, and it also came along in time to rescue the idea of the nation-state. The political organization of a modern nation must be morally justified, and in many former colonial countries new generations of leaders found increasing difficulty in rallying support from the masses on the basis of a vision of society that mirrored that of the failing old colonial powers. Many of these countries might have descended into anarchy, been conquered by neighboring states, or come under the hegemony of a large international power if it were not for the insulation provided by religious nationalism. In Eastern Europe and the former Soviet Union, religious and other forms of ethnic nationalism might well have blocked Gorbachev's vision of a new secular, nonsocialist empire to replace the vast Soviet Union.

THE GLOBALIZATION OF RELIGIOUS REBELLION

In the first decade of the twenty-first century, the contestation between secular and religious forces was cast in a global frame of reference. The significant moment in this development was September 11, 2001. Though most of the nineteen hijackers who boarded the four commercial airplanes involved in the attacks on the World Trade Center and the Pentagon on that fateful day were Saudis, the planning for the conspiracy was global. It involved scores of activists in multiple countries from Afghanistan to Germany to the United States. Moreover, the goals of the jihadi networks were increasingly transnational. Originally jihadi leaders like Khalid Shaikh Mohammad and bin Laden had fixated on local issues—in bin Laden's case, on Saudi Arabia. He was concerned especially about the role of the United States in propping up the Saudi family and, in his mind, America's exploitation of the oil resources of the country. He then adopted a broader critique of Middle Eastern politics, following the general jihadi perspective of Maulana Maududi, Sayyid Qutb, and other Muslim political thinkers who rejected all forms of Western political and social influence in the region. Increasingly the goal of bin Laden's and the other jihadi activists was to get American influence not just out of Saudi Arabia but out of the whole Muslim world. This meant a confrontation of global proportions on multiple fronts.

Hence September 11 was just one of a series of jihadi terrorist attacks that occurred in the years before and after that date. All of them were aimed at bringing to public consciousness the notion that the world was at war. The attacks seemed puzzling to the surviving victims and to those who witnessed them, since they did not seem motivated by any clear political objective. Though bin Laden had declared war on the United States in his famous *fatweh* of 1996, it was largely an invisible conflict, a great confrontation that lay largely within the imaginations of the jihadi activists, until September 11, 2001, brought it to public attention.

The response of the American political leadership following September 11 was dramatic and historically transformative. The televised pronouncements of President George W. Bush on both September 11 and even more decisively on the following day made clear how he and his administration were going to interpret the attack: they adopted the jihadi terms. Rather than viewing the terrorist acts as criminal deeds by a gang of thugs, the U.S. leaders adopted some of the major elements of bin Laden's view of the world and saw them as skirmishes in a global war. The simmering new Cold War of the 1990s had become hot and exploded into a real war, the first of the twenty-first century.

The new war also received a name. It was dubbed the "War on Terror" by U.S. officials and the American news media. The war was also characterized as the "struggle against radical Islam," and indeed the Muslim aspects of the religious encounter with the secular state became the single concern of Western policy makers, despite the persistence of Christian militants in America, Hindu and Sikh activists in India, Jewish extremists in Israel, and violent Buddhists in Sri Lanka and Thailand. Yet only the Muslim activists shared an ideological perspective that was global in its encounter with the West and transnational in its network of activists. Its actions were brutal and violent. So too were the American attempts to suppress it, and the heavy-handed approach created further cycles of violence in response.

Within a month after the September 11, 2001, attacks, the U.S. military bombarded Afghanistan, lending its support to an alliance of Afghan rebels who sought to topple the Taliban regime. Because the Taliban had harbored bin Laden, many observers saw this as a justified response to the events of 9/11, though many in the Muslim world thought it was an excessive military invasion aimed more at the Taliban than at the transnational terrorists. At the same time, U.S. involvement in the Philippines in support of the attempt to control radical Muslim groups was also perceived as an anti-Muslim military exercise.

Iraq became the most significant theater in the U.S. "war on terror," and the single largest catalyst for global anti-American anger. The invasion and occupation of the country in 2003 was initially justified as an attempt to find and destroy weapons of mass destruction (though none were found). But throughout the Muslim world the Iraq invasion was widely perceived as an attempt to control Middle East politics and its economic resources. Many saw it as part of America's war on Islam. Those who perceived it this way were apt to accept the al-Qaeda vision of a global war and to morally justify what was regarded as a defense of the Muslim faith—if necessary through violence.

Terrorist acts associated with jihadi Muslim activists increased dramatically around the world in this decade. The arena of terror became transnational. Some of the acts were indirectly aimed at Israel—such as an attack on a synagogue in Tunisia and on Israeli-populated hotels in Egypt's Red Sea resorts. Other acts were against Western cultural influence in Muslim countries far from the Middle East, such as the assault on Bali resorts in 2002 and the 2003 bombing of Jakarta hotels. Still others were against governments thought to oppress Islam—such as India with regard to its policies against the Muslim separatist movement in Kashmir, the situation that was likely behind the Mumbai train blasts in 2006.

But the most spectacular attacks were those related directly or indirectly to the coalition of American-led forces in Iraq. In addition to those incidents in Iraq itself (including a United Nations headquarters and sites sacred to Shi'a Muslims) were those far from Baghdad—the Madrid train bombings in 2004, for instance, that killed almost two hundred; and the London subway and bus bombings in 2005 that took the lives of more than fifty commuters. Another plot was intercepted in 2006 that might have killed hundreds in midair commercial airplanes as they crossed the Atlantic from London to destinations in the United States. When the conspirators were apprehended, most turned out to be British citizens—expatriate Pakistanis and other Muslims living in the United Kingom.

Many of the Muslim activists in Europe were inflamed not only about European countries' support for the U.S.-led military coalition in Iraq, but also about European attitudes toward the Muslim immigrant community. The resentment of some elements of the expatriate community boiled over into violence. Among the more incendiary moments were the tensions following the assassination of the Dutch filmmaker Theo van Gogh in November 2004, the rage of violence by North African and Arab youth in France that left over a thousand automobiles torched across the country in 2004, and the protests earlier that same year over the French government's attempt to ban the wearing of headscarves by Muslim women living in France. An international outcry followed the September 2005 publication of cartoons by a Danish newspaper that were deemed offensive by many Muslims, and in the first months of 2006 riots broke out across the world.

The actions of Muslim militants associated with Hamas in Palestine and Hezbollah in Lebanon also persisted into the twenty-first century. Though their activities were not transnational in scope, their ideology and much of their support came from kindred Muslim supporters in other parts of the Shi'ia world (in the case of Hezbollah), and from Sunni regions (in the case of Hamas). By the middle of the decade many supporters of the largely local Hamas movement had begun espousing the rhetoric of global jihad. The Hezbollah position in the 2006 war with Israel in southern Lebanon was hailed throughout the Muslim world. In Iraq the violence against the U.S.-led occupation force and the new American-protected government also became much more than a resistance struggle against a foreign occupation. Under the leadership of Abu Musab al-Zarqawi, the movement forged an alliance with al-Qaeda and aimed at destroying Shi'a political power as well as American military force.

In the twenty-first century a new arena for radical religious activism was created through the Internet. Through password-protected private sites and publicly-accessible recruitment sites and chat rooms, the ideological net of radical jihad was cast around the world. New acts of violence emerged from small cells of activists mobilized through Internet sites but not controlled or coordinated by any single command. Thus the virulence of religious radicalism metastasized throughout the planet through cybernetworks. Among a diversity of groups, from minority immigrant communities in London to Chicano prison gangs in California, jihadi rhetoric became a vehicle of social protest. The new Cold War was waged not only on a geographical battlefield but also on the intellectual terrain of cyberspace. Yet, like the old Cold War, the ideological confrontation always carried the threat of bloodshed.

WHY RELIGION?

But was the conflict essentially about religion? There is no question that many of the movements against the secular state were expressed in strident religious terms. Yet this does not necessarily make the movements either for or about religion. In a widely-discussed book published in 2006, *Dying to Win,* Robert Pape examined the most brutal form of violence associated with religious activism, suicide bombing, and argued that in these cases religion was not the motive.[3] Looking at a broad swath of cases of suicide activists in recent years, Pape concluded that they were not motivated by a blind religious fervor as much as by a calculated political attempt. The primary motive has been to defend territory. Pape accurately pointed out that until 2003, most suicide bombings were conducted not by a religious group but by a secular ethnic movement, the Tamil Tigers in Sri Lanka.

Pape based his conclusions on an analysis of the database maintained by the Chicago Project of Suicide Terrorism. He provided a demographic profile of over 460 male and female suicide bombers—though they are mostly men. They are not, he argued, "mainly poor, uneducated, immature religious zealots or social losers," as they have sometimes been portrayed. What they have in common is the sense that their territory or culture has been invaded by an alien power that cannot easily be overthrown. In this desperate situation of social survival they turn to the simplest and most direct form of militant engagement, using their own bodies as bombs. Contrary to the perception of many observers, suicide bombers are not religious loners but are usually part of large militant organizations with well-honed strategies aimed at ousting foreign control from what they consider their own territory. The concessions made to such organizations in the past by the governments who have been opposed to them have given the organizations behind suicide bombings the confidence that their strategies work and are worth repeating. Rather than seeing these activists as religiously-motivated crazies, Pape saw them as strategists making rational calculations for political gain.

I think that Pape is largely correct. Yet religious language and ideas do play an important role, though not necessarily the initial one. The conditions of conflict that lead to tension are usually matters of social and political identity—issues regarding who a people are, and what makes them cohere as a moral community. Often this is manifested as a defense of the homeland, as Pape describes it, a protection of territory or culture that is perceived to be under control by an outside power. At some point in the conflict, however, usually at a time of frustration and desperation, the political and ideological contest becomes "religionized." Then what was primarily a worldly struggle takes on the aura of sacred conflict. This creates a whole new set of problems.

Most movements of religious rebellion—including Sikhs in the Punjab; Muslim separatists in Kashmir; the Buddhist antigovernment protesters in Sri Lanka; the Aum Shinrikyo movement in Japan; the Islamic revolution in Iran; Sunni jihadi movements in Egypt, Palestine, and elsewhere in the Middle East; Messianic Jewish movements in Israel; Catholic and Protestant militants in Northern Ireland; the Christian militia in the United States; and the transnational movement of jihadi activists around world—share some common similarities. Though each group was responding to its own set of local issues, in all cases these were communities that perceived themselves to be fragile, vulnerable, and under siege.

They also shared a common ideological component: the perception that the modern idea of secular nationalism had let them down. They were convinced that the secular state was insufficient to protect their communities or provide the moral, political, economic, and social strength to nurture them. They had lost faith in secular nationalism. In many cases the effects of globalization were in the background as global economic and communications systems undercut the distinctiveness of nation-state identities. In some cases the hatred of the global system was overt, as in the American Christian militia's disdain of the "new world order" and the jihadis' targeting of the World Trade Center. Thus, underlying their political activism was a motivating "cause"—if such a term can be used—that was not a yearning for a specific political goal but the gnawing sense of a loss of identity and control in the modern world.

This sense of social malaise is not necessarily a religious problem, but it is one for which religion provides a solution. Hence in each of these cases, religion became the ideology of protest. Particular religious images and themes were marshaled to resist what were imagined to be the enemies of traditional culture and identities: the global secular systems and their secular nation-state supporters.

There were other similarities among these cases. In each of them those supporters who embraced radical anti-state religious ideologies felt personally upset with what they regarded as the oppression of the secular state. They experienced this oppression as an assault on their pride, and felt insulted and shamed as a result. The failures of the state—though economic, political, and cultural—were often experienced in personal ways as humiliation and alienation, as a loss of selfhood.

It is understandable, then, that the men (and they were usually men) who experienced this assault on their identity and pride would lash out in violence—the way that men often do when they feel frustrated and humiliated. Such expressions of power are meant to at least symbolically regain their sense of manhood.[4] In each case, however, the activists channeled these feelings of violence through images of collective violence borrowed from their religious traditions: the idea of cosmic war.

The idea of cosmic war was a remarkably consistent feature of all of these cases. It is a powerfully restorative image for social malaise. Those people whom we might think of as terrorists often think of themselves as soldiers. They are engaged in attempts to restore their sense of power and control in what they imagine to be sacred battles. Acts of religious terror serve not only as tactics in a political strategy but as symbolically empowering sacred deeds. These are performances of violence, enacted to create a moment of spiritual encounter and personal redemption. Religious violence is especially savage and relentless, since its perpetrators see it not just as part of a worldly political battle but as part of a scenario of divine conflict.

So although religion may not be the problem, the religious response to the problem of identity and control in the modern world is often problematic. When antimodernism, anti-Americanism, and antiglobalization are expressed in the drama of religious struggle, religion brings in a whole new set of elements. For one thing, religion personalizes the conflict. It provides *personal rewards*—religious merit, redemption, the promise of heavenly luxuries—to those who struggle in conflicts that otherwise have only social benefits. It also provides *vehicles of social mobilization* that embrace vast numbers of supporters who otherwise would not be mobilized around social or political issues. In many cases, it provides an *organizational network* of local churches, mosques, temples, and religious associations into which patterns of leadership and support may be tapped. It gives the legitimacy of *moral justification* for political encounter. Even more important, it provides *justification for violence* that challenges the state's monopoly on morally sanctioned killing. Using Max Weber's dictum that the state's authority is always rooted in the social approval of the state to enforce its power through the use of bloodshed—in police authority, punishment, and armed defense—religion is the only other entity that can give moral sanction for violence and is therefore inherently at least potentially revolutionary.

Religion's images of *cosmic war* add further complications to a conflict that has become baptized with religious authority. The notion of cosmic war gives an *all-encompassing worldview* to those who embrace it. Supporters of Christian militia movements, for instance, described their "aha!" experience when they discovered the Christian Identity worldview, a totalizing ideology that helped them make sense of the modern world, their increasingly peripheral role in it, and the dramatic actions they could take to set the world right. It gives them roles as *religious soldiers* who can literally fight back against the forces of evil. When the template of spiritual battle is laid upon a worldly opposition, it dramatically changes the perception of the conflict by those engaged in it, and it vastly alters the way that the struggle is waged. It *absolutizes the conflict* into extreme opposing positions and *demonizes opponents* by imagining them to be satanic powers. This absolutism makes compromise difficult to fathom and holds out the promise of *total victory* through divine intervention. A sacred war that is waged in a godly span of time need not be won immediately, however. The *time line of sacred struggle is vast,* perhaps even eternal.

I once had the occasion to point out the futility—in secular military terms—of the Islamic struggle in Palestine to Dr. Abdul Aziz Rantisi, the late leader of the political wing of the Hamas movement. It seemed to me that Israel's military force was such that a Palestinian military effort could never succeed. Dr. Rantisi assured me that "Palestine was occupied before, for two hundred years."[5] He explained that he and his Palestinian comrades "can wait again—at least that long." In his calculation, the struggles of God can endure for eons. Ultimately, however, they knew they would succeed. In the religious frame of reference a defeat is never really a defeat, since in the vast timeline of sacred warfare ultimately the righteous side will succeed.

So religion can be a problematic aspect of contemporary social conflict even if it is not *the* problem, in the sense of the root causes of discontent. Much of the violence in contemporary life that is perceived as terrorism around the world is directly related to the absolutism of conflict. The demonization of enemies allows those who regard themselves as soldiers for God to kill with moral impunity. In many cases they feel that their acts will give them spiritual rewards.

Curiously, the same kind of thinking has crept into some of the responses to terrorism. The "war on terrorism" that was launched by the United States government after September 11 is a case in point. To the degree that the war references are metaphorical, and meant to imply an all-out effort in the manner of previous administrations' "war on drugs" and "war on poverty," they are understandable attempts to marshal public support for security measures and police surveillance. The September 11 attacks were, after all, hideous acts that deeply scarred the American consciousness, and one could certainly understand that a responsible government would want to wage an all-out effort to hunt down those culpable and bring them to justice.

But among some public commentators and politicians who espoused a "war on terrorism," the militant language was more than metaphor. God's blessing was imagined to be bestowed on a view of confrontation that was, like all images of cosmic war, all-encompassing, absolutizing, and demonizing. It led to the invasion and occupation of two Muslim countries and justified an amendment of civil rights for the purpose of surveillance and exacting information from prisoners of war. What was problematic about this view was that it brought an impatience with solutions that required the slow procedures of systems of justice—even if these were ultimately more effective in locating terrorists and less provocative in creating more acts of violence. The war rhetoric demanded instead the quick and violent responses that lent simplicity to the confrontation and a sense of divine certainty to its resolution. Alas, as the escalating violence in Iraq bore testimony, such a position could fuel the fires of retaliation, leading to more terrorism instead of less.

The role of religion in this literal "war on terrorism" has, in a curious way, been similar to religion's role in the cosmic war imagined by those perpetrating the terrorism that it was attempting to counter. In both cases religion was a problematic partner of political confrontation. Religion brought more to the conflict than simply a repository of symbols and the aura of divine support. It problematized the conflict through its abiding absolutism, its justification for violence, and its ultimate images of warfare that demonize opponents and cast the conflict in transhistorical terms.

WHY NOW?

Though there have been instances of religious rebellion throughout history—from the Taiping Rebellion to the millenarian Christian movements of medieval Europe—the current crop of religious activists is so frequent, so globally ubiquitous, as to insist on an answer to the question, why now? One clue to the answer, it seems to me, is in the ubiquity of religious activism—it occurs in every religious tradition, in every part of the globe. Another clue lies in the historical context. The religious activism of the present comes at a time when the ideological competition of the Cold War is ending, an anticolonial critique in the formerly Third World is being revived, and a Westernized form of hegemonic economic and cultural globalization is on the rise. These historical currents present serious challenges to the credibility of the Enlightenment idea of moral politics shaped in discrete nation-states and buttressed through concepts of secular nationalism shrouded in moral superiority. The result is a collapse of confidence in secular politics around the world. This "loss of faith in secular nationalism," as I have described it, is the fertile ground in which new religio-political movements can grow, for they provide the sense of moral authority and the clarity of communal identity that the old secular nationalism is perceived as having abandoned.[6]

Those on the secular nationalist side, however, do not usually understand or appreciate this moral critique. In a book written shortly after the fall of the Cold War, I expressed the fear that ideological stereotypes can arise on both sides of the imagined secular-religious divide that might create an intractable Cold War mentality.[7] I titled my book with the warning phrase, *The New Cold War?*—with an emphasis on the question mark. When Samuel Huntington came out with his essay "The Clash of

Civilizations?" some months after my book was published, I feared that the public might confuse my thesis with his, though our positions were almost diametrically different.[8] Fortunately most readers have understood me to say that there is not a historical clash of civilizations, but that the historical context of our times has led to a crisis of confidence in secular political institutions.

The future trajectory of this religious activism is unclear. The religiously related political movements that have entered the public arena from the late 1970s through the first decade of the twenty-first century have had diverse careers. Several religious revolutions have been attempted—including the Taliban's harsh regime in Afghanistan and the brief rise to power of the Islamic Courts Council in Somalia—but Iran remains the only long-term example of a successful attempt to establish a religious state. It has founded a political order based on religious ideology, fanned the fires of nationalism with religious zeal, enacted laws that privilege particular religious ideas and practices, and brought into the sphere of political influence clerics whose only credentials were their theological acumen. Even in Iran, though, the main business of government has been the same as anywhere else—providing a stable and just political order, and supporting economic development. These aspects of mundane politics have no particular religious claim. Moreover, the influence of the clergy and religious ideology in Iran has waxed and waned since the 1979 revolution.

In other countries, religious movements have assimilated into the political process in a nonrevolutionary way. They have become political parties, or used their political support to back particular candidates. The Hindu religious nationalist movement that supports the Bharatiya Janata Party (BJP) in India has scored huge electoral successes in both state and national parliaments. In Palestine, the Hamas movement transformed itself into a political party and soared to victory in the 2006 parliamentary elections. In other cases religious rebellions have been brutally suppressed before they have had a chance to take the reins of power. The Sinhalese arm of the radical JVP movement in Sri Lanka was essentially killed off in the 1990 military action against the movement, but it then resurfaced in later years. In India, rebellious Sikhs were killed in the thousands along with large numbers of armed police in a protracted ten-year war. It ended early in the 1990s, as much from exhaustion and infighting as from the government's militancy. Eventually many villagers who were weary of all the violence refused to give the Sikh militants safe shelter.

Elsewhere factionalism weakened a good number of other movements, including the Christian militia in the United States, opposition nationalist churches in the Ukraine, Shi'a factions in Lebanon, and rival Muslim groups in the resistance movement in Palestine. In Iraq, extremist groups of Shi'a and Sunni Muslims have set about killing one another in a violence that shifted the pattern of militancy in the post-Saddam era from anti-occupation insurgency to civil war. These developments give rise to the possibility that some movements might end up turning against themselves as infighting essentially destroys them from within. In other cases the violence of rebellious religious movements was bridled through legal means. In Japan, after the 1995 nerve gas attacks in the Tokyo subways, the Aum Shinrikyo was placed under extensive government surveillance. All of the major participants were arrested and after lengthy trials were sentenced to long prison terms and more.

Perhaps the most successful conclusion to movements of terrorism through nonviolent means was the Good Friday Agreement in 1998 that brought the troubles of Northern Ireland onto a path of peace. The Northern Ireland solution brought an end to violence that terrified London, Belfast, and other cities for decades. It showed the value of not responding in kind to provocative terrorist attacks and letting the patient process of negotiation and compromise work out a solution of accommodation. The agreement called for both Protestant and Catholic communities in the region to have guaranteed representation through a commission supported by both the state of Ireland and the United Kingdom.[9] Could other violent situations be settled in a manner similar to Northern Ireland's Good Friday Agreement? It would not take a huge stretch of imagination to think that it could, especially when the issue is largely over contested land.

Yet other movements have abandoned political activism altogether as the futility of their efforts encouraged their leaders to turn towards other ventures. In the case of the Christian militia in the United States, there is some indication that the enormity of the violence perpetrated by Timothy McVeigh in bombing the Oklahoma City Federal Building in 1995 had a sobering effect on the right-wing Christian movement in the rest of the country. Yet another factor in diminishing the role of the violent religious right after the Oklahoma City bombing was the fact they were largely ignored by the public authorities and the news media. Neither the prosecution or the defense side of Timothy McVeigh's much publicized trial made any effort to link McVeigh with the larger underworld of the Christian militant movements in the United States. The absence of media attention served to further marginalize them from public attention.

By contrast, when a similar sort of terrorist attack resulted in the catastrophic collapse of the World Trade Center and damage to the Pentagon on September 11, 2001, the connections to radical Islam became the central issue. Within days, the al-Qaeda network became identified as America's most vicious foe and Osama bin Laden the Hitler of the new world war. When American leaders adopted bin Laden's rhetoric of religious war and vaunted him to the level of its global foe, they inadvertently promoted his image and ideas throughout the Muslim world. It is possible that this might have emboldened al-Qaeda even more. The paradoxical effect of the "war on terror" might well have been the increased proliferation of terrorism. The popularization of jihadi ideology as an anti-American posture of protest may have been due in no small part to U.S. policy that elevated it into the role of a global enemy.

Hence to a large degree the future of religious rebellions against the secular state depends not only on the rebellious religious movements but also on the way that government authorities respond, especially in Europe and the United States. It is important to recall that much of the passion behind the religious rebels' positions has come as a response to what they have perceived as the West's attitude of arrogance and intolerance toward them. If they could perceive the West as changing its attitude—respecting at least some aspects of their positions—perhaps their response would be less vindictive. It is this sensitivity that has been behind some of the more cautious moments in European and U.S. responses to acts of terrorism. In Spain, for instance, one response to the Madrid bombings was an attempt by the Spanish government to be more hospitable to the Muslim minority living in the country.

Attitudes are difficult to sway, however, and the frequency of acts of terrorism associated with the radical jihadi movement led to a certain Islamophobia in Europe and the United States. Like the old Cold War, the perception was one of Western civilization under siege, attacked by a hostile and alien force. This in turn led to the notion that all Muslim activists—or even all Muslims—were the same. Policies based on this perception widened the gulf between the two sides, just as they did during the Cold War, and even more violence was the result. Though one U.S. State Department official warned that "we have to be smarter in dealing with Islam than we were in dealing with communism thirty or forty years ago," the animosity between secular and religious politics settled into something of a new Cold War.[10]

The "war on terrorism" became a self-fulfilling prophecy. America became an enemy in large part because of policies that made it appear as if it was indeed the enemy that some religious radicals imagined. The trajectory of religious terrorism in the years following the Bush administration are a part of the larger dynamics of global political order in a post–Cold War world, in which not only the strategies of religious rebels but the policies intended to counter it are the elements that shape the future of this global encounter between religious forces and the secular state.

NOTES

1. A more thorough discussion of these issues in their broad historical context may be found in my book *Global Rebellion: Religious Challenges to the Secular State* (Berkeley and Los Angeles: University of California Press, 2008), from which some excerpts have been taken for this essay.

2. Imam Abu Kheireiddine, quoted in Kim Murphy, "Islamic Party Wins Power in Algeria," *Los Angeles Times*, December 28, 1991, A1.

3. Robert Pape, *Dying to Win: The Strategic Logic of Suicide Terrorism* (New York: Random House, 2005).

4. I explore the topic of male empowerment as a factor in violence in the section "Why Guys Throw Bombs," in *Terror in the Mind of God: The Global Rise of Religious Violence* (Berkeley and Los Angeles: University of California Press, 2003), 198–209.

5. Interview with Dr. Abdul Aziz Rantisi, cofounder and political leader of Hamas, Khan Yunis, Gaza, March 1, 1998.

6. Mark Juergensmeyer, *The New Cold War? Religious Nationalism Confronts the Secular State* (Berkeley and Los Angeles: University of California Press, 1993), 11.

7. Juergensmeyer, *The New Cold War?*

8. Samuel P. Huntington, "The Clash of Civilizations?" *Foreign Affairs*, summer 1993. A revised, enlarged version of this essay was published without the question mark in the title as *The Clash of Civilizations and the Remaking of World Order* (New York: Simon and Schuster, 1996).

9. I analyze the Northern Ireland peace agreement as an example of nonviolent conflict resolution in a time of terror in my book *Gandhi's Way: A Handbook of Conflict Resolution* (Berkeley and Los Angeles: University of California Press, rev. ed., 2006).

10. A "senior Administration official" quoted in Robin Wright, "U.S. Struggles to Deal with Global Islamic Resurgence," *Los Angeles Times*, January 26, 1992, A1.

8. Gendered Tropes and the New World Order

Cowboys, Welfare Queens, and Presidential Politics at Home and Abroad

Eileen Boris

Slamming the foreign policy of George W. Bush as "failed cowboy diplomacy," Presidential candidate Barack Obama linked the presumptive Republican nominee, John McCain, to the shoot-first-and-refuse-to-talk posturing of the man they both hoped to succeed. "For all of their tough talk, one of the things you have to ask yourself is, what are George Bush and John McCain afraid of? . . . I am not afraid that we will lose some propaganda fight with a dictator," the Democrat declared.[1] Obama evoked, albeit in a counter-hegemonic manner, gendered tropes that haunted him throughout the 2008 campaign. McCain, in turn, accused Obama of his own "cowboy diplomacy" when it came to the North American Free Trade Agreement, which the Democrat would renegotiate.[2]

Such representations of cowboys and warriors had signaled national longings and fears for more than a century. What kind of performance of masculinity must a president embody? Need a president be a cowboy to go after the latest band of outlaws on the world stage? Should he be "imperial," with a style fitting an empire? Even after the withdrawal of candidate Hillary R. Clinton, the contest would become, as the feminist writer Susan Faludi explained through terms that fully reinforced such frameworks, "an epic American gender showdown."[3]

John McCain, all agreed, had lived the captivity narrative of the war hero. As Faludi noted, "Although Senator McCain didn't rescue any helpless maidens, he outdid even Daniel Boone in averting emasculating domination" by surviving more than five years' imprisonment by the North Vietnamese. Obama, in contrast, "will not be cast as the avenging hero in 'The Rescue' any time soon—and not because of the color of his skin or his lack of military experience. He doesn't seem to want the role."[4] But he apparently has had little choice. The more ominous prediction of Stan Goff in *The Huffington Post* seemed to be coming true during summer 2008, when the Illinois senator seemed to waffle on Iraq withdrawal and voted to absolve communications companies for illegal wiretaps. "[N]ow that two men are running, we will see the essence of gender as a thoroughgoing system of male dominance—and masculinity constructed as conquest, as McCain forces Obama to demonstrate his membership in the death cult called masculinity," Goff lamented.[5] And, to the chagrin of some feminists, in a much-publicized address on Father's Day Obama took up the cause of fatherhood responsibility, a position associated with conservatives who sought to end welfare for poor single mothers.[6]

Over the course of the twentieth century, as the United States became an urban, industrial society and moved from its earlier imperialist ventures through an internationalist foreign policy toward post–Cold War empire, gendered and racialized tropes captured the national ideal of independence, associated with white and free men who had the economic resources to act on their own accord. The disdained opposite, dependence, became associated with the unfree, women, the old and the young, paupers, and people of color—that is, those needing support or too degraded to become independent. These relations we find most tellingly embodied in the icons of the cowboy and the welfare queen, symbols of the nation and the anti-nation.

Too often scholars of the United States consider domestic policy (at home) apart from foreign policy (abroad).[7] This essay breaks with that scholarly division of labor by suggesting one set of connections based on two cultural/political archetypes, the cowboy and the welfare queen, which were/are simultaneously gendered and racialized. Political leaders both deployed cowboy iconography and were recognized for good or ill as displaying characteristics associated with a mythic American West in which this heroic figure tames the wilderness and crusades against evil, violent outlaws. The myth largely ignores that the cowboy acted to wipe out the rightful indigenous inhabitants of the land.[8] The welfare queen, in contrast, was a label that detractors gave to poor women, undeservedly growing fat off of government largesse. It has existed as a verbal tag or a name printed or implied under a photograph that otherwise, and with another caption, would merely serve as a picture of a black woman.[9] Drawing upon newspaper accounts, blogs, speeches, and iconographic representations, this essay traces the ways that modern presidents since Lyndon B. Johnson have deployed these icons to push independence as a national virtue in spite of their apparently different political positions. Indeed, the languages of independence and dependence have provided an easy vocabulary for policy making that aspires to moral heights, leading to a performativity that traps those who utter the tropes of their predecessors into policy grooves not necessarily of their own choosing.[10]

These types, of course, represent constructions. Actual cowboys, those who herded cattle on the ranching frontier, composed a multicultural workforce whose position as wage earners dependent on employers hardly appears salient in the national imagery, never mind media representations.[11] Until recently, the majority of women on welfare were white; most of these poor single mothers spent less than two years receiving public aid before returning to employment.[12] But just as the cowboy as a symbol of white male individualism has represented worthy American manhood, so the welfare queen has stood for a despised black womanhood.[13] Behind the image of the cowboy stands the workings of Empire; behind the portrait of the welfare queen lies the punishing of poor women, often African American or Latina, for their motherhood, sexuality, and lack of dependence on husbands. The problem with the welfare queen is that she parlayed her dependence on the state into independence from men and employment (that is, work as commonly understood.) [14] Like the enemies who would make the nation dependent by withholding a vital resource—oil—and who require disciplining through "cowboy diplomacy," welfare dependents have become the primitive other, politically assaulted, responsible for national decline, who need taming through cowboy social policy. The 2008 presidential election both reflected these icons and upended them with the distinctively non-cowboy persona of Barack Obama.

AN IMPERIAL COWBOY: LBJ

The presidential cowboy rode onto the national stage during the United States' imperialistic extension of its boundaries across the West and beyond the Pacific. He temporarily became discredited with the morass of the Vietnam War.[15] Lyndon Baines Johnson combined expansionist foreign policy with domestic reform to improve the lives of the less fortunate. Nonetheless, the dependency of mothers and children taken for granted in 1900 no longer held by the 1960s. Not only did a growing women's movement demand the end to workplace discrimination and equal pay for equal work, but the face of welfare in the political imagination had undergone a racial transformation from the white widow to the black "matriarch," as Daniel Patrick Moynihan—an adviser to both LBJ and Richard Nixon and later a U.S. Senator—named female-headed families, no matter the persistence of unequal treatment of women of color who applied for public assistance.[16] It no longer was clear that mothers with small children belonged with the frail elderly and the permanently and totally disabled among the unemployables or were deserving of public assistance. The meaning of dependency changed, and so did government support, when the color of dependency became black.[17]

To the problem of poverty, Johnson brought martial metaphors. Riding a horse on his Texas ranch, LBJ embodied the cowboy image, even though the former teacher had been a politician since the 1930s and his persona was much more one of a Washington insider.[18] He relished his presentation as a cowboy; he sought to be photographed in the saddle. But later he felt that the Eastern establishment dismissed him because of his cowboy persona.[19] Certainly the image has stuck. Millinery Web sites continue to offer broad Stetsons as LBJ cowboy hats.[20] In his conduct of the Vietnam War, commentators still remember cowboy characteristics, such as "shoot first" and go at it alone. In advising George W. Bush to follow Johnson's lead, *USA Today* founder Al Neuharth reinforced both men's association with the cowboy: "LBJ, after mismanaging the Vietnam War that so bitterly divided the nation and the world, decided he owed it to his political party and to his country not to run for re-election. So, he turned tail and rode off into the sunset of his Texas ranch." George W. Bush, he implied, should follow suit.[21]

Johnson justified foreign policy in terms of national independence; stopping communism was necessary to maintain freedom. In his 1964 State of the Union address, he declared that "we must strengthen the ability of free nations everywhere to develop their independence and raise their standard of living, and thereby frustrate those who prey on poverty and chaos. To do this, the rich must help the poor—and we must do our part."[22] This goal paralleled that of domestic policy to enhance the independence of the most impoverished within the nation. But with Vietnam, the cowboy's self-reliance had morphed into an "arrogance of power."[23]

When it came to welfare and dependency, Johnson's Great Society modernized the New Deal. Thirty years before, Franklin Delano Roosevelt, a polio survivor dependent on others for mobility, had equated independence with employment. "Continued dependence upon relief induces a spiritual and moral disintegration fundamentally destructive to the national fiber," Roosevelt proclaimed in 1935. "To dole out relief in this way is to administer a narcotic, a subtle destroyer of the human spirit."[24] LBJ remained true to the New Deal's preference for work over relief when designing the War on Poverty to offer "a hand-up, not a hand out," which would assist "taxeaters" to become "taxpayers."[25] Training and education programs proliferated. But in encouraging maximum participation of the poor through community action and promoting civil rights, the War on Poverty helped to spark a nationwide welfare rights movement that demanded a decent standard of living, reproductive freedom, and fair treatment by the state itself. These poor, single, predominantly African-American mothers rejected the equation of welfare with dependency and instead sought welfare as a right of citizenship.[26] In response, the 1967 amendments to Social Security required recipients of Aid to Families with Dependent Children (AFDC), commonly referred to as "welfare," to work off their benefits through "workfare" programs that were to give them experience and training to handle jobs in the private economy and thus end welfare dependency.

"PROJECT INDEPENDENCE"

Tropes of independence and dependence pervaded the official discourse of Johnson's successor, Richard M. Nixon. Nixon himself was no cowboy—unlike Johnson or Ronald Reagan, he didn't ride horses and his claim to real masculinity always remained suspect. He was Tricky Dickie, the vice-presidential candidate who cried during the 1956 "Checkers" speech while pleading to retain his slot on the ticket despite having taken inappropriate campaign contributions.[27] Nixon associated independence abroad with ending dependence at home, but he was a political realist and geared above all to reelection. So he sometimes spoke of interdependence as well.

Richard Nixon, the foreign policy president, turned to welfare dependency, attacking its corrosive impact as harshly as he responded to any hint of American dependency abroad. "A country that does not take care of its domestic problems is not going to have an effective position abroad," Moynihan, then a presidential assistant, noted in August 1969. Nixon just had introduced a sweeping and ultimately unsuccessful plan to overhaul AFDC.[28] AFDC "deepened dependency by all too often making it more attractive to go on welfare than to go to work," the president charged.[29]

As part of a political scheme to capture southern white voters for the Republican party, Nixon sought to direct government funds to poor white male-headed families over black single mothers. Nixon promised that the poor would gain "the opportunity to guide their own destinies" and "a way of independence through the dignity of work."[30] His Family Assistance Plan (FAP) would institute a guaranteed basic annual income. But in doing so, the government would require employment or work from adult recipients, exempting only mothers of small children, still seen as worthy of government aid. Following the Work Incentive Program of 1967, states were able to require recipients to work for their payments, what came to be called "workfare." Welfare rights activists charged that such forced work was slavery, the ultimate dependence, and that Nixon's proposed annual income was too low to support an urban northern family. Along with trade unions, they helped to "zap FAP," and the president himself abandoned the program to defeat after 1972.[31] Nixon, however, may never have believed in his own program. As he commented to White House aides the previous May in the characteristically crude language captured by his secret tapes, "We're going to (place) more of these little Negro bastards on the welfare rolls at $2,400 a family . . . let people like Pat Moynihan and Leonard Garment [his attorney] and others believe in all that crap. But I don't believe in it . . . work, work, throw 'em off the rolls. That's the key."[32]

Nixon's foreign policy introduced questions of interdependence, which then were subject to more robust political debate than after the end of the Cold War, when the United States was presumably left as the world's lone superpower. In 1973, while the Yom Kippur War was waged between Israel and its Arab neighbors, U.S. reliance on Middle Eastern petroleum would lead to an oil embargo, gas lines, and an energy crisis—that is, to oil dependence.[33] The oil crisis came amid Watergate and U.S. defeat in Vietnam.[34] Nixon responded with "Project Independence," declaring that "the United States of America as the greatest industrial power of the world with 7 per cent of the world's people and using 30 per cent of the world's energy shouldn't have to depend on any other country for energy that provides our jobs and our transportations and our light and our heat. We can become self-sufficient."[35]

Talk of oil dependence, independence, and interdependence pervaded the press, including the nation's foremost newspaper, the *New York Times.* Some proposed increased interdependence. News articles declared "Self-Sufficiency May Be Only a Mirage," and columnists questioned, "A Fortress America?" asking, "Alone or Together?"[36] Letters to the editor suggested internationalizing oil resources. One correspondent emphasized the need for U.S.-European interdependence, lest a Soviet-Arab stranglehold suffocate European growth. Another writer even invited Europe to join "Project Independence" as an equal partner, paying its share of the cost, of course.[37] Early in 1974, however, the *Times* editorialized, "'Project Independence'—to make this country independent of unreliable foreign sources for its essential energy needs—should begin with an overhaul of the tax laws that have resulted in Condition Overdependence," that is, inducements to U.S.

companies, like the oil depletion allowance, that encouraged expanded foreign production over domestic development. Domestic and foreign policy depended on each other.[38]

Meanwhile, Secretary of State Henry Kissinger engaged in "shuttle diplomacy." Kissinger saw the United States as generating cooperation among allies; he proposed that the Europeans, North Americans, and Japanese work together to develop "an initial action program for collaboration in all areas of the energy problem."[39] At the World Energy Conference in Washington in early February 1974, Kissinger pointed to "the energy crisis" as "indicat[ing] the birth pangs of global interdependence." But French Foreign Minister Michel Jobert questioned this assumption, seeing in Kissinger's vision regional independence rather than global interdependence: "We must not appear before the entire world as seeking to define alone a 'new course' which would inevitably lead to a confrontation or a conflict with the producing countries and maybe with all the developing countries." Jobert urged, "Let us not seek to establish or to impose a new world energy order."[40] Kissinger would implore Europe "to work with the United States for a new world order," *Times* writer James Reston argued. France, however, suggested a sinister plot on the part of the United States to regain its dominance over other industrial nations and "would go it alone," only highlighting in Reston's analysis the ridiculousness of "selfish nationalistic interests."[41] In essence, as Reston earlier had explained, "Kissinger . . . switch[ed] the emphasis from Project Independence to Project Interdependence."[42]

The notion of "interdependence" within a Cold War alliance system that recognized U.S. supremacy existed within its diplomatic repertoire, even if the concept of "interdependence" remained absent from promotion of "workfare" over welfare. But as the historian Natasha Zaretsky convincingly argues, the oil crisis symbolically linked the national appetite for oil, including the overconsumption of middle-class families and wage-earning women of "convenience" foods and appliances, with lack of restraint exhibited by poor mothers and "the Arab oil sheik," two "racialized notions of dependency."[43] Independence through homes, thus, replaced notions of interdependence within them.

REAGAN'S LEGACIES

It was Ronald Reagan, not Richard Nixon, who crafted a "new world order." Historians have argued that Reagan "lived in a world of myths and symbols, rather than facts and programs."[44] During the 1980 presidential campaign, advisers toned down the impression that he "would 'put on a six-shooter and take Iran'" or that "'he's flinty-hearted and would kick all the blacks off welfare.'"[45] In foreign policy, he actually gave great latitude to advisers, which undoubtedly helped usher in the Iran-Contra scandal. Despite Central American misadventures, he managed to negotiate arms reduction, setting the basis for, first, détente with Mikhail Gorbachev and, then, the end of the Cold War with the collapse of the Soviet Union.[46]

The actor Ronald Reagan actually had played few cowboys, although his favorite Hollywood films were "adventure and action," involving "escape and rescue." The public associated him with the small screen's *Death Valley Days*; as the Old Ranger selling 20-Mule Team Borax. This representation as a Western outsider barely camouflaged his salesmanship of corporate goods. Reagan left television to run for governor, a post he won after promising toughness against civil rights, antiwar, student, and other outbursts against "law and order." After two terms in Sacramento, he bought a ranch in Santa Barbara county, where photographers could picture him in the saddle and cutting brush. [47] As president he drew upon that past in fashioning an imaginary as the sheriff who would bring the bad guys—the Soviet Evil Empire—to justice.[48] Voters described him as "a man who, when he says something, sticks to his guns." He recalled "a John Wayne type of thing . . . the Cavalry." One 1984 poll had respondents describing him with "terms like 'bravado,' 'swagger,' 'swashbuckle,' 'tough guy,'" in contrast to effete Democrats.[49] No less than the general public, scholars and journalists have delighted in painting him as "tall in the saddle."[50] He became known for "cowboy capitalism," or what one "free market" proponent defined as "policies of low tax rates, deregulation, free trade, price stability, and massive entrepreneurship." Reaganomics, the name given to his combination of tax cuts and reductions in domestic spending, then, would encourage individual action without government presence, behavior associated with the freedom of the range, with the cowboy's West.[51]

Reagan rode to political prominence by fanning resentment against the "welfare queen." As California's governor, he linked big government, high taxes, and welfare fraud. "Public assistance should go to the truly needy not the truly greedy," he claimed, as he pledged to end cheating by undeserving poor black and brown single mothers—by replacing social workers, who, he charged, coddled the poor, with eligibility clerks and forcing recipients to work for their benefits.[52] The crime of the undeserving poor was manipulating the system, deliberately having children for a higher relief check, in contrast to the disabled, ill, and elderly, whose dependency came from no fault of their own. These other clients of public assistance remained, like children, naturally dependent. In contrast, the poor mother on welfare became, as the historian Rickie Solinger has shown, "the symbol of *the dependent woman who makes bad choices.*"[53] During Reagan's two terms as governor, California tightened welfare eligibility rules, instituted workfare and "birth control training," and refused to implement federal directives, including those promulgated by the Nixon administration, that required more generous benefits—until unfavorable court decisions forced compliance.[54]

The story of the "welfare queen" became a staple of the presidential campaign trail. During the New Hampshire primary in 1976, Reagan incorporated into his stump speech the tale of a Chicago woman charged with welfare fraud by an "Illinois investigation." This woman "has 80 names, 30 addresses, 12 Social Security cards and is collecting veterans' benefits on four nonexisiting deceased husbands," he proclaimed. She received "welfare under each of her names," overall obtaining $150,000 in "tax-free cash income." But like many lines recited by the former actor, this one turned out to be an exaggeration. The woman in question, Linda Taylor, indeed seemed to have collected a disproportionate amount from the government, but not nearly to the extent portrayed by Reagan. She apparently used four aliases to receive $8,000. The police later confiscated "her Cadillac limousine," which they believed "was used to transport a fur coat, television set, diamond ring," and other goods that signaled her bad consumer choices as well as waste of taxpayer dollars.[55] But, thanks to Reagan, this forty-seven-year-old woman became the prototypical woman on welfare who treated herself royally as a "pig at the trough."[56] Later, Reagan would parlay voter resentment of welfare to increase the number of investigations for fraud and thus the policing of poor families. Meanwhile, he enacted deep cuts in social programs, including food stamps and aid to the disabled, transforming even the deserving poor into the undeserving.[57] Reagan promoted work requirements to end dependence out of the belief that "we can only measure our success by the number of people we have removed from the welfare rolls and made self-sustaining citizens—not the number we have added."[58] But the wages available to those leaving welfare rarely lifted their families out of poverty.[59]

Once a liberal strategy to increase women's independence, employment became a conservative weapon to punish female sexuality and reinforce the low-wage labor force. In the 1990s, Republicans portrayed President Bill Clinton as "soft" on foreign policy, but he certainly took a hard line when it came to welfare dependency. Though he asked for increases in child and health care, his rhetoric appropriated Republican themes, encouraging opponents who would punish the autonomy of women under the guise of "family values" and who never accepted aid to poor solo mothers in the first place.[60] During the 1992 campaign he promised to "end welfare as we know it," and in his first address as president he called to "end welfare as a way of life and make it a path to independence and dignity." As the 1996 election loomed, Clinton continued to deploy the old tropes. "We can break the vicious cycle of welfare dependency," he urged. "It should be pro-work, pro-family, pro-independence, responsible. Welfare should be a second chance, not a way of life."[61]

The resulting legislation replaced AFDC with TANF (Temporary Assistance for Needy Families). It forced recipients to take any job, even one below minimum wage, eliminating credit for higher education as a work activity as well as making poor mothers leave the home for other labor. It also limited social assistance to no more than five years in a lifetime, established a family cap restricting poor women's reproductive freedom, and continued the attempt to garnish the wages of poor men to reimburse the state for assisting the mothers of their children. Reacting to fears that pregnant women crossed the border to deliver in the United States, thus automatically making their children citizens, Congress further excluded immigrants from benefits. Some states used their own monies to cushion these provisions, which became more restrictive under the following George W. Bush administration.[62] TANF reauthorization a decade later curtailed state flexibility by increasing the number of work hours, restricting what counts as work, and cutting child care and other family supports. To further reduce welfare dependency, George W. Bush proposed a massive $1.5 billion pro-marriage initiative and pushed prevention of motherhood. Marrying off poor single mothers to men, or at least forcing men to take fatherhood support seriously, would make women independent of public support.[63] His policies would reverse what welfare rights activist Johnnie Tillmon over thirty years before described as "trad[ing] *a* man for *the man.*"[64]

Clinton, the antiwar protestor, could not escape the cowboy designation any more than his predecessor, the well-manner George H. W. Bush, who, in his first year of office, had appeared a "modest, sober, selfless steward" rather than a cowboy. But Bush Senior certainly proved that he was "no policy wimp," and, after Iraq's invasion of Kuwait, became a real "Rambo," the Cold War update of the gunslinger, even as he built a multinational consensus for troop deployment to the Persian Gulf.[65] Though some charged Clinton with dependency on European allies, he too was castigated for going it alone when it came to Bosnia and was accused of being "trigger-happy."[66] The persistence of oil dependency—"an energy policy which basically has given up the goal of energy independence," as one former energy secretary explained—led Clinton's secretary of state to speak in terms of outlaw regimes as much as would the administration of George W. Bush.[67]

REAGAN REDUX?

During his presidential campaign, George W. Bush declared, "I started as a cowboy. Now I'm a statesman."[68] Images of Bush II using his appropriation of the cowboy archetype both hail and mock the past. A button for sale on a Web site devoted to Republican party memorabilia places Bush in a white Stetson next to Ronald Reagan in a similar iconic hat. Emblazoned with the words, "My Heroes Have Always Been Cowboys," this button seeks to transfer the enthusiasm and affection of party faithful from Reagan to G. W. Bush, a son who aspires to be more like the "Gipper" than his own father.[69] Declaring "I'm glad that my President is a cowboy," Rush Limbaugh compared the two as good guys recognized by their white hats as fighters against evil.[70] Bush Junior apparently shares Reagan's proclivity for make-believe, as well as his economic conservatism and New Right social positions. Like Reagan, this Bush purchased his ranch in anticipation of running for higher office and the ranch has functioned as a stage set for image-making. But this Bush, unlike Reagan, is no horse rider. In Crawford, he drives a good-ol' boy pick-up truck and reports circulate that he actually is frightened of horses.[71]

The cowboy moniker has stuck with Bush II. Where Republican partisans during the contested 2000 election in Florida proclaimed "This Country Needs Cowboys, Not Smarty Pants," a few years later antiwar protestors at home and abroad held signs like the one in Glasgow, Scotland, declaring far less favorably, "Bush Is a Cowboy."[72] The *Los Angeles Times* likened his March 2003 ultimatum to Saddam Hussein to "a Wild West sheriff warning the bad guys to get out of town." It was "giving Saddam and his boys 48 hours to get out of Dodge."[73] But the cartoonist Charles Pugsley Fincher scorned "Cowboy Bush's Cowboy Plan for Terrorists" as a bad replay of the movies.[74] "Old West Cowboy Ethic" may have remained "the American Way to Fight Evil," but, for Europeans, the cowboy has become the "symbol of reckless irresponsibility."[75] Hans Ulrich Klose of the German parliament complained, "the way he talks, this provocative manner, the jagging of his finger at you . . . It's Texas, a culture that is unfamiliar to Germans. And it's the religious tenor of his arguments."[76] As the war began, the *Ventura Country Star* [California] described his lack of European support as, "If Bush is the cowboy sheriff, he's riding without a posse."[77] Democratic opponents lamented his go-it-alone behavior, with Connecticut Senator Chris Dodd insisting that we must not "act like a unilateral cowboy."[78] The libertarian *Santa Barbara News Press* concluded, "George W. Bush's brand of cowboy justice hasn't served the country well;" his going at it alone had undermined the United States' position in the world.[79] When the military stepped up testing antimissile weapons, one *Washington Post* columnist quipped, "George Bush, Space Cowboy."[80]

George W. Bush may have distorted "the Cowboy Code," as a *Village Voice* columnist claimed, by failing to protect the little guy and the weak, or to stick by his word and be truthful, or to work hard while maintaining dignity.[81] But his foreign policy came to stand for "cowboy diplomacy," so that when it appeared that he was consulting with allies, *Time* magazine announced "The End of Cowboy Diplomacy," with a cover featuring a big Stetson with the presidential seal and a pair of boots sticking down from it. Bush II apparently floated notions of interdependence only when, as the Realpolitik *Washington Post* columnist Charles Krauthammer explains, "there is something the allies will actually help accomplish, or . . . there is nothing to be done anyway, so multilateralism gives you the cover of appearing to do something."[82] Still other commentators countered that "Cowboy Diplomacy Is Not Dead Yet."[83] The cowboy remained an icon of masculinity, independence, and action.

The welfare queen also persisted as a descriptor of poor single mothers but migrated to additional referents, others who illegitimately get rich from public funds. Thus, in receiving foreign aid, South Korea goes to the top of the U.S. State Department's "foreign policy welfare queens." As the state with the most federal assistance per capita, Alaska has become "a welfare queen."[84] Meanwhile, the political left hurls "welfare queen" as an epithet at corporations for undeservingly dipping into public coffers. Thus, in paying workers so little that they have to rely on food stamps, Medicaid, and the earned income tax credit, Wal-Mart has transferred costs of doing business onto taxpayers, while other companies, like Boeing, live off federal contracts. An Arizona Green party chapter compared support of "the welfare mother" with that of the "corporate welfare mother," who costs the government billions of dollars more.[85] Such designations reinforce the negativity of welfare and thus legitimate the term in its original signification of the dependency of poor black mothers.

THE MORE THINGS CHANGE, THE MORE GENDER REMAINS

The 2008 presidential election was a history making event, with the first white woman and first black man as serious candidates. Yet the tired gendered tropes of the cowboy and welfare queen pervaded the contest. In offering hope and a new politics beyond left and right, red and blue states, and Washington ways, Barack Obama may have sought to move beyond these expressions of independence and dependence through calls for national interdependence and grassroots mobilization. But, as a black man raised by a single mother, Obama found himself tossed into the troubled waters of stereotype. So much of his appeal came from a life story that cast him as the son abandoned by his father and brought up by women, a tale that fed into welfare queen and matriarchy narratives. The uniqueness of his biography—a white Kansas mother who meets his African father in multicultural Hawai'i—separated him from the usual tale but also identified him with the family problem of black America. He has emphasized his comfort being around women; he is, as Susan Faludi put it, "the young man in the bower of a matriarchy—raised by a 'strong' mother, bolstered by a 'strong' sister, married to a 'strong' wife and proud of his 'strong' daughters," and, we might add, protected by his loving, though sometimes racially insensitive, grandmother.[86] His call for "fathers to realize that responsibility does not end at conception" came as an offer of "help to all the mothers out there who are raising these kids by themselves." In reinscribing the heterosexual family, Obama embraced reigning norms even as elsewhere he defended gay rights.[87]

He had to avoid appearing to be too much of a black man, since to conjure up manhood and blackness reinforced racialized gendered messages used to excuse racism.[88] Popular culture long has associated black men with danger, crime, sexual assault, and outlaw power. Obama had to display a feminine side to counter his black maleness. Thus, a contributor to the MOJO *(Mother Jones)* blog perceptively commented, "This—Obama is a 'woman' cuz he's all nice and stuff—seems like yet another example of how Obama isn't 'really' black. (He can't be. He isn't scary.) That makes him acceptable to whites since 'black' men are dangerous and uncooperative and, to put it mildly, not team players."[89] Others praised this softer turn. In *Newsweek,* Martin Linsky, a professor at Harvard's Kennedy School, paid him the dubious compliment of being "the first serious woman candidate for president in the same way that Bill Clinton was the first black president"; that is, his demeanor could substitute for the real thing and feed the illusion of change without crossing a political taboo.[90] Obama reflected women's ways of knowing, the kind of gendered traits universalized as expressions of "female difference." According to Linsky, he displayed "a commitment to inclusiveness in problem solving, deep optimism, modesty about knowing all the answers, the courage to deliver uncomfortable news, not taking on all the work alone, and a willingness to air dirty linen."

Distracters, on the other hand, questioned his strength and indirectly his manhood. He was a talker, as opposed to a doer. The *New York Times* columnist Maureen Dowd asked during the Democratic primaries, comparing Obama to his main rival, Hillary Clinton, "Will Hillzilla Crush Obambi?"[91] This association of the Illinois senator with the innocent fawn looking for his mother not only was infantilizing but characterized him as weak. As the campaign wore on, Clinton morphed into a white working-class hero—she had "the strength to take on tough problems" and possessed "'testicular fortitude,'" said the head of the Sheet Metal Worker's Union.[92] But Dowd retained gender skepticism. She concluded after Clinton failed to end the contest after Super Tuesday, "Hillary was so busy trying to prove she could be one of the boys—getting on the Armed Services Committee, voting to let W. go to war in Iraq, strong-arming supporters and donors, and trying to out-macho Obama—that she only belatedly realized that many Democratic and independent voters, especially women, were eager to move from hard-power locker-room tactics to a soft-power sewing circle approach."[93]

Conservative television and radio commentators continued to question his masculinity. After Obama's "metrosexual" rival John Edwards, who couldn't get beyond his image as "the Breck girl," left the race, Obama bore the brunt of conservative homophobia.[94] Some of his missteps, from a disastrous attempt at bowling to attacking rural white Pennsylvanians before a San Francisco fundraiser, fed into the "elite" and "effete" label that opponents pinned on the Ivy League educator-writer. Obama was "prissy," "a sissy boy," "like kind of a wuss," "wimpy," and thus hardly "a real man." To reports about the setting up of Obama book clubs, a brilliant organizing strategy, Tucker Carlson declared in the summer of 2007, "Well, everybody knows that a book club is no place for a man. So why has Barack Obama suddenly turned into Oprah?" To which his guest replied, "Obama has violated the trust of men everywhere . . . It makes you wonder what he won't compromise of himself. Are we going to have mani/pedi parties next?"[95]

If Obama was another sister, then his wife, Michelle, was an angry black woman, too strong for her (or his) own good. While the conservative columnist Michelle Malkin discussed media portrayals of Michelle Obama on Fox News, a visual flashed across the screen calling the Princeton- and Harvard-trained lawyer "Obama's baby mama." Responded Joan Walsh in Salon.com, "Do you try to explain that 'baby mama' is slang for the unmarried mother of a man's child, and not his wife, or even a girlfriend?" The comment thus entered the chat cycles in which online as well as television commentators repeated the slur, what African Americans interpreted as a willful ignorance of black life and culture.[96] By transforming Barack into an irresponsible stud, Michelle became just another welfare queen—just as Obama made his Father's Day appeal to black men.

PERSISTENT ICONS

Tropes of independence and dependence are powerful precisely because they tap into historical memories and lend themselves to multiple readings or manipulations. But we need not construct a new world order—or conduct presidential campaigns—on the basis of old gendered (and racialized) myths. Feminist theorists of care, and other advocates for social justice, offer an alternative to such binary oppositions; we have emphasized interdependence over the dyad of dependence/independence.[97] In this sense, Barack Obama tapped into a new form of masculinity, redefining manhood and not only black manhood. But whether he will turn out to slay the welfare queen as well as the cowboy by offering new visions for home and abroad was up for debate as the 2008 campaign headed down the home stretch. The persistence of gender wars—that were racialized and nationalized as well—was more likely, no matter who would walked into 1600 Pennsylvania Ave.

NOTES

I would like to thank my research assistants Jill Jensen, Leandra Zarnow, Lizzie Lamoree, and Janiene Langford, as well as Giles Gunn and Carl Gutiérrez-Jones for their suggestions and for inviting me to present at the conference from which this article originated. An earlier version appears as "On Cowboys and Welfare Queens: Independence, Dependence, and Interdependence at Home and Abroad," *Journal of American Studies* 41 (December 2007): 599–621.

1. Maria Garilovic, "Obama Slams McCain's 'Cowboy Diplomacy,'" CBS News, May 19, 2008, at http://www.cbsnews.com/blogs/2008/05/19/politics/fromtheroad/entry4108388.shtml, accessed July 10, 2008.

2. Andrew Ward, "McCain Attacks Obama's 'Cowboy Diplomacy,'" FT.com, June 20, 2008, at http://www.ft.com/cms/s/0/43b5746a-3efb-11dd-8fd9–0000779fd2ac.html, accessed July 11, 2008.

3. Susan Faludi, "Think the Gender War Is Over? Think Again," *New York Times*, June 15, 2008.

4. Faludi, "Think The Gender War is Over?"

5. Stan Goff, "Elections and the Death Cult," *Huffington Post*, June 6, 2008, at http://www.huffingtonpost.com/stan-goff/elections-and-the-death-c_b_105598.html, accessed July 10, 2008.

6. Maria Gavrilovic, "Obama's Father's Day Message," CBS News, June 15, 2008, http://www.cbsnews.com/blogs/2008/06/15/politics/fromtheroad/entry4181891.shtml, accessed July 11, 2008. On feminist opposition to fatherhood initiatives, see Anna Marie Smith, *Welfare Reform and Sexual Regulation* (New York: Cambridge University Press, 2007).

7. This division is particularly true in women's and gender history. For a critique, see Laura Briggs, "Gender and U.S. Imperialism in U.S. Women's History," in *The Practice of U.S. Women's History: Narratives, Intersections, and Dialogues*, ed. S.J. Kleinberg, Eileen Boris, and Vicki L. Ruiz (New Brunswick, N.J.: Rutgers University Press, 2007), 146–60.

8. Feminist historians have undermined this myth. For a review of the literature, see Susan Armitage, "Turner's Ghost: A Personal Retrospective on Western Women's Literature," in *The Practice of U.S. Women's History*, 126–45.

9. Martin Gilens, *Why Americans Hate Welfare: Race, Media, and the Politics of Anti-Poverty Policy* (Chicago: University of Chicago Press, 1999).

10. Here I extrapolate from Joan W. Scott, "'Experience,'" in *Feminists Theorize The Political*, ed. Judith Butler and Joan W. Scott (New York: Routledge, 1992), 22–40; and Judith Butler, "Critically Queer," in *Bodies That Matter* (New York: Routledge, 1993), 226–42.

11. Don Santina, "Cowboy Imagery and the American Presidency: Ride 'Em Brush Cutter!" *CounterPunch*, December 19, 2005, at http://www.counterpunch.org/santina12192005.html, accessed September 1, 2006; David E. Lopez, "Cowboy Strikes and Unions," in *The American West: The Reader*, ed. Walter Nugent and Martin Ridge (Bloomington: Indiana University Press, 1999); Dee Garceau, "Nomads, Bunkies, Cross-Dressers, and Family Men: Cowboy Identity and the Gendering of Ranch Work," in *Across the Great Divide: Cultures of Manhood in the American West*, ed. Matthew Basso, Laura McCall, and Dee Garceau (New York: Routledge, 2001), 149–65; Simon M. Evans, Sarah Carter, and Bill Yeo, eds., *Cowboys, Ranchers and the Cattle Business: Cross-Border Perspectives on Ranching History* (Boulder: University Press of Colorado, 2000); R. Philip Loy, *Westerns in a Changing America, 1955–2000* (Jefferson, N.C.: McFarland, 2004); and Richard Slotkin, *Gunfighter Nation: The Myth of the Frontier in Twentieth-Century America* (New York: Athenaeum, 1992).

12. Rickie Solinger, *Beggars and Choosers: How the Politics of Choice Shapes Adoption, Abortion, and Welfare in the United States* (New York: Hill and Wang, 2001), 143.

13. Ange-Marie Hancock, *The Politics of Disgust: The Public Identity of the Welfare Queen* (New York: New York University Press, 2004); Holloway Sparks, "Queens, Teens and Model Mothers: Race, Gender and the Discourse of Welfare Reform," in *Race and the Politics of Welfare Reform*, ed. Sanford Schram, Joe Soss, and Richard C. Fording (Ann Arbor: University of Michigan Press, 2003), 171–95; Wahneema Lubiano, "Black Ladies, Welfare Queens and State Minstrels: Ideological War by Narrative Means," in *Race-ing Justice, En-gendering Power: Essays on Anita Hill, Clarence Thomas and the Construction of Social Identity*, ed. Toni Morrison (New York: Pantheon Books, 1992), 323–63; Martha Fineman,

"Images of Mothers in Poverty Discourse," *Duke University Law Journal* 2 (1991): 274–95.

14. Gwendolyn Mink, *Welfare's End* (Ithaca: Cornell University Press, 1998).

15. Ronald Takaki, *Iron Cages: Race and Culture in 19th-Century America* (New York: Oxford University Press, 1990), 253–89; Mathew Frye Jacobson, *Barbarian Virtues: The United States Encounters Foreign Peoples At Home and Abroad, 1876–1917* (New York: Hill and Wang, 2000).

16. Jennifer Mittelstadt, *From Welfare to Workfare: The Unintended Consequences of Liberal Reform, 1945–1965* (Chapel Hill: University of North Carolina Press, 2005), 107–54; Anna Marie Smith, *Welfare Reform and Sexual Regulation* (New York: Cambridge University Press, 2007).

17. "Percent African American in Newsmagazine Pictures of the Poor, 1950–1992 (compared with true percent black)," table in *Welfare: A Documentary History of U.S. Policy and Politics*, ed. Gwendolyn Mink and Rickie Solinger (New York: New York University Press, 2003), 538.

18. Robert A. Caro, *The Path to Power: The Years of Lyndon Johnson* (New York: Knopf, 1982); Santina, "Cowboy Imagery and the American Presidency."

19. George Christian quoted in Douglas Quenqua and Sherri Deatherage Green, "W's Ranch Spurs Homely Feel to President's Image," *PRWeek USA* , September 3, 2001, at http://www.sherrigreen.com/W's%20ranch.htm, accessed September 1, 2006.

20. http://www.cowboyhatstore.com/stetsonfelt_index/openroad_LBJ_index.htm; http://www.millerhats.com/lbj_catalog/lbj.html, accessed September 1, 2006.

21. Al Neuharth, "Should Cowboy Bush Ride into the Sunset?" *USA Today*, May 13, 2004, at http://www.usatoday.com/news/opinion/columnist/neuharth/2004-05-13-neuharth_x.htm, accessed September 1, 2006.

22. Lyndon B. Johnson, "Annual Message to the Congress on the State of the Union, January 8, 1964," at www.lbjlib.utexas.edu/johnson/archives.hom/speeches.hom/640108, accessed September 2, 2006.

23. J. William Fulbright, *Arrogance of Power* (New York: Vintage Books, 1966).

24. Franklin D. Roosevelt, "Annual Message to the Congress," January 4, 1935, in *Public Papers and Addresses of Franklin D. Roosevelt*, ed. Samuel I. Rosenman (New York: Random House, 1938?), 4:19.

25. James T. Patterson, *America's Struggle against Poverty in the Twentieth Century* (Cambridge, Mass.: Harvard University Press, 2000), 132; Christopher Weeks, *Job Corps: Dollars and Dropouts* (Boston: Little, Brown and Co., 1967), 130–31.

26. Felicia Kornbluh, *The Welfare Rights Moment: New York City and the Nation, 1960–1975* (Philadelphia: University of Pennsylvania Press, 2007); Premilla Nadasen, *Welfare Warriors: The Welfare Rights Movement in the United States* (New York: Routledge, 2005).

27. David Greenberg, *Nixon's Shadow: History of an Image* (New York: W. W. Norton, 2003); Richard Bradley, *American Political Mythology from Kennedy to Nixon* (New York: Peter Lang, 2000).

28. "Moynihan Applauds Nixon on Welfare," *New York Times*, August 11, 1969, 24. On Nixon's welfare proposal, see Jill Quadagno, "Race, Class, and Gender in the United States Welfare State: Nixon's Failed Family Assistance Plan," *American Sociological Review* 55 (1990): 11–28.

29. "Excerpts from Nixon Message to Congress on Welfare Plan," *New York Times*, August 12, 1969, 18.

30. James M. Naughton, "The Presidency: He Proposes a New Way of Helping the Poor," *New York Times*, August 10, 1969, E1.

31. Nadasen, *Welfare Warriors*, 157–86; Eileen Boris, "When Work Is Slavery," in *Whose Welfare?* ed. Gwendolyn Mink (Ithaca: Cornell University Press, 1999), 37–38.

32. James Warren, "Nixon on Tape Expounds on Welfare and Homosexuality," *Chicago Tribune*, November 7, 1999, "Perspective," 2.

33. Edward D. Berkowitz, *Something Happened: A Political and Cultural Overview of the Seventies* (New York: Columbia University Press, 2006), 12–31, 61–65.

34. For the fullest discussion of the oil crisis, see Natasha Zaretsky, *No Direction Home: The American Family and the Fear of National Decline, 1968–1980* (Chapel Hill: University of North Carolina Press, 2007), especially chapter 2, "Getting the House in Order: The Oil Embargo, Consumption, and the Limits of American Power," 71–104. See also Zaretsky, "In the Name of Austerity: Middle-Class Consumption and the OPEC Oil Embargo of 1973–1974," in *The World the 60s Made: Politics and Culture in Recent America*, ed. Van Grosse and Richard Moser (Philadelphia: Temple University Press, 2003), 138–61.

35. "Transcript of Nixon's Question and Answer Session With A.P. Managing Editors," *New York Times*, November 18, 1973, 62.

36. Harry Schwartz, "Self-Sufficiency May Be Only a Mirage," *New York Times* December 9, 1973, 260; Anthony Lewis, "A Fortress America?" *New York Times*, December 3, 1973, 39; James Reston, "Alone or Together?" *New York Times*, December 16, 1973, 243. (All page numbers are from Proquest edition.)

37. Letters to the Editor, *New York Times*, November 18, 1973, 238 (Proquest edition).

38. "The Taxes on Oil," *New York Times*, January 21, 1974, 26.

39. Reston, "Alone or Together?" 243.

40. Bernard Gwertzman, "Kissinger Offers 7-Point Program on World Energy," *New York Times*, February 12, 1974, 1, quotes at 20.

41. James Reston, "Two Cheers for France," *New York Times*, February 15, 1974, 33.

42. Reston, "Alone or Together?" 243.

43. Zaretsky, *No Direction Home*, 95.

44. Michael Schaller, *Reckoning with Reagan: America and Its President in the 1980s* (New York: Oxford University Press, 1992), 122.

45. Howell Raines, "Reagan Words Often Conflict with Strategy," *New York Times*, July 13, 1980, 1, quote at 12.

46. Schaller, *Reckoning with Reagan*, 149–78; Gil Troy, *Morning in America: How Ronald Reagan Invented the 1980s* (Princeton, N.J.: Princeton University Press, 2005).

47. Santina, "Cowboy Imagery and the American Presidency." For the governorship, see Lou Cannon, *Reagan* (New York: Putnam, 1982).

48. Robert Dallek, *Ronald Reagan: The Politics of Symbolism* (Cambridge, Mass.: Harvard University Press, 1984), 21; Michael Rogin, *"Ronald Reagan," The Movie, and Other Episodes in Political Demonology* (Berkeley and Los Angeles: University of California Press, 1987), 38.

49. James Combs, *The Reagan Range: The Nostalgic Myth in American Politics* (Bowling Green, Ohio: Bowling Green State University Popular Press, 1993), 50–51.

50. Schaller, *Reckoning with Reagan*, 119. The cover of this study has Reagan in a cowboy shirt riding a horse.

51. Larry Kudlow, "Saddle Up with the Dollar: Cowboy Capitalism Will Take Care of the Greenback," November 16, 2004, at http://www.nationalreview.com/kudlow/kudlow200411160821.asp, accessed September 3, 2006; Olaf Gersemann, *Cowboy Capitalism: European Myths, American Realities* (Washington, D.C.: Cato Institute, 2004), unfavorably compares European economic decline to America's cowboy capitalism.

52. Committee to Re-Elect Governor Reagan, press release on Labor Day address, September 7, 1970, 3, GO 186, Research File, Health and Welfare, Welfare 1970 (4/5), Ronald Reagan Presidential Library, Simi Valley. For Reagan vs. social workers, see Eileen Boris and Jennifer Klein, *Organizing Home Care,* chapter 4, manuscript in author's possession.

53. Solinger, *Beggars and Choosers,* 148.

54. Cabinet Staff Meeting, November 22, 1968, GO 25, Cabinet Meeting Minutes, November 1968 [2/2], 2–3, National Archives at Ronald Reagan Presidential Library; Bill Boyarsky, "Reagan Proposes $100 Million Cutback for Welfare in State," *Los Angeles Times,* March 20, 1970, 1; Philip Hager, "State Offers New Plan on Welfare to Avert Fund Cutoff," *Los Angeles Times,* October 30, 1970, A3.

55. "'Welfare Queen' Becomes Issue in Reagan Campaign," *New York Times,* February 15, 1976, 51; "'Welfare Queen' Loses Her Cadillac Limousine," *New York Times,* February 29, 1976, 42; "Chicago Relief Queen Guilty," *New York Times,* March 19, 1977, 8; Solinger, *Beggars and Choosers,* 179–80.

56. For Reagan's language used in the early 1970s, see Johnnie Tillmon, "Welfare Is a Woman's Issue," in *Welfare,* ed. Mink and Solinger, 375.

57. Robert Pear,"3 Key Aides Reshape Welfare Programs," *New York Times,* April 26, 1982, B8.

58. Ronald Reagan, "Welfare Is a Cancer," *New York Times,* April 1, 1971, 41.

59. Frances Fox Piven, "Welfare and Work," in Mink, *Whose Welfare?* 83–99.

60. R. Kent Weaver, "Ending Welfare as We Know It: Policymaking for Low-Income Families in the Clinton/Gingrich Era," in *The Social Divide: Political Parties and the Future of Activist Government,* ed. Margaret Weir (Washington, D.C.: Brookings, 1998), 361–416.

61. William J. Clinton, State of the Union address, February 17, 1993, http://www.washingtonpost.com/wp-srv/politics/special/states/docs/sou93.htm; William J. Clinton, "The President's Radio Address," May 18, 1996, John Woolley and Gerhard Peters, *The American Presidency Project* (online, Santa Barbara, Calif.: University of California [hosted], Gerhard Peters [database]). http://www.presidency.ucsb.edu/ws/?pid=52834, accessed September 4, 2006.

62. Mink, *Welfare's End;* see also the essays in Mink, ed., *Whose Welfare?*

63. Editorial, "Marriage Skills, Federal Style," *Christian Science Monitor,* January 23, 2004, 10; "Welfare Rolls Continue to Fall," *HHS News,* February 9, 2006, http://www.acf.hhs.gov/news/press/2006/welfare_rolls_decline_june_05.htm, accessed September 4, 2006.

64. Tillmon, "Welfare," 374.

65. Charles Krauthammer, "When the Going Gets Tough, We Will Need a Captain," *The Atlanta Journal-Constitution,* February 8, 1989, A15; Stephen Kurkjian, "Bush Proves He's No Policy Wimp," *Boston Globe,* December 31, 1989, A3; Charley Reese, "Ultimatum to Iraq a Blunder That Boxes in Bush and Hussein," *The Orlando Sentinel,* August 26, 1990, G2; Lynn Garner, "Bush Dubbed 'Rambo' in Cool Reception to Energy Plan on Capitol Hill," *The Oil Daily,* February 22, 1991, 2.

66. "Globo-Cop Glop," *The Progressive* 59 (December 1995): 9–10; John Hall, "Nation's Forces—and Maybe Its Fate—in Hands of Others," *Richmond Times-*

Dispatch, April 17, 1994, F2; David Limbaugh, "It's also foreign policy . . . and TV Drama," *The Washington Times*, April 3, 1999, C1.

67. Laura Mecoy, "U.S. May Feel Effects of Invasion at Gas Pump," *Sacramento Bee*, August 3, 1990, A24: Robin Wright, "Fighting the Fires of Islam," *Los Angeles Times*, July 4, 1993, M-1; Marilyn Greene, "Iran, Iraq, Libya Are Targeted on Terror," *USA Today*, March 31, 1993, 4A; Maura Reynolds, "The State of the Union Address," *Los Angeles Times*, January 29, 2003, A1.

68. Quoted in Infact Report, "Cowboy Diplomacy: How the US Undermines International Environmental, Human Rights, Disarmament and Health Agreements," http://www.infact.org/cowboyd.html, accessed August 30, 2006.

69. "My Heroes Have Always Been Cowboys," button #21197, *RepublicanMarket.com*, at http://www.republicanmarket.com/store/home, accessed August 28, 2006.

70. "This Cowboy," *Rushonline.com*, http://www.rushonline.com/halloffame/thiscowboy.htm, assessed July 11, 2008.

71. Alex Spillius, "George Bush the Texan Is 'Scared of Horses,'" *Telegraph.co.uk*, September 21, 2007, at http://www.telegraph.co.uk/news/worldnews/1563773/George-Bush-the-Texan-is-%27scared-of-horses%27.html, accessed July 10, 2008.

72. "What the World Needs Now," in Wayne Lutz, "Joe Hoeffel, Anti-Cowboy," *The Tocquevillian Magazine*, March 18, 2004, http://www.tocquevillian.com/articles/0173.html; contrast with http://www.submitresponse.co.uk/archives/march/march-Pages/Image3.html, last accessed September 6, 2006.

73. Reed Johnson and Gayle Pollard-Terry, "Bush's Speech: One for the Ages? Maybe," *Los Angeles Times*, March 19, 2003, E-1.

74. http://www.theillustrateddailyscribble.com/daily.scribble.pages.05/06.30.05.html, accessed September 6, 2006.

75. Andrew Bernstein, "Old West Cowboy Ethic Is the American Way to Fight Evil," *Insight on the News*, April 1, 2003, 50–51.

76. David E. Sanger, "To Some in Europe, the Major Problem Is Bush the Cowboy," *New York Times*, January 24, 2003, 1.

77. Tom Teepen, "If Bush Is the Cowboy Sheriff, He's Riding without a Posse," *Ventura County Star*, March 21, 2003, B12.

78. Quoted in John Potter, "Bush Gives Cowboys Bad Image," *The Billings Gazetter*, March 10, 2003.

79. "Leadership over Damage Control," *Santa Barbara News Press*, April 14, 2004, A10.

80. Dan Froomkin, "George Bush, Space Cowboy," *WashingtonPost.com*, February 21, 2008, at http://www.washingtonpost.com/wp-dyn/content/blog/2008/02/21/BL2008022101414.html, assessed July 11, 2008.

81. Erik Baard, "George W. Bush Ain't No Cowboy," *Village Voice*, September 28, 2004, at http://www.villagevoice.com/news/0439,baard,57117,1.html, accessed September 2, 2006.

82. Charles Krauthammer, "The Comeback Kid: Multilateralism," *Santa Barbara News-Press*, August 29, 2006, A11.

83. Mike Allen and Romesh Ratnesar, "The End of Cowboy Diplomacy," *Time*, July 17, 2006, posted July 9, 2006, http://www.time.com/time/magazine/article/0,9171,1211578-1,00.html, accessed August 17, 2006; Jim Lobe, "Cowboy Diplomacy Is Not Dead Yet," July 15, 2006, at http://www.antiwar.com/lobe/?articleid+9310, accessed August 29, 2006.

84. Doug Bandow, "Foreign Policy Welfare Queen," October 22, 2005, at http://www.cato.org/pub_display.php?pub_id=5146; Charles Soto, "Alaska Is Such a Wel-

fare Queen," *clnet News*, February 28, 2006, at http://news.com.com/5208-1034-0.html?forumID=1&threadID=14425&start=0, both accessed August 29, 2006.

85. See, "Corporate Welfare, The Shame Page," http://www.progress.org/banneker/cw.html; "Wal-Mart, the Welfare Queen," http://blog.wakeupwalmart.com/ufcw/2005/04/walmart_the_wel.html; Mary, "Boeing: Corporate Welfare Queen," *The left coaster*, December 7, 2003, at http://www.theleftcoaster.com/archives/000860.php, accessed August 29, 2006.

86. Barack Obama, *Dreams from My Father: A Story of Race and Inheritance* (New York: Times Books, 1995); Faludi, "Think the Gender War Is Over?"

87. "Obama's Father's Day Speech," reprinted at http://www.huffingtonpost.com/2008/06/15/obamas-fathers-day-speech_n_107220.html, accessed July 11, 2008; Obama mentioned the rights of gays and lesbians in his standard stump speech. See, Associated Press, "Michelle Obama Links Gay Rights to Civil Rights," June 27, 2008, at http://elections.foxnews.com/2008/06/27/michelle-obama-praises-clinton-in-new-hampshire, assessed July 11, 2008.

88. Arica L. Coleman, "Does Barack Obama Have Testicular Fortitude?" *History News Network*, June 2, 2008, at http://hnn.us/articles/51000.html, accessed July 10, 2008. See also Steve Estes, *I Am A Man!: Race, Manhood, and the Civil Rights Movement* (Chapel Hill: University of North Carolina Press, 2005).

89. Debra Dickerson, "If Obama Is a Woman, and I Vote for Clinton, Am I a Man?" *MOJO Blog*, February 28, 2008, at http://www.motherjones.com/mojoblog/archives/2008/02/7432_hed_if_obama_is.html, accessed July 11, 2008.

90. Martin Linsky, "The First Woman President?" *Newsweek*, February 26, 2008, at http://www.newsweek.com/id/115397, accessed July 11, 2008.

91. Maureen Dowd, "Will Hillzilla Crush Obambi?" *New York Times*, December 13, 2006.

92. Fernando Suarez, "Union Boss Says Clinton Has 'Testicular Fortitude,'" CBS News, April 30, 2008, at http://www.cbsnews.com/blogs/2008/04/30/politics/fromtheroad/entry4059528.shtml, accessed July 10, 2008.

93. Maureen Dowd, "¿Quién Es Less Macho?" *New York Times*, February 24, 2008.

94. Brian Montopoli, "John Edwards and the Case of the 'Breck Girl' Comment," CBS News, April 24, 2007, at http://www.cbsnews.com/blogs/2007/04/24/publiceye/entry2722181.shtml, last accessed July 11, 2008; Maureen Dowd, "Running with Scissors," *New York Times*, April 21, 2007.

95. Flaudi, "Think the Gender War Is Over?" "Still More Carlson on Obama: 'Why Has Barack Obama Suddenly Turned into Oprah?'" *Media Matters*, http://mediamatters.org/items/200707130009, accessed July 10, 2008.

96. David Bauder, "Fox News Refers to Michelle Obama as 'Baby Mama,'" *FoxNews.com*, June 13, 2008, at http://www.foxnews.com/wires/2008Jun13/0,4670,TVFoxObama,00.html, accessed July 10, 2008; Adrienne Washington, "Black Women Rally to Michelle," *Washington Times*, July 5, 2008; Rex W. Huppke, "Perception Problem: When Outsiders Look in on Black America," *Chicago Tribune*, July 6, 2008.

97. For example, Joan Tronto, *Moral Boundaries: A Political Argument for an Ethic of Care* (New York: Routledge, 1993); Selma Sevenhijsen, *Citizenship and the Ethics of Care: Feminist Considerations on Justice, Morality and Politics* (New York: Routledge, 1998); Wendy Sarvasy, "Social Citizenship from a Feminist Perspective," *Hypatia* 12, no.1 (1997): 54–74; and Madonna Harrington Meyer, ed., *Care Work: Gender, Labor and the Welfare State* (New York: Routledge, 2000).

9. Air Raids

Television and the War on Terror

Lisa Parks

The term "air raid" typically conjures the sound of a whining siren or the massive destruction wrought during World War II as pilots plunged toward European cities from London to Dresden, carpeting them with firebombs. But for several reasons the term is relevant to the most recent round of global warfare as well. First, the term designates atmospheric and electromagnetic spaces as fundamental parts of the battlefield and serves as a reminder that armed struggles occur in the signal territory. Second, the air raid metaphorically evokes the process by which elected officials have historically sold off the publicly owned broadcast spectrum to commercial interests that have granted more and more airtime to corporate and militaristic perspectives, as evident in television news after 9/11. Finally, the air raid implies the possibility of a surprise attack, a reversal of power by an unexpected force, and in this sense it is suggestive of hegemonic power plays that shape world history. I begin with this term, then, because it usefully evokes post-9/11 conditions such as the intensifying relations between media and military institutions, the production of wartime atmospherics in everyday life, and the political contestations that necessarily underpin the U.S. war on global terror.

The George W. Bush administration's policy of waging ongoing war on global terror inaugurated a paradigm of episodic warfare that played out first in Afghanistan and then in Iraq. Speculations about the location of the administration's next war—whether in Iran, Syria or North Korea—abounded in the press. The very structure of warfare has taken on uniquely televisual patterns, not only by virtue of the practice of embedding commercially paid broadcast journalists inside of armed personnel carriers, but also with cable news' recurring spokespersons/characters, settings, plotlines, and sponsors, presented twenty-four hours a day, seven days a week. Having said this, it would be irresponsible, I think, to treat television news simply as a monolith, since, in producers' efforts to condense and contain complex historical events, the medium is invariably leaking at the seams. War is way too complex for TV's small cadre of character parts, way to unwieldy for its short attention span, and way too dismal for its steady diet of feel-good spectacles. This is why episodic warfare is inevitably punctuated by internal media crises such as the eviction of reporters Peter Arnett and Geraldo Rivera from the war in Iraq, the panic over airing brutal images from Fallujah or Abu Ghraib prison, or the crisis over the circulation of photos of soliders' flag-covered caskets returning to Dover Air Force Base.

Liberal and leftist intellectuals tend to be highly critical of television news, but few ever watch it and as a result their critiques often lack specificity and detail. In order to draw attention to some of these details, I critically examine a selection of cable news content after the strikes on the World Trade Center and the Pentagon on September 11, 2001 and during the U.S. war against Afghanistan. I contrast the programming of Oxygen with the coverage of networks such as CNN and Fox News in order to evaluate whether this relatively new women's multimedia network was able to articulate feminist discourses of demilitarization in the context of a political climate that discouraged debate and suppressed dissent in favor of rapid-fire calls for military intervention. After 9/11, U.S. cable television networks such as CNN and Fox News adopted the command and control logics of military institutions, hired retired military officials as news reporters, created Hollywood-like catchlines such as "America Strikes Back," reduced complex events to good-versus-evil polarities, and exacerbated public fear and paranoia to rationalize U.S. military retaliation. Oxygen's paucity of conventional news resources and liberal feminist agenda, however, had the effect of positioning its coverage—even if temporarily—outside of and apart from dominant television news discourses, enabling the network to formulate forms of coverage that circulated voices of dissent from women in the United States and abroad. After describing U.S. cable news coverage after 9/11, I turn to a discussion of more literal air raids—the U.S. bombings of Al Jazeera stations in Kabul and Baghdad in 2001 and 2004—and I suggest that these attacks can be understood as continuous with the dominant coverage paradigm of CNN and Fox News, since they, too, suppressed dissent, but in the most violent and even fatal terms. The U.S. attacks on Al Jazeera represent a troubling mobilization of state-sanctioned violence, information management, and media capitalism to quash the only Arab satellite television network consistently dedicated to the evaluation of democratic principles throughout the Arab world.[1]

MILITARY OPTIONS AND NETWORK VIGILANTISM

The 9/11 attacks were notorious for interrupting the flows of commercial entertainment, whether late-night TV talk shows, Disneyland rides, or Hollywood movie releases, but they actually revitalized satellite and cable television news channels as viewers clustered around their sets to watch history unfold. The demand for post-9/11 news pumped life back into CNN, sent the ratings of Fox News skyrocketing, and put Al Jazeera on the global media map. It also created opportunities for lesser-known cable channels such as Oxygen. In a highly competitive multichannel environment, cable news networks seize upon historic events such as 9/11 and the wars in Afghanistan and Iraq to add value to their brand names by introducing special programming, experts, personalities, audiovisual perspectives, graphics, and styles of reporting. Since it would be impossible to discuss all of the coverage after 9/11, I have elected to focus on what might be called signature programming—that is, programming that came to be associated with the brand names of three different networks, CNN, Fox News, and Oxygen.

Although post-9/11 coverage differed across the networks, the major cable players such as CNN and Fox News established what might be considered a dominant paradigm. This can be understood, for instance, as taking shape in the CNN show *Military Options,* which began after September 11 and lasted throughout the U.S. war in Afghanistan. Hosted by the owl-eyed correspondent Wolf Blitzer and also by Miles O'Brien, *Military Options* typically featured retired military commanders explaining new weapons systems and maneuvers in the Afghan war theater, CNN Pentagon and White House correspondents summarizing press conferences, and experts and officials interpreting declassified U.S. military intelligence. CNN added several military experts to its pool of personalities, including retired generals Wesley Clark, David Grange, George Joulwan, and Don Shepperd, who made regular appearances in late 2001.

While the program's title seems to suggest a show dedicated to deliberation of various "military options," its formulaic assimilation of military spokespersons, technological vantage points, and rhetoric valorized only one option—a full-fledged attack on Afghanistan. The show, in other words, was not so much about "options" as it was a resounding endorsement of U.S. military decisions made behind closed doors and without substantive public or congressional debate. (Wolf Blitzer even went so far as to claim antiwar demonstrations were unpatriotic.)

Cynthia Enloe suggests that militarization is "a step by step process by which a person or a thing gradually comes to be controlled by the military or comes to depend for its well-being on militaristic ideas."[2] What was striking after 9/11, though, was the degree to which television's militarization did not transpire as a step-by-step process; rather, it seemed to happen virtually overnight. Paul Virilio characterizes this quick shift as the "replacement rate" of totalitarian systems, writing that under such systems "the collective murder and ritual sacrifice of innocents . . . would no longer be hidden activities but unavoidable daily spectacles."[3] Though the militarization of television arguably began in early-twentieth-century experiments that included its deployment in Nazi Germany, the speed with which militaristic rhetoric permeated U.S. cable news networks after 9/11 was startling. The military discourse of command and control was instantly transposed upon that of broadcast journalism.

Most of the CNN correspondents providing the hard stories on the frontlines were men, but the veteran reporter Christiane Amanpour sent stories from Islamabad and Kabul, and Kyra Phillips went to the region to investigate Navy operations. Female anchors such as Joie Chen delivered coverage from CNN headquarters in Atlanta. Chen may not have been deployed to the warfront, but she regularly meandered through an immersive map of Afghanistan projected on the studio floor while she interviewed former commanders from "the War Room." In one segment, she interviewed retired Major General Don Shepperd about U.S. attacks on Kandahar and Jalalabad. In these segments, coverage is organized through the alternation of broadcast correspondence and military command in a way that is fully gendered. Chen politely asks questions, pointing to various sites on the map, and the authoritative white male military expert details U.S. assaults, mentioning the artillery used, the direction of the attack, and the anticipated effect. The two stand upon and crouch around the map of Afghanistan as if playing a strange hybrid of the board games *Twister* and *Risk.* The sequence immerses the news anchor and military commander together in the war theater in a way that symbolically anticipates the practice of "embedded reporting," which found fuller expression during the war in Iraq. We might also consider what it means for viewers to see an Asian-American woman occupying a world map with a white U.S. military commander explaining strategies for U.S. domination of the East. The repetition of such sequences commandeers Asian-American femininity as a complicit partner in U.S. global militarism, as opposed to an active investigator of the conditions that might necessitate it.[4]

Perhaps it was the remoteness of military and cartographic views on

CNN that made Geraldo Rivera's on-location stint for Fox News in late 2001 seem so utterly sensational. Rivera, who claimed he couldn't bear to stay on the sidelines during a big story, left his job at CNBC on November 16, 2001, and headed for Afghanistan three days later. As Rivera explained, "the war on terrorism is the biggest story of our times [and] I've got to get out there. And when you're an anchor, you're literally anchored. I had to break the chain."[5] On November 19 Rivera went to Afghanistan and by early December he was sending live satellite transmissions from outposts in the White Mountains near Tora Bora where U.S. "daisy cutters" were trying to "flush Al Qaeda fighters out of the caves." Hired as Fox's "hot spot" correspondent, Rivera was assigned to capture footage of Osama bin Laden the moment he emerged from the caves defeated. Rivera positioned himself as the perfect man for the job, stating "I'm feeling more patriotic than at any time in my life. Itching for justice, or maybe just revenge."[6]

In one segment Geraldo appears in an Afghan hat and military jacket standing on a hilltop near Tora Bora. He has timed his report so that he can present live views of U.S. aircraft dropping their payload on nearby caves. He looks up at the sky and explains that he has been watching similar flyovers all day and wants to share with U.S. viewers what retaliation looks like up close. Geraldo orders his camera operator to shoot the sky and as we watch a plane circle over a target several times, Rivera excitedly proclaims, "He's just about to do it! He's gunna unload it any second. I've been watching this all day! They're gunna unload it right now and destroy all the bad guys' hideouts in that mountain over there!" We watch for more than a minute as the camera pans and strains to keep U.S. aircraft in view, but the attack never happens. Rivera, demoralized, assures his audience that the bombings have been happening all day and are bound to happen again, just not right now.

In his Tora Bora coverage Geraldo monitors B-52 bombers crisscross the sky, crawls around the desert in military garb, befriends Afghan rebels, and fends off flying bullets caught in the crossfire. In short, he functions more like a sports enthusiast than a war reporter and is ultimately deployed to the frontline to support a discourse of U.S. retaliation and revenge, to confirm that U.S. bombs were indeed falling from the sky and striking al-Qaeda hideouts near Tora Bora. Days after U.S. aircraft attacked the caves, Geraldo and his crew wandered inside to expose what he called the "rats nest." Rivera boasted that he was proud to spend a couple of nights in Osama's caves because, as he put it, it was "symbolic of what I think is a tremendously underappreciated victory."[7] Later, when asked why Osama bin Laden and his cohort had still not been found, Rivera explained, "I believe that these guys are all hunkered down, like the sissies they are, hiding under some one's skirt in Pakistan."

Just as CNN's *Military Options* valorized military officials and their views and interpretations of events, Fox News used *Geraldo Rivera Reports* to endorse U.S. military retaliation as a platform, and to provide affirmative and spectacular views of it. And while CNN's coverage produced a gendered address through its integration of male military commanders and a deferential Q&A format, Geraldo's segments generated a cranked up militarized masculinity, one that reveled in gonzo-style reporting, unapologetic revenge, and macho vigilantism. Acting as if a soldier of words, Rivera (and others on the Fox News Channel) consistently feminized the enemy, referring to them as sissies, wimps, and rats. But Rivera was not limited to the sword of his tongue. He positioned himself as one of TV journalism's rare warriors, insisting "I'm very fit. I still box . . . I'd like to find a reporter who can outdistance me . . . Courage has never been my problem. Brave men run in my family."[8]

Briefly, then, CNN's *Military Options* and Fox's *Geraldo Rivera Reports* advance a dominant paradigm of coverage that privileges technologized military vantage points and vengeful warfront reporting. This paradigm, of course, reinforces U.S. separation from the world. CNN integrates the command and control discourse of military officials to manage information from a strategic distance and produces in-studio simulations in a way that displaces war's embodied effects. And Geraldo may be close to the battlefield, but his desire for revenge and compulsive use of demeaning language obscures his vision and compromises his ability to report from such a proximity. This televisual discourse, which I have described elsewhere as *distant vision up-close*, can have the effect of structuring and affirming isolationist sensibilities, insulating U.S. viewers from animosity and outrage directed toward the United States. In fact, the close-up distance that television news affords, I would argue, is directly related to the fact that many U.S. citizens were shocked and dismayed to discover on 9/11 that the U.S. had enemies with such contempt. This shock itself was a symptom of U.S. viewers/citizens' detachment from and ignorance about our place in the world and about the historical effects of our state's military, economic, and cultural actions.

AN AIR OF RESISTANCE: OXYGEN

Oxygen's post-9/11 coverage is significant in this context because it differed from the dominant paradigm in two ways. First, it showed women debating and evaluating military options, and consistently calling for peaceful resolutions at time when most Americans and U.S. cable networks did not dare do so. Second, Oxygen's coverage structured a negotiated practice of feminist demilitarization. The women who appeared on the network's live 9/11 specials ardently questioned and critiqued U.S. militarism, while in general Oxygen's cable programming and Web content encouraged viewers to cope with 9/11 through conventionally feminine tropes of shopping, beauty, and health, and motherhood.

I will limit my discussion to two live-via-satellite specials transmitted just after 9/11. The first, *United We Stand: National Town Hall Meeting* aired on September 17, 2001, from Oxygen's studio in New York. The program, broadcast without commercial interruptions, featured a panel of U.S. feminists including Gloria Steinem, Kim Crenshaw (sociologist), Cheryl Mills (former Clinton adviser), Eve Ensler (author of *The Vagina Monologues* and political activist), among others. Hosted by former CNN International correspondent May Lee and comedian Stephanie Miller, the discussion ranged widely. After mentioning that Bush thought the Taliban was a rock band during his presidential campaign, Steinem discussed the phenomenon of blowback and the fact that the United States had given Osama bin Laden $3 billion over the past decade. Crenshaw explained how racial profiling and civil rights violations were impacting Arab Americans, and asked "After the Oklahoma City bombing did FBI go around arresting young white men and Persian Gulf War veterans?" Women in the studio audience had a chance to voice their opinions as well. A young Afghan-American woman stood up and emotionally cautioned, "If we retaliate we better be willing to be accountable for those who die in the attacks! We better realize that Afghani women and children will die! Let's not pretend! Let's talk about it in the media!" And an Israeli woman explained that after having served in the Israeli army, she fully supported U.S. military retaliation since terrorism must be stopped at all costs. The panelists and audience were seated against a backdrop of American flags, which blanketed this televised feminist dialogue in a diorama of red, white, and blue. On the one hand, such iconography conjoined feminism with patriotism, blending these sometimes incommensurable positions and making them part of a broader national agenda. On the other hand, it suggested that feminist antiwar sentiments had to be mired in a visual field of flag-waving in order be aired and taken seriously.

Oxygen's discussion of the U.S. war against Afghanistan continued in a live international satellite broadcast called *World Wide Women Responding to the Crisis* aired from London on October 4, 2001. This ninety-minute special, hosted by the well-known British talk show host Kaye Adams, featured prominent guests such as the writer and human rights activist Isabelle Allende; the human rights lawyer Asma Jahanghir; Zinzi Mandela, a businesswoman and the daughter of Nelson Mandela; and Rabbi Julia Neuberger. It also included live feeds from Sarajevo, Moscow, and Paris, as well as New York as May Lee, the host of the network's flagship show *Pure Oxygen,* chimed in. The program aired only in the United States. Oxygen wanted its viewers to have an opportunity to hear what women from around the world had to say about the 9/11 attacks and the prospect of U.S. military retaliation. Again, the perspectives ranged widely. Jasmine, a British Indian woman born in Uganda, stressed again and again how the events of 9/11 were adversely impacting Muslim communities worldwide, insisting "I want no revenge I want justice!" An Irish journalist who had covered IRA terrorist attacks in the UK compared them to 9/11 to suggest that such violence has occurred recently in other Western countries. Both Zinzi Mandela and Asma Jahanghir urged viewers to consider possibilities other than military retaliation. The program also integrated prerecorded segments revealing how 9/11 was impacting the lives of Muslim women in North London, and what life was like in Sarajevo after the war in Bosnia. In other words, the Oxygen special allowed women from different countries, ethnic backgrounds, and occupations to discuss alternatives to U.S. military intervention and encouraged U.S. viewers to think twice before following the nationalistic party line.

Reactions to the live satellite program spilled over onto Oxygen's Web site and numerous viewers posted comments triggered by the broadcast. Responses to Oxygen's special programming ranged widely as well.

> "I want to know why everyone flies an American flag when people from 80 countries were killed . . . "
>
> "I have been waiting for some news program to openly discuss some very uncomfortable truths about American Governmental policies world wide for the past 50 years . . . "
>
> "since I was a little girl . . . all I heard was Bomb Iraq . . . Bomb Iran . . . or damn raghead . . . or sandniggers . . . PLEASE . . . Leave me out of YOUR hate . . . THIS American Does NOT support the attacks to Afghanistan and NO I don't back up Bush . . . he's an ignorant hick who is leading YOU to hate . . .
>
> "What's up with this show going past it's scheduled time lot. I wanted to see Xena . . . "

As Oxygen used live satellite transmission to publicize women's discussions of 9/11 and the war in Afghanistan, the new network sustained itself during this precarious time with conventional programming geared toward women. What resulted was a bizarre flow of originally scheduled shows, implying that women should carry on with business as usual, interspersed with 9/11 public service announcements, video memorials, and panicky tickers. During the yoga program *Inhale,* viewers were encouraged to breath deeply and assume postures while a ticker ran across the bottom of the frame encouraging them to visit Oxygen.com for tips on how to cope with the tragedy. The Oxygen Web site encouraged women to make "patriotic purchases" and listed twenty ways to spend $20, suggesting this was a way to tell the terrorists "Ha! You can't dictate our lives." Items on the list included twenty lottery tickets, a share of stock, a bottle of wine, a doll, split a membership to Costco, a jump rope, a box of truffles, and lipstick.[9] To cope with 9/11 Oxygen encouraged viewers to "soothe their souls" with "grief and forgiveness rituals" and to "rebuild the USA one share at a time." New links appeared on the site such as "caring for kids" and "help and healing." While these traumatic events no doubt required a healing process, Oxygen addressed women in conventionally feminine ways as consumers and mothers as opposed to political activists and policy makers, implying women could shop or jump rope their way out of this global political quagmire. Thus, even as Oxygen created viable public forums for feminist political speech, its flow, structure, and Web site content interpellated female viewers as "feel-good feminists" who were more concerned about making good investments and making flags fashionable than resisting U.S. militarization. I don't mean to suggest that Oxygen did not play an important political function in this climate, but rather I want to highlight how this new commercial women's network mitigated or tempered antiwar feminisms to sustain itself in a political economy in which dissent became dangerous.

THE U.S. BOMBINGS OF AL JAZEERA

Thus far I have explored some of the ways U.S. cable networks represented the war in Afghanistan, emphasizing the military options, network vigilantism, and patriotically negotiated feminisms that emerged after 9/11. Yet the commandeering of the airwaves took more violent forms as well. It involved literal "air raids" when the U.S. military bombed the facilities of Al Jazeera and other Arab television networks as part of the war on terror. The U.S. bombings of Al Jazeera can be understood as an extreme and violent extension of the militarism and vigilantism that emerged in the discourse of U.S. cable news networks after 9/11. The suggestions reiterated in cable newscasts that the United States only had military options, that retaliation and revenge were necessary and spectacular, and that political dissent was unpatriotic created a climate that had the effect of authorizing the United States to take unprecedented military actions in the airwaves.

Although Al Jazeera emerged in 1996, five years before 9/11, most Westerners became familiar with the Arab satellite television network only after it broadcast videotapes from Osama bin Laden and al-Qaeda, and began reporting on the war on terror as it played out first in Afghanistan and then in Iraq. Partly financed by the Emir of Qatar, Al Jazeera, which means "island" or "peninsula" in Arabic, generated coverage of wartime events in ways that differed from those of U.S. cable networks, in part because of reporters' familiarity with and deeper understanding of Muslim countries and their histories. Further, since Al Jazeera's reporters speak and read Arabic languages they could eavesdrop on militias, communicate with civilians, and venture into conflict zones to expose grim scenes of U.S. invasion and occupation.[10] Over time Al Jazeera came to be seen as the Arab world's equivalent to CNN. After the network broadcast messages from bin Laden and al-Qaeda, the Bush administration publicly condemned the network as the "mouthpiece of Osama Bin Laden" and insisted Al Jazeera was being used by al-Qaeda to distribute coded messages to supporters around the world.[11] Against such accusations, it is important to note that Al Jazeera had already become popular throughout the Arab world in the years before 9/11 because the network exposed human rights abuses, showed live coverage of political events, discussed women's rights under Islam, and criticized government parties in a region where the broadcast media is largely under state control.[12] Al Jazeera's motto is "the opinion and the counter-opinion," and its management claims to be committed to free debate, the elimination of taboos, and the awakening of rigid societies.[13]

Despite Al Jazeera's reputation for trying to educate the Arab world about democracy, the network became a U.S. military target only two months after 9/11. On November 13, 2001, the U.S. military dropped a 500-pound bomb smack into the network's Kabul station just before the Northern Alliance's seizure of the city. Although no employees were killed, the network's broadcast facilities were destroyed along with some employees' homes. As the BBC reporter William Reeve covered the event live from his nearby office, he was loudly interrupted by the explosions. Footage of Reeve ducking beneath his desk to avoid fallout from the blast reportedly played again and again on BBC TV, symbolizing the precarious position of broadcast journalists in the war on terror.[14] The attack was also covered live by the Al Jazeera reporter Taysur Alluni, one of the few correspondents on the ground when the United States invaded Afghanistan in 2001. Incidentally, Alluni is now in a Spanish prison after being charged, with U.S. pressure, by a Spanish court as being a member of al-Qaeda.[15]

On April 8, 2003, the U.S. military engaged in a similar attack in Baghdad, not only striking Al Jazeera's broadcast facilities, but those of another Arab network, Abu Dhabi (of the United Arab Emirates), as well as the Palestine hotel where many international correspondents were known to have been staying. The U.S. military killed three journalists that day including Tariq Ayoub of Al Jazeera, Taras Protsyuk of Reuters, and Jose Cuso of the Spanish network Telecino. The events culminated in a press conference during which Tariq Ayoub's wife, Dima Tareq Tahboub, implored the international community to investigate the attacks and to "please tell the truth," as her husband had "died trying to reveal the truth to the world" as a journalist.[16] In addition to speaking at the press conference via phone, she published an editorial in the *Guardian* (UK) six months after her husband's death describing her traumatic loss and condemning the U.S. attacks:

> In Bagdhad during the war, the coverage of al-Jazeera again focused mainly on the daily suffering and loss of ordinary people; and again the Americans wanted their crimes and atrocities to pass unnoticed. The two bombs they dropped on al-Jazeera's Baghdad office were the ones that killed my husband. Then the Americans opened fire on Abu Dhabi television, whose identity was spelled out in large blue letters on the roof. The next target was the Palestine hotel, the headquarters of world media representatives—an American tank fired a shell and two more journalists were killed. Thus the U.S. tried to conceal evidence of its crimes from the world and kill the witnesses . . . My husband and the others were killed in broad daylight, in locations known to the Pentagon as media sites.[17]

Dima Tareq Tahboub's appeal for a thorough investigation was accompanied by critiques from members of the international press community, Reporters without Borders, and the Committee to Protect Journalists.[18]

Just as troubling as the physical destruction of Arab networks' broadcast facilities is the unexplained arrest and detention of Al Jazeera's employees by U.S. troops.[19] In addition to Alluni (mentioned above), in December 2001 a Sudanese cameraman working for Al Jazeera, Sami Muhyideen al-Haj, was apprehended by U.S. military and eventually taken to detention facilities in Guantánamo Bay, where, according to his lawyer, Clive Stafford Smith, he has been beaten, denied treatment for throat cancer, and subject to shifting allegations by U.S. officials.[20] In November 2003 the Al Jazeera employees Salah Hassan and Suheib Badr Darwish were detained and tortured in Abu Ghraib prison and then released more than a month later.[21] In January 2006 U.S. troops arrested Al Jazeera's Kabul correspondent, Waliullah Shaheen, the cameraman Nasir Hashimi, and the driver Mahmood Agha in Afghanistan for allegedly filming too close to U.S. military headquarters.[22]

In addition to destroying the facilities of Al Jazeera and killing and detaining its employees, the United States has initiated its own Arab media enterprises as well. After the war in Iraq began, the United States began beaming the nightly newscasts of the U.S. networks ABC, CBS, NBC, Fox News, and PBS into Baghdad as bombs fell from the sky.[23] As Christian Parenti suggests, the U.S. hostility toward Al Jazeera "is best viewed in the context of the escalating, multimillion-dollar regional media war between Al Jazeera and the U.S. government." [24] In an effort to combat Al Jazeera's popularity the U.S. government allocated $62 million in 2004 to launch a Virginia-based Arab language satellite television network called Al Hurra, which means "the free one."[25] The *Washington Post* called the new satellite network the "most expensive effort to sway foreign opinion over the airwaves since the creation of Voice of America in 1942."[26] Al Hurra's signal reaches a potential audience of 120 million in 22 countries. In 2004 USAID also funded the development of the first commercial television network in Afghanistan, Tolo TV, which airs Western-style programming influenced by MTV and has reportedly caused much controversy among Muslim officials.[27]

U.S. military officials first claimed that neither of the attacks on Al Jazeera was intentional, but evidence to the contrary has emerged. In 2005 Great Britain's *Daily Mirror* leaked a five-page transcript detailing a conversation between Prime Minister Tony Blair and George W. Bush. In it Bush made explicit his intention in April 2004 to order the military bombing of Al Jazeera headquarters in Doha, Qatar, in the midst of the U.S. campaign in Fallujah. Even though Blair managed to persuade Bush against such an attack, the leak revealed it was certainly plausible that the Bush administration would have ordered prior attacks on Al Jazeera in Kabul and Baghdad. After interviewing top U.S. officials for his book *The One Percent Doctrine,* the investigative journalist Ron Suskind confirmed that the U.S. bombings of Al Jazeera were deliberate.[28] Such information has provided families of Al Jazeera employees and other journalists killed or injured in U.S. attacks the incentive to proceed with lawsuits against the U.S. government.

The U.S. bombings of Al Jazeera are significant for several reasons. First, the attacks establish a troubling precedent in that the United States has singled out a media corporation and its employees as military targets. Never before have private transnational media companies and their workers been subject to a series of overt U.S. military assaults and detentions. This is particularly disturbing to journalists whose livelihoods depend on a modicum of security when covering military conflicts. The BBC anchor Nic Gowing insists that reporters have every right to cover wars and peacekeeping operations, yet points to a disconcerting trend whereby "a lot of the military—particularly the American and the Israeli military—do not want us there . . . security forces in some instances feel it is legitimate to target us with deadly force and with impunity."[29] Indeed, as former U.S. Secretary of Defense Donald Rumsfeld insisted, there is no distinction between civilian and military targets in a total war against terrorism.[30] This means that any target is a fair target: any journalist can be detained or killed, any television station destroyed.

Second, the attacks on Al Jazeera make clear that a total war on terror is intertwined with the global media economy. After bombing Al Jazeera, the United States launched its own Arab satellite television network, Al Hurra, and has supported the formation of a commercial network in Afghanistan, TV Tolo. Thus, in addition to destroying Al Jazeera facilities and apprehending its employees, the United States has developed its own enterprises to compete with Arab media corporations, even if Al Hurra is, as one journalist put it, "widely regarded as a laughingstock in the middle east."[31] The U.S. positioning in the Arab media market is so audacious that it led one political satirist to concoct a sardonic article with the headline, "Fox News Buys Al-Jazeera."[32]

Third, the Al Jazeera bombings have serious gender implications. Al Jazeera not only employs many Arab women but regularly airs programs such as *Only for Women, Everywoman, The Opposite Direction,* and *Religion and Life,* which address gender and sexual issues that are of interest to Arab women and men alike.[33] The network has also broadcast news features that assess how the wars in Afghanistan and Iraq have uniquely impacted women's lives. After 9/11 Bush administration officials often invoked women's treatment under Islam and in the Arab world as one of the rationales for U.S. military intervention, yet that same administration has managed to destroy facilities of the Arab satellite television network most consistently committed to discussing such issues. One effect of the

U.S. bombing of Al Jazeera, then, is to exhibit a disregard for the voices and experiences of Arab and Muslim women and to threaten the publicization of their concerns in the international mediasphere.

Finally, the bombings of Al Jazeera expose the Bush administration's cynicism about the relationship between television and democracy. How can the airwaves be imagined as spaces of free deliberation, debate, dissent, evaluation, and opposition if they are at the same time targeted as sites of physical annihilation and economic competition? It is clear that the Bush administration is more interested in demonizing and replacing Arab media networks than supporting existing networks based in the Middle East. As the editors of *The Nation* boldly put it, "If a President who claims to be using the U.S. military to liberate countries in order to spread freedom then conspires to destroy media that fail to echo his sentiments, he does not merely disgrace his office and soil the reputation of his country. He attacks a fundamental principle, freedom of the press—particularly a dissenting and disagreeable press—upon which that country was founded."[34]

Yet the Al Jazeera bombings not only represent a dramatic blow to the concepts of a free press and dissent, they also point to the devaluation in the correspondence between television and democracy. Leftist and liberal intellectuals largely abandoned the dream of democratic television the moment the medium became a form of mass consumer culture. Right-wing conservatives hope to use television to build a free, capitalistic, and Christian world. But surely there must be more subtle ground to explore here. Political leaders of Middle Eastern states have referred to satellite channels like Al Jazeera as an "off-shore democracy" because it offers a unique platform to communicate with policy makers and the wider public without going through ordinary government channels. Further, the satellite television network operates as a deterritorialized and transnational entity that poses difficult and challenging questions to traditional and authoritarian states and leaders throughout the world.[35] The point here is not necessarily to celebrate Al Jazeera over CNN or Fox News, but rather to push for further consideration of the different ways in which "television" and "democracy" are defined and functioning in different parts of the world in the midst of the war on terror.

In this essay I have explored the relationship between television and the war on terror. It has emerged in the way Joie Chen is positioned to throw softball questions at military experts while standing on a map, in Geraldo Rivera's solo macho vigilantism, in Oxygen's negotiation of women's antiwar positions with consumerism, beauty, and patriotic motherhood, and in the U.S. bombings of Al Jazeera. The air raids have involved practices of militarization, vengeance, suppression, and annihilation. Above all, they have involved a different disposition toward dissent. The reduction of dissent in cable news reports and the destruction of Al Jazeera's property and the death, injury, and detention of its employees are all part of the same matrix of intolerance and violence. Air raids are no longer limited to sirens in the sky; they now range from ideological positions enunciated in the electromagnetic spectrum to the elimination of property and personnel required to broadcast the news in the first place.

The question that remains is this: Given all that has happened since 9/11, could television in the United States or elsewhere ever be imagined as helping to facilitate a thoughtful and peaceful resolution to the war on terror? Or will the airwaves continue to fuel and become a stage for international polarities and corporatized war games? One thing is certain. An active correspondence between television and democracy could only ever surface in the United States with further critical and public investment in the medium. As it stands, television is too often thought of as a lost cause. Perhaps we can understand the U.S. bombings of Al Jazeera not only as a raid, but also as a rallying cry for more scholarly and public attention to television news in the United States and abroad.

NOTES

1. For a discussion of the various ways Arab satellite television networks operate, see Naomi Sakr, *Satellite Realms: Transnational Television, Globalization and the Middle East* (London: I. B. Tauris, 2001).

2. Cynthia Enloe, *Maneuvers: The International Politics of Militarizing Women's Lives* (Berkeley and Los Angeles: University of California Press, 2000), 3–4.

3. Paul Virilio, *Ground Zero* (London: Verso, 2002), 25.

4. In general there has been a troubling appropriation of U.S. people of color after 9/11—whether Hispanic and black Americans serving in higher proportion on the frontlines in Afghanistan and Iraq, or officials such as Colin Powell and Condoleezza Rice serving as "erudite" spokespersons for the Bush administration and alleviating crises in the wake of Texan diplomacy. In the news media there are thus ample reminders of African-American social mobility, yet simultaneously there have been unprecedented violations of civil liberties against Arab and South Asian–American citizens and residents of the United States. News representations have constructed a post-9/11 racial politics in which civil liberties appear to have been afforded to black Americans while those for other communities of color are challenged or denied.

5. "Geraldo Rivera Goes from CNBC to Fox," November 2, 2001, available at http://www.foxnews.com/story/0,2933,37898,00.html, accessed Nov 3, 2004.

6. Ibid.

7. Interview with Geraldo Rivera on *Hannity and Colmes,* October 4, 2002.

8. Gail Shister, "Rivera on a Mission as Fox News War Correspondent," *Philadelphia Inquirer,* November 6, 2001, available at http://www.indybay.org/news items/2001/11/07/1085951.php. Despite his bravado, Rivera was expelled from Iraq after drawing lines in the sand indicating U.S. and enemy positions during a live news report while he was embedded with the U.S. military.

9. The full list included twenty lottery tickets, the offer of taking a friend to the movies, a magazine subscription, a share of stock, a bottle of wine, a doll, a split membership to Costco, two candles, a jazz CD, a box of truffles, a jump rope, mascara, lip balm, and a manicure. Next to the list was an image of a woman with closed eyes in a bubble bath.

10. "US Uses Napalm in Fallujah," *Al Jazeera,* November 28, 2004. The media watchdog group FAIR offers an analysis of Al Jazeera's coverage and the responses generated by U.S. media at http://www.fair.org/index.php?page=3114.

11. "Al Jazeera Kabul Offices Hit in US Raid," BBC News, November 13, 2001, available at http://news.bbc.co.uk/2/hi/south_asia/1653887.stm, accessed October 20, 2006.

12. For further discussion of these issues see, Hugh Miles, *Al-Jazeera: The Inside Story of the Arab News Channel That Is Challenging the West* (New York: Grove Press, 2005).

13. For more nuanced and detailed perspectives on Al Jazeera, see Rick Zednik, "Perspectives on War: Inside Al Jazeera," *Columbia Journalism Review* 2 (March/April 2002), and the documentary film *Control Room* (2004; dir. Jehane Noujaim).

14. Matt Wells, "How Smart Was This Bomb?" *The Guardian,* November 19, 2001, available at http://www.guardian.co.uk/waronterror/story/0,1361,597067,00.html, accessed October 20, 2006.

15. John Cherian, "Bombing Out Dissent," *Frontline* 23, no. 2 (January 28–Febrary 10, 2006), available at http://www.flonnet.com/fl2302/stories/20060210001305600.htm, accessed October 20, 2006.

16. This footage was available on http://www.youtube.com in a clip called "The Murder of Tarek Ayub (A U.S. War Crime)," posted by Halifaxion, June 23, 2006, and subsequently removed for terms-of-use violations. It was excerpted from the documentary *Control Room.* As of this writing it could be accessed at http://www.dailymotion.com/video/x1em68_us-war-crime-the-murder-of-tarek-ay_news.

17. Dima Tareq Tahboub, "The War on Al-Jazeera," *The Guardian,* October 4, 2003, available at http://www.guardian.co.uk/world/2003/oct/04/iraq.iraqandthe media.

18. "Reporters without Borders Outraged at Bombing of Al-Jazeera Office in Baghdad," *Reporters without Borders* Web site, April 8, 2003, available at http://www.rsf.org/Reporters-Without-Borders-outraged.html.

19. The Pentagon awarded a $16.7 million contract to the Rendon Group to monitor media in the Islamic world and charged it to keep a close watch on Al Jazeera bureaus and correspondents in particular (Cherian, "Bombing Out Dissent"). In addition to detentions and monitoring, Al Jazeera was banned and threatened with expulsion by the Coalition Provisional Authority and Iraqi Governing Council for "destabilizing the occupation" with its reporting. "Iraqi Officials Ban Al Jazeera," Al Jazeera Web site, February 1, 2004.

20. For a detailed discussion of al-Haj, see Joel Campagna, "Sami al-Haj: The Enemy?" *CPJ: A Publication of Committee to Project Journalists,"* available at http://cpj.org/reports/2006/10/prisoner.php.

21. Christian Parenti, "Al Jazeera Goes to Jail," *The Nation,* March 29, 2004, available at http://www.thenation.com/doc/20040329/parenti.

22. "Al Jazeera Employees Arrested in Afghanistan," Radio Free Europe, January 1, 2006, available at http://www.rferl.org/content/article/1064338.html.

23. Karen DeYoung and Walter Pincus, "US to Take Its Message to Iraqi Airwaves," *Washington Post,* May 11, 2003, A17.

24. Parenti, "Al Jazeera Goes to Jail."

25. Ibid.

26. Ellen McCarthy, "Va.-Based, U.S.-Financed Arabic Channel Finds Its Voice," *Washington Post,* October 15, 2004, A01.

27. Ben Arnoldy, "Kabul's Must-See TV Heats Up Culture War in Afghanistan," *The Christian Science Monitor,* May 10, 2005, available at http://www.csmonitor.com/2005/0510/p01s03-wosc.html, accessed November 5, 2006.

28. Ron Suskind, *The One Percent Doctrine* (New York: Simon and Schuster, 2006), 138. Suskind confirmed this finding in an interview with CNN's Wolf Blitzer on June 20, 2006; see http://transcripts.cnn.com/TRANSCRIPTS/0606/20/sitroom.02.html.

29. Quoted in Steve Weissman, "Dead Messengers: How the U.S. Military Threatens Journalists," http://www.truthout.org, February 24, 2005.

30. Quoted in Cherian, "Bombing Out Dissent."

31. Abigail Lavin, "Is Al Jazeera Planning to Bring English-Language News to an American Audience?" *The Weekly Standard,* September 20, 2006, available at http://www.weeklystandard.com/Utilities/printer_preview.asp?idArticle=12722&R=EDFF90A, accessed November 7, 2006.

32. Andy Borowitz, "Fox News Buys Al-Jazeera," *Newsweek,* February 1, 2005. Available at http://www.newsweek.com/id/48428.

33. This coverage has been especially important to a diverse, international Arab community that has felt their representations and positions misconstrued, caricatured, and gravely reduced in Western media. For a broader history of these issues, see Edward Said, *Orientalism* (New York: Vintage, 1978).

34. Jeremy Scahill, "The War on Al Jazeera," *The Nation,* December 19, 2005, available at http://www.thenation.com/doc/20051219/scahill, accessed November 6, 2006.

35. See Sakr, *Satellite Realms,* 4; Miles Hugh. *Al Jazeera: The Inside Story of the Arab News Channel That Is Challenging the West* (New York: Grove Press, 2005); Marc Lynch, *Voices of the New Arab Republic: Iraq, Al-Jazeera, and Middle East Politics Today* (New York: Columbia University Press, 2005); and the documentary *Control Room.*

10. Culture, U.S. Imperialism, and Globalization

John Carlos Rowe

The return of what was once termed gunboat diplomacy in the first decade of the twenty-first century as part of the "new global order" endorsed repeatedly and abstractly by George H. W. and now George W. Bush's regimes could not have occurred without the prior work of culture. In what follows, I make a simple, important point: U.S. cultural production, the work of what Horkheimer and Adorno termed "the culture industry," conditioned American citizens to accept the undisguised militarism and jingoistic nationalism driving U.S. foreign policy.[1] In its inevitably globalized forms, the U.S. culture industry continues to produce the deep divisions between local resistance and subaltern imitation so characteristic of colonial conflicts from the age of traditional imperialism to the neo-imperialisms of our postindustrial era. And the culture industry today does its work in ways that encompass a wide range of nominally different political positions, so that in many respects left, liberal, and conservative cultural works often achieve complementary, rather than contested, ends. In this respect, little has changed since Horkheimer and Adorno argued in 1944: "Even the aesthetic activities of political opposites are one in their enthusiastic obedience to the rhythm of the iron system."[2]

As the U.S. military raced toward Baghdad, there was considerable criticism of the "embedded reporters" allowed to report the war under the special conditions imposed by the Pentagon and Department of Defense. Most of the criticism assumed that such reporting was biased or censored. When a *Newsweek* photographer was caught doctoring on his laptop a photograph of an encounter between Iraqi civilians and U.S. military personnel, his firing seemed to vindicate the news magazine of prejudice. Antiwar activists circulated two photographs of Iraqi demonstrators tearing down a monumental statue of Saddam Hussein in Firdos Square, Baghdad: the first was a familiar photograph in the news of demonstrators beating on the sculpture's foundation and then, with the help of an Abrams tank, toppling the hieratic image of the defeated dictator. In the second photograph, not displayed in the popular press or evening news, the camera provides a wide-angle view of the scene at the square, where access roads have been blocked by the U.S. military and the "populist" demolition of the statue has been theatrically stage by U.S. forces. In a third photograph circulated on the Internet, the same Iraqis actively involved attacking the Baghdad statue are shown "one day earlier" in Basra, where they are preparing to board U.S. military aircraft for transport to Baghdad—identified in this photograph as members of the "Iraqi Free Forces."[3]

Such exposures of U.S. military propaganda during the war have continued in news coverage of the putative "rebuilding" of the political and economic infrastructure in Iraq. The debate regarding who was actually responsible for the disinformation regarding "Weapons of Mass Destruction" used as the principal justification for the invasion of Iraq is the most obvious example of public concern regarding the federal government's veracity. For such propaganda to be successful, there must be a willing audience, already prepared for certain cultural semantics adaptable to new political circumstances and yet with sufficient "regional" relevance as to make possible the very widespread confusion between Saddam Hussein and Osama bin Laden, between a secular Iraqi state tyranny and an Islamic fundamentalist guerrilla organization. How was it possible that such a preposterous war could be permitted by Congress and by the U.S. population? The answer is not simply that the Bush administration ignored the numerous international protests of the preparations for war and its eventual conduct. Nor is the answer simply that when the war began, the Bush administration controlled the news and staged symbolic events to fool the public, although there is plenty of evidence to support these claims. The cultural preparations for a "just war" and for the U.S. as global "policeman" did not occur overnight; they are our cultural legacy from the Vietnam War and integral parts of our emergence as a neoimperial nation since 1945. Central to this legacy is the conception of the United States as a discrete nation that nonetheless has a global identity and mission. Although traditional imperialism works by way of expansion from a national center, U.S. imperialism since Vietnam has worked steadily to "import" the world and to render global differences aspects of the U.S. nation—in short, to internalize and "hypernationalize" transnational issues.

It is commonplace, of course, to criticize the United States as one of the several first-world nations to employ cultural media to market its products around the world. Neocolonialism generally connotes some complicity between a "multinational corporation covertly supported by an imperialist power," to borrow Chalmers Johnson's definition, and thus implies some entanglement of economic, political, and military motives.[4] The globalization of consumer capitalism and the commodities of first-world economies (often manufactured elsewhere) are identified as specific targets by political movements as different as "Slow Food" in Italy, Earth First!, and al-Qaeda. Although the arcades and other defined shopping areas were developed in nineteenth-century Europe—Paris, Milan, Berlin, and other metropoles—the shopping mall is an American spinoff. With its emphasis on the "city-within-a-city," the linkage of entertainment and consumption, the faux cosmopolitanism of its "international" and regionally specific shops (Cartier, Mont Blanc, Nieman Marcus, Saks Fifth Avenue, "Texas Souvenirs") and its ubiquitous, often international "food courts," the American shopping mall was developed in the 1960s and refined over the past forty years. Such megamalls as Minneapolis' Mall of America, Houston's Galleria, and Southern California's South Coast Plaza have redefined the public sphere as the site of consumption and commodification both of products and consumers.

Whether directly exported by U.S. business interests or developed by multinational corporations to look like its U.S. prototypes, the international mall is often traceable to U.S. funding, design, and marketing sources or models. A PBS *Frontline* report, "In Search of Al Qaeda," which aired on November 21, 2002, includes footage of a shopping mall in Riyadh, Saudi Arabia, which is physically indistinguishable from European and American malls and includes many of the same stores.[5] Of course, the reporter calls attention to the presence of the Mu'tawah or religious police, who stroll through this mall looking for unveiled women or illicit liaisons between unmarried men and women. "In Search of Al Qaeda" is a fine attempt by *Frontline* to explain the animosity felt by many different groups in the Arab world toward the United States. The mall in Riyadh represents quite clearly one common source of resentment: the rapid Americanization of Saudi Arabia and the tacit demand that everyday Muslim practices be adapted to the demands of the global market. From one perspective, the Mu'tawah operate comfortably within this typical mall, with its long, open corridors and the insistent appeal of its transnational commodities. In another view, the religious police seem already defeated by the cultural rhetoric of the mall, which encourages romance and consumption in the same free-wheeling space. As Anne Friedeberg has argued, the mall links consumer and psychic desires in ways that depend crucially on "the fluid subjectivity of the spectator-shopper."[6]

Commodities are neither passive nor politically innocent; they are perpetually active in the specific kinds of desires they produce in consumers and work by means of the social psychologies of commodity fetishism analyzed by Marx in *Capital* and reification elaborated by Lukács in *History and Class Consciousness.*[7] Specific consumer desires can also be traced back to hierarchies of specific kinds of capitalist labor. In modern, industrial economies, stores displaying high fashion and leisure-class products, such as designer clothing for women and luxury products for successful men, were central. The traditional display windows with their mannequins of elegantly dressed and sexually alluring women belong to the era of the large department stores, and while they are still a part of the postmodern mall they are challenged by stores displaying the most elaborate array of computerized bodily extensions and miniaturizations, labor-saving devices, and high-tech tools promising greater access to the primary source of wealth and power: the control and manipulation of information and its assorted hermeneutic and representational protocols. In the crush of the crowds defining the public space of the mall, the consumer is promised some individuality apart from just what forces him/her through the doors of his/her local "Circuit City." Such identity depends, of course, on its promise of communication, but not so much *with* other people, especially those who may be different from this consumer, but *apart* from others in the notable privacy of postmodern life. The new laptops and PDAs are prized for allowing us to negotiate the crowd as we travel through it, but then saving from this mob our informational work, which can be stored, sifted, and processed in the privacy of our own homes. Of course, the peculiar desire for representational power and authority fetishized in computer hardware and software is rapidly displacing the public sphere created by the late-modern desire for more traditional commodities, such as fashion and luxury items. The mall is "morphing" into the Internet, an imaginary space so rapidly commercialized as to terrify even the most recalcitrant critic and sometime defender of consumer capitalism.

In spite of the admirable efforts of intellectuals to find emancipatory possibilities in the new technologies—alternatives to traditional social forms and practices certainly do exist today—the speed with which the Internet has been commercialized and hierarchized is symptomatic of the huge inequities dividing corporations that can afford access, individuals who merely use the technology (and are thereby used by it), and the majority of the world's population left entirely out of the new communicative practices. In *What's the Matter with the Internet?,* Mark Poster recognizes most of these problems while stressing the "underdetermined" character of new digital technologies and thus their availability for new transnational politics: "The Internet affords an opportunity for a contribution to a new politics [and] . . . may play a significant role in diminishing the hierarchies prevalent in modern society and in clearing a path for new directions of cultural practice."[8] In *Ambient Television,* Anna McCarthy acknowledges the ideological consequences of television's portability and publicity in achieving a culture of surveillance such as Foucault predicted, but she also imagines critical alternatives and interventions capable of disrupting and in some cases even transforming unidirectional television.[9] Such alternatives, however, are pushed increasingly to the margins of the Internet and television. Most television scholars agree that the "post-network era" has reconfigured the industry only by allowing more corporate giants to share the wealth of television programming. "Niche" television and "target audiences" have led to a wider variety of television only within certain limits of the liberal-to-conservative political spectrum. Radical television, such as Dee Dee Halleck's Paper Tiger Television, goes virtually unwatched, is financially marginal, and is supported primarily by extramural grants. The networks long ago succeeded in defeating "public access cable" as a populist alternative to one-way television, and the short-term future of "interactive" television, especially when integrated with computers and the Internet, is likely to be little more than an extension of the enormously profitable video-game market.

We yearn for each new electronic device, but the vast majority are finally useless to most consumers either because they do not know *how* to use them or have *no use* for them in the first place. What lures consumers to new digital technologies is the general promise of *social communication*—ironically just the ideal offered by Marx and Engels in *The German Ideology*—but it is a false promise that substitutes complex programming and upgrades for socially meaningful communication.[10] Designed to serve business and commercial needs, and predicated on the increasing privatization of the public sphere whereby the illusion of sociability is simulated in the radical alienation and paradoxical exclusivity of the home office, commuter vehicle, or commercial airline's reserved seat, such devices produce specific desires structured by their ideological motivations. The imperial imaginary thrives upon these desires, which, once initiated, are difficult to reverse or purge. Cultural apologists for the "Americanization" of the globe, like Francis Fukuyama, imagine that such homogenization will take us to that "end of history" fantastically dreamt by Hegel and other protomoderns, because such conditions will produce a political consensus.[11] Fukuyama is certainly right that one-way globalization is likely to result in an international consensus, even if it is one we can hardly condone, which we know will be not only excruciatingly tedious but finally "inhuman," and will require periods of incredible, unpredictable violence.

Such criticism of what may generally be termed a "postmodern economy" focused on information, communications, and entertainment products, including their integrated research and development components, may seem strangely anachronistic when applied to the contemporary global situation. Today, we confront the revival of traditional imperialism as the United States towers over all other human communities and exerts its unchallenged power in the most flagrantly militaristic manner. Not since the British empire ruled the world by force and fear in the late eighteenth and nineteenth centuries has there been such undisguised rule by military power. While recognizing important differences between contemporary U.S. global rule in the twenty-first century and that of the British in the nineteenth century, Chalmers Johnson traces a historical genealogy from British to U.S. imperial policies, especially in such critical regions as the Middle East and Southeast Asia.[12] In Somalia and most of Africa, Kosovo, Serbia, Cuba, Nicaragua, Panama, Salvador, Colombia, the Philippines, North and South Korea, Afghanistan, Israel and Palestine, Saudi Arabia and the Gulf states, Iraq, and Iran, the United States works by open military action or threats. Such situations hardly appear to have much to do with the postmodern economics analyzed by theorists of postindustrial or late capitalist practices, such as Ernest Mandel, Fredric Jameson, and David Harvey.

But there is an important relationship between the emergence of U.S. military power, along with the complementary threats of inequitable and repressive policies toward peoples (especially but not exclusively non-U.S. citizens) at home and abroad, and the capitalization of "cultural exports" ranging from Hollywood entertainment and television programming to digital technologies and their protocols for communication and work. John Gallagher and Ronald Robinson's theory of "free-trade imperialism" is now half a century old and was formulated long before the postmodern economy came to dominate global relations by restructuring other forms of economic production and trade (especially devastating for the "industrialized" developing nations, now cast in the shadow of new, privileged forms of capitalization).[13] The thesis of "free-trade imperialism" still explains a good deal about how traditional imperial military power should emerge with such prominence and frequency as a "foreign policy" at the very moment when globalization seems the nearly inevitable consequence of U.S. economic triumphalism. Contemporary critics of U.S. foreign policy like Chalmers Johnson have also recognized that "free trade" is often used as a rationalization for the conduct of multinational corporations and for the U.S. government's development of "client states" like Israel and, until recently, South Korea.[14]

Gallagher and Robinson refute traditional theories that imperialism—their principal example was British imperialism in Africa—proceeded historically from military conquest to the consolidation of colonial rule, only to be legitimated and transformed slowly through economic development. Gallagher and Robinson argue that "free-trade" policies generally *preceded* historically the militarization of colonies and that such military force was required only by the failure to negotiate trade agreements between metropolitan and colonial centers. Military force is thus held in reserve, not out of humane considerations, of course, but primarily for reasons of practicality and economy, while the imperial power promotes trade agreements—either for raw materials or finished products—with the appearance of favorable and equitable terms to colonizer and colonized. It is only when this illusion of "free-trade" is shattered that military force is required to reimpose imperial "order," when the appearance of free trade can be resumed, under whose guise what in fact usually occurs is demonstrably inequitable exploitation of natural or human resources of the colony. As they write: "The usual summing up of the policy of the free trade empire as 'trade, not rule' should read 'trade with informal control if possible; trade with rule when necessary.'"[15]

Is this not the situation we are witnessing today in the Gulf and in other strategic locations around the world? At present, the relationship between the United States and the Peoples Republic of China can be described accurately as one operating according to the logic of "free-trade imperialism," as China's economy booms in large part thanks to the exploited labor required to manufacture products for the U.S. export market.[16] One of the assumptions of Fukuyama's approach to globalization is that the "end of history" will bring an end of warfare and national struggle, that the "global village" and world peace are inextricably linked. From this perspective, whatever the cost of globalization in the mediocrity and uniformity of personal lives is more than compensated by the security achieved. In view of the everyday fear experienced by the majority of humankind, the sacrifices are well worth the enormous gains achieved by U.S. global hegemony. In his neoliberal defense of the United States' exercise of power around the world in its own "defense," Robert Kagan reaches a similar conclusion, albeit one that involves his condemnation of both the European Union and the United Nations—the closest competitors for U.S. global hegemony at the present moment.[17]

Late capitalism thrives on fear, even employing fear as a principal marketing strategy. In the depressed U.S. economy of the past few years, one of the rare bright spots has been the booming market for self-defense goods, especially high-tech gadgets, in response to 9/11 and the assorted xenophobic anxieties, such as the mailing of anthrax, it prompted. In his documentary *Bowling for Columbine* (2002), Michael Moore attributes violence in the U.S. primarily to a culture of fear propagated by the news media and federal government. If we accept the general outlines of his argument, then the globalization of U.S. cultural capital will involve the exportation of precisely this "culture of fear," a phenomenon we have witnessed as complementary with the increase in U.S. military actions as the Bush administration took seriously its role as global policeman of the new world order. I want to propose, then, a dialectical relationship between cultural or free-trade imperialism and military imperialism that is mediated by way of a "culture of fear" that helps market late-capitalist products and encourages, rather than diminishes, military conflicts in the place of international diplomacy.

The history of this dialectic is understandably as long as that of modernity itself, especially if we trace modernity back to the voyages of exploration and conquest of the late fifteenth and early sixteenth centuries. Modernization begins not so much with the technologies used to achieve such conquests—no new technology was, in fact, invented just for the voyages of exploration—but with the imagining of other worlds and peoples. It is commonplace to speak of how easily the early explorers substituted one people for another, as Columbus mistook Caribs and Arawaks for "Indians" of the Far East (and the name continues to this day, albeit often contested by Native Americans and First Peoples). But there is a shorter history that tells us a good deal about this dialectic, especially in its present deployment in world politics, and that history begins with the military failure of the United States in Vietnam in the early 1970s. Beginning in that moment, U.S. culture attempted to explain and rationalize the war in a wide range of media and from virtually every possible political perspective. Sorting out these diverse outlooks on the Vietnam War remains crucial work for cultural and political critics, but the general impression this cultural work offers is that of the re-narrativization of a military and colonial failure into a foundation for subsequent military ventures in the

Caribbean, Central America, the Persian Gulf, Africa, and the warring republics of the former Yugoslavia.

What appeared in the mid- to late 1970s to be a series of critical interpretations of U.S. involvement in Vietnam—such films as *Coming Home* (1978), *The Deer Hunter* (1979), and *Apocalypse Now* (1980)—were replaced by films and television programs that appropriated the liberal rhetoric of these predecessors but incorporated it into compensatory narratives intent on imaginatively fighting the war again and winning. Sylvester Stallone's "Rambo" character is the locus classicus of just such heroic conventions. John Rambo fights the Vietnamese, the Russians, and other foreign enemies in the Rambo films, but he also combats *Americans* in ways that clearly anticipate the contemporary "nationalization" of global issues in U.S. mass media. The opening scene of the first film, Ted Kotcheff's *Rambo, First Blood* (1982), establishes John Rambo's motivation for fighting the local police department and eventually the National Guard called in to hunt him down. As the opening credits roll, Rambo walks down a charming Northwest dirt road to a modest house on the edge of a lake. The African-American woman, who is hanging her wash on a clothes line and who centers a sublime prospect of natural beauty, is the mother of Rambo's best friend in Vietnam, Delmar Berry. In the opening dialogue of the film, Rambo learns from Delmar's mother that his friend has died of cancer, a victim of the Agent Orange sprayed as a defoliant in Vietnam. I have elsewhere interpreted how Rambo consequently appropriates the civil rights, antiwar, and countercultural movements of the late 1960s and early 1970s to legitimate the militarism he represents in *Rambo: First Blood*.[18]

In the second film, George P. Cosmatos's *Rambo, First Blood, Part II* (1985), Rambo's rage is directed at the CIA's reliance on high technology rather than human agency. In the concluding scene of the film, Rambo fires the large automatic weapons he has used on his mission into Vietnam to destroy the computer command center of the CIA in Thailand, and then he releases a primal scream to accompany this ritualized destruction of the new automated warfare he clearly condemns as inhuman. Ironically, the Emersonian self-reliance and natural identity of Rambo in both films is set in explicit contrast with the automated militarism employed by the Department of Defense and Pentagon in the first and second Gulf wars, which for many people were culturally justified by the revival of militaristic values exemplified by the Rambo character. There is a direct line from the fictional John Rambo to Brigadier General Vincent Brooks, "the six-foot-plus, Hollywood-handsome African American spokesman for Central Command" during the second Gulf war, who at Camp as-Sayliyah's state of the art, "$ 1.5 million, made-for-TV 'Coalition Media Center,' . . . gave hundreds of journalists his daily edited presentations."[19]

Never very precisely defined as a culture, geopolitical region, history, or people, "Vietnam" became a flexible term, so that the war refought in cultural fantasy could take place at home in such films as Louis Malle's *Alamo Bay* and Walter Hill's *Southern Comfort* (1981), or in other global hot spots, such as the Grenada of Clint Eastwood's *Heartbreak Ridge* (1986), or Central America in Mark Lester's *Commando* (1985), or Afghanistan in Peter McDonald's *Rambo III* (1988), where John Rambo fights valiantly with the Afghan *mujahideen* against the Soviets. Of course, the anticolonial resistance movement in Afghanistan, supported by CIA advisers and U.S. funds and weapons, would in the mid-1990s align itself with the Taliban (Students of Islam), which in turn would host Osama bin Laden and al-Qaeda.[20] Screening *Rambo III* today in the United States is a bizarre experience, as the viewer watches John Rambo learning and even participating in the folk rituals, such as horse racing, of Afghan "freedom fighters" who by 2001 would be our unequivocal enemies in that now nearly forgotten U.S. colonial enterprise in the oil-rich regions southeast of the Caspian Sea, including Uzbekistan, Turkmenistan, and Afghanistan.

Contemporary with these films and such fictional television programs as *China Beach* and *Miami Vice* or documentary series such as HBO's *Soldiers in Hiding* were military "tie-ins," which traded official sites as movie sets and insider information about military procedures for films that promoted military heroism and honor, such as *An Officer and a Gentleman* (1982), *Top Gun* (1986), and the many spinoffs, which have by now helped establish a cinematic and televisual genre (see, for example, the popular *JAG* [Judge Advocate General]). What came to be termed "the Vietnam effect" extended its aura to draw parasitically upon other wars, so that the recent revival of World War II as a topic in films, television docudramas, and print narratives (fiction, biography, and oral histories) had as much to do with the large-scale revision of the Vietnam War (and U.S. imperialism in Southeast Asia) as it did with such nominal historical markers as the fiftieth anniversary of D-Day or memorials for the end of World War II. Billed as antiwar films, often because of their graphic and thus alienating violence, films like Steven Spielberg's *Saving Private Ryan*, Terrence Malick's *Thin Red Line* (1998), and John Woo's *Wind Talkers* (2002) helped remilitarize the United States not only because they drew on the conventions of World War II heroism and military success but also because each in its own way borrowed liberal, often explicitly pacifist, sentiments for its purposes. Thus the lieutenant (Tom Hanks) leading the soldiers assigned to rescue Private Ryan is a schoolteacher unwilling to risk human lives unnecessarily and obliged merely to do the unpleasant but necessary job of civilian soldier. Officers in *Thin Red Line* disobey orders from above when they put their troops at unreasonable risk, and the Navajo "wind talkers" in John Woo's film challenge the racism of their fellows soldiers. All end up fighting, however, thereby linking a "just war" thesis with liberal and antiwar sentiments. My point that combat films with radically different political perspectives often contribute equally to pro-military sentiments is confirmed by Anthony Swofford in his recent memoir of the Gulf War, *Jarhead.* Describing U.S. soldiers' fascination with antiwar films about the Vietnam War, Swofford concludes: "But actually Vietnam War films are all pro-war, no matter what the supposed message, what Kubrick or Coppola or Stone intended. . . . The magic brutality of the films celebrates the terrible and despicable beauty of their fighting skills. Fight, rape, war, pillage, burn. Filmic images of death and carnage are pornography for the military man."[21]

Criticized by intellectuals for a variety of reasons—direct efforts to relegitimate U.S. military force, part of a general return to "masculine" values in reaction to the women's rights movement, more complex efforts to co-opt and thus defuse the sort of anti-war dissent that did contribute significantly to ending the Vietnam War—mass media rarely addressed these questions directly. Populist media and documentary filmmakers, including the surprisingly popular Michael Moore and less visible producers of "alternative" television, such as Paper Tiger's Dee Dee Halleck, rarely address the subtlety with which the mass media have employed the rhetoric of their political opponents. In Moore's *Roger and Me,* the CEO of General Motors is a classic capitalist hypocrite and thief; in *Bowling for Columbine,* the president of the National Rifle Association is the senile, foolish, and contradictory Charlton Heston. Only demystify!

There are important exceptions, of course, such as Barry Levinson's *Wag the Dog* (1998) and David O. Russell's *Three Kings* (1997), both of which criticized the nationalist propaganda and media control that allowed the George H. W. Bush administration to wage the Gulf War with little public scrutiny and the illusion of an "international coalition" of allied forces. *Wag the Dog* is based on the premise that a "war" we are waging against Albania is entirely fabricated by a Washington spin-doctor (Conrad Bream, played by Robert De Niro) with the help of a Hollywood producer (Sidney Motss, played by Dustin Hoffman) to distract public attention from a sexual harassment charge against the incumbent president two weeks away from his reelection. *Wag the Dog* brilliantly satirizes the increasing control the U.S. federal government has exercised over news reporting of its foreign military ventures. In many respects, *Wag the Dog* seems merely to elaborate in Hollywood film satire the claims made by Jean Baudrillard in his deliberately iconoclastic *La Guerre du Golfe n'a pas eu lieu* (1991).[22]

In a very different fashion, *Three Kings* attempted to peel away the mask of patriotic dedication in the Gulf War by exposing the greed of the U.S. soldiers for Kuwaiti gold looted by the invading Iraqi army as a metaphor for U.S. self-interest in controlling the oil-rich Gulf. I admit that the pacifist and populist sentiments of *Three Kings* are noteworthy, especially in a period when Hollywood films were targeted increasingly at 12–17-year-old moviegoers, who pay the most dollars per person of any age group in the United States. The grisly scene of an M-16 bullet penetrating human intestines in slow motion and producing the green bile that will slowly and painfully kill the victim is far more effective than the slow-motion melodrama of U.S. troops dying on the beaches of Normandy during the D-Day invasion in *Saving Private Ryan.*

Nevertheless, both *Wag the Dog* and *Three Kings* rely on a narrative of Americanization that plays a significant role in the general public's understanding of globalization and anticipates how post-9/11 film and television would rely on similar processes of nationalizing international problems to "channel the nation back to normalcy—or at least [to] the normal flows of television and consumer culture," as Lynn Spigel puts it.[23] *Wag the Dog* does this cultural work in an obvious manner by locating all of the action of the film in the United States; the imprisoned soldier (Denis Leary), who is picked to simulate an actual U.S. soldier "downed" by hostile gunfire in Albania and miraculously "rescued," has to be picked up by the media team from his maximum-security military prison in Texas. The liberal politics of *Wag the Dog* make what I have termed "hypernationalization" an explicit theme in the film, so that we are expected to understand immediately the irony of the Hollywood producer Motss and the Washington insider Bream inventing an international crisis to cover a domestic sexual scandal. The film satirizes Americans' chronic ignorance of world events, thanks to news structured around entertainment and commercialism, but it also reinforces the assumption that the United States is the center of the world and that even a "fictional" war can have meaning and value, as long as it is waged by the United States. Carefully structured news stories about the second Gulf war seem to have followed the example of *Wag the Dog,* despite its satiric and countercultural intentions. The "saving" of Jessica Lynch, the U.S. soldier wounded and captured by Iraqi troops during the U.S.-British invasion, follows just such a narrative of Americanization, from her heroic rescue by U.S. Special Forces through her medical treatment and debriefing at a U.S. military based near Frankfurt to her triumphant return to her hometown in Palestine, West Virginia. Rather than *Wag the Dog*'s satire overwhelming and thus neutralizing the "Jessica Lynch" story on the evening news, Jessica Lynch's narrative, now made into a television biopic, has undone the irony of Barry Levinson's film, especially its "rescued soldier" device.

More conventionally, *Three Kings* challenges self-interested U.S. militarism and foreign policy in the Gulf by condemning the command-structure of the U.S. military and countering it with the populist pacifism and humanitarianism of the "three kings," who finally live up to their biblical titles by guiding dissident Iraqis and their families to their "promised land" across the border in Iran. The familiar imperial narrative of U.S. paternalism, of the "white-man's burden," plays itself out once again in terms almost identical with those criticized so thoroughly in nineteenth-century imperial narratives. The dissident Iraqis who save Archie Gates (George Clooney), Troy Barlow (Mark Wahlberg), Chief Elgin (Ice Cube), and Conrad Vig (Spike Jonze) from attack by the Republican Guard turn out to be primarily intent on "get[ting] rid of Saddam," in order to "live life and do business," as their leader Amir Abdullah (Cliff Curtis) says.

The film criticizes consumer capitalism and its globalization, but advocates on the other hand the value of small businesses. When Troy Barlow is captured and tortured by Republican Guards, he is made to drink crude oil poured into his mouth propped open with a CD case. The consumer goods stolen from Kuwait and heaped in poorly guarded Iraqi bunkers exemplify the meretriciousness of multinational globalization—the tape and CD players in their unopened boxes, tangled skeins of jewelry, heaps of cell phones, and other consumer "junk" are visually effective, but the political dissidents these three kings will eventually save are committed to modest but meaningful businesses, such as hair-styling. Following a nearly schematic narrative of "education," the three remaining kings (Conrad Vig dies and is prepared for a Muslim burial) use the gold they have stolen from the Iraqis (who have stolen it from the Kuwaitis) to "buy" safe passage for the political dissidents into the relative safety of Iran. The final scene of the film in which the border crossing is enacted, replete with sentimental waves and sympathetic looks between the dissidents and the enlightened U.S. soldiers, is difficult to watch from a post–Iraq War vantage point, where various commentators are already clamoring to expand the U.S. invasion and occupation of Iraq to include Iran.

The sympathy these U.S. soldiers establish with the Iraqi dissidents is certainly intended by David O. Russell to counter the Orientalist demonization of Arab peoples so common in U.S. mass culture since the nineteenth century, intensified as part of the build-up for the first Gulf War, and driven to near cultural hysteria in the months following the attacks on 9/11.[24] Yet the Iraqi dissidents are represented in what seem to be deliberately ambiguous regional, ethnic, and religious terms. The mercenary U.S. soldiers enter southern Iraq in quest of the stolen Kuwaiti gold, so the political dissidents they encounter in the aftermath of the first Gulf War would most likely be Shi'ite dissidents, similar to those who appealed to George H. W. Bush for military assistance and staged an unsuccessful rebellion against Saddam Hussein in the weeks following the conclusion of that war. Yet there is considerable cinematic evidence to conclude that the Iraqi dissidents are Kurds. Hair-dressing, for example, is a traditionally respected profession among the Kurds, so that one of the dissidents' plans to return to that profession hints at Kurdish affiliations, displaced of course from the main Kurdish population centers in northern Iraq to the film's setting in southern Iraq. Saddam Hussein's government did forcibly "resettle" Kurds in the South (including many who were murdered and buried in mass graves there) during the Anfal, the genocidal "ethnic cleansing" the Iraqi dictator conducted prior to the first Gulf War.[25]

The deliberate confusion of different dissident groups in Iraq seems intended not only to achieve cinematic economy, but also to make these dissidents more accessible to the four U.S. soldiers. These soldiers represented in the film offer a sample of U.S. multiculturalism: Chief Elgin is a devout Christian African American, Conrad Vig is an uneducated southern white racist, Archie Gates is a white career soldier taking early retirement, and Troy Barlow a model WASP. To be sure, the representativeness of this group is very narrow, but their respective sympathies with the Iraqi dissidents perform a narrative of cultural hybridity that unmistakably argues for greater understanding of other peoples as an alternative to unilateral globalization and to U.S. militarism. Chief Elgin appears to abandon Christianity for Islam, and he dons the traditional Arab male *kaffiyeh* ("head covering") to announce his conversion. Conrad Vig learns about Islamic burial practices, overcomes his racism toward Chief Elgin by way of their shared interest in Islam, and is eventually prepared for an Islamic burial of his own. In fact, when the dissidents cross the border into Iran, they are carrying his body with them for a proper burial on the other side. The protagonists learn to sympathize with and understand not historically and regionally specific groups of Iraqis, but generalized "Arab" and "Muslim" types. In this way, the four Americans act out liberal multiculturalism, which is often criticized for what Lisa Lowe terms its contribution to the "ideological representation of the liberal imperialist state."[26] Thus the cinematic experience of viewing in 2004 the concluding scene of Iraqi dissidents crossing the border into the relative freedom of Iran is not a prophecy from 1997 of how the Bush administration would turn to military power again in 2003 because it failed to follow the humane and politically liberal advice of *Three Kings.* Instead, the liberal ideology, itself deeply invested in U.S. nationalism, helped produce the circumstances that would make the Bush administration's invasion of Iraq a military and colonial reality and the "logical next step" of this foreign policy covert or military efforts at "regime change" in Iran.

What has been particularly noteworthy in U.S. mass media since the terrorists attacks of September 11 and during the invasion of Iraq has been a new twist on these old themes, but a turn that is compatible with them and readable as part of a history stretching from the Vietnam era to the present in the gradual, ineluctable control of the news and entertainment media by the U.S. government. Fiction and nonfiction television has understandably paid great attention to the related events of 9/11 and the justification of U.S. military intervention in Iraq. Lynn Spigel describes in some detail how "traditional forms of entertainment" reinvented "their place in U.S. life and culture" after 9/11, initially by reducing the number of violent films released and replacing them on television with "family fare."[27] Spigel goes on to argue that very quickly after this period of self-censorship, Hollywood and television turned instead to familiar historical narratives to stabilize the myths of national cohesion and reaffirm a teleological narrative about the American experience.[28] Spigel's fine study confirms my own sense that Hollywood and television quickly recycled old mythic narratives about America, rather than drawing the opposite conclusion: that the terrorist attacks of 9/11 indicate that Americans need to know far more about the world they are so intent upon "globalizing." As if in direct response to this promise of greater attention to the other peoples of the world, the media began to incorporate "terrorism" into the United States and strip it of its international threat. Like President Bush's continual efforts to link Iraq directly with al-Qaeda, the nationalizing of terror helped defuse its transnational, inchoate, and thus truly terrifying power. The containment of terror on contemporary U.S. television follows the logic of the cultural imperialism I have been tracing thus far, but now with the claim that the best weapons against such "terror" are those of traditional U.S. democracy: the fairness of the law and the populism of an American people that exceeds party politics.

Since the 1987–88 television season, NBC's *Law and Order,* now the main title for three separate television programs, has worked out fictional solutions to much-publicized cases in criminal law in the United States.[29] Starring Sam Waterston as the lead prosecutor of the district attorney's office in New York, the program makes moral claims specific to the medium of television and distinguishes itself thereby from the continuing spate of police and crime shows, which rely primarily on the urban public's anxieties about living in an increasingly dangerous America and world. The program is structured in two parts: in the first half-hour, police detectives investigate a crime, arrest a suspect, and present their case to the DA's office; in the second half-hour, the chief prosecutor, Jack Mc Coy (Waterston), and his attractive Assistant DA, Serena, bring the case to trial and judgment. Although the detective and legal work do not always coincide, the errors in the system seem to confirm the overall checks and balances built into the police-judicial system, as it is referred to in the voice over prologue to the program.

Here I want to digress for a moment to anticipate my larger argument. I disagree with Michael Moore's repeated claim in *Bowling for Columbine* that it is primarily the news media, rather than entertainment television and film, that have shaped the atmosphere of fear in the United States, resulting in more than 11,000 gun deaths per year. Citing how other societies, like Canada and Japan, where gun deaths are less than 1,000 per year, still generate large audiences for violent films, television programs, and video games, Moore contends that in such societies even adolescent viewers can suspend their disbelief in fiction programs and understand the difference between fantasy and reality. But in the United States, there is a long tradition of confusing fiction and reality in the mass media, primarily for the purposes of maximizing the commercial advantages of each mode. We hardly need the examples of recent "reality television" to remind us that television thrives on what Baudrillard long ago defined as the "hyperreal," a phenomenon seemingly explained best by the way television gives us the illusion of heightened knowledge and authority over an otherwise baffling real. *Law and Order* certainly has this effect on its viewers, which may account for its huge success on network television otherwise challenged significantly by cable channels, such as Lifetime and Oxygen, targeting specific market shares and trying to break up network hegemony in the so-called post-network era.

I have argued elsewhere that the socially conscious television of the early 1970s, such as Norman Lear pioneered in *All in the Family,* was transformed in the 1980s into much more conventional "moral problem solving" within the existing legal and social boundaries of U.S. democracy.[30] *All in the Family* argued that racial and ethnic bigotry could not be overcome entirely by the law, but required changes in personal values. *Sanford and Son* joined that argument to claim that class and racial antipathies were inextricably bound together in psychological habits difficult but still possible to change. But *Law and Order* imagines that equality under the law, despite notable aberrations in U.S. legal history, is our best defense against injustices tied to class, race, ethnicity, gender, or sexuality. The cultural shift is clearly from television committed to political and social reform to television concerned with defending existing institutions, as indeed the title of the program—a slogan of conservative Republican campaigns for the past thirty-five years—suggests.

The episode of *Law and Order* I want to analyze focuses on the murder of a popular professor of anthropology, Louise Murdoch, who is also the head of a community advocacy center for Muslim women, and the eventual arrest and trial of a young American male, Greg Landen, who has converted to Islam. Of course, the most infamous American convert to Islam on October 2, 2002, the date this episode was first broadcast, was John Walker Lindh, the so-called American Taliban, who had left his upper-middle-class home in Marin, California, to study Arabic and thus the Qu'ran in Yemen and Pakistan and then to join the Taliban in Afghanistan. Two days after this episode aired, Lindh was sentenced to a twenty-year prison term in a plea bargain that reduced the charges against him to "one count of providing services to the Taliban and one count of carrying explosives during a felony."[31] In his sentencing hearing, Lindh was tearful and apologetic, denying he had any intention of taking up arms against the United States, and his divorced parents stood by him throughout his arrest and trial.

Lindh is certainly the historical model on which the character of Greg Landen in *Law and Order* is based, but very important changes are made in his character and history. First, the young man in *Law and Order* despises his parents, the legal system, and America in general, so that his courtroom tirades as he takes over his own legal defense for purposes of political propaganda remind the viewer of news accounts of Zacarias Moussaoui, the accused "twentieth" hijacker in the 9/11 attacks, who also insisted on serving as his own legal counsel and used the courtroom as a bully-pulpit. Testifying in his own defense, Landen makes some very reasonable connections between al-Qaeda's possible motivations and the historical motivations of oppressed minorities in the United States to resist domination:

> Since 1990, [the U.S.] has occupied our holy lands. . . . America doesn't respect any culture but its own. . . . America is a country that was born out of the mass murder of native Americans and built on the backs of Africans. If the native Americans could have defended themselves by flying planes into buildings, don't you think they would have? If the slaves could have freed themselves by becoming martyrs, don't you think they would have? And it wouldn't have been terrorism; it would have been self-defense.[32]

In Muslim male dress and beard, Greg Landen is exoticized and Orientalized, even though his testimony echoes reasonable arguments made by many intellectuals in response to 9/11. In addition to his physical appearance, Landen is also alienated by his father, who is shown in the courtroom shaking his head from side to side and mouthing the unheard word, "no," as his son testifies.

The young man's target in *Law and Order* is not the capitalist authority symbolized by the World Trade Towers in New York City or the military authority of the Pentagon, but a woman professor of anthropology, who has devoted her life to liberal social change and exemplifies that work in her diversification of the American university. Equating global terrorist attacks, such as al-Qaeda's on the United States (or Israel, France, or Indonesia), with "domestic terrorism" within the United States, such as Timothy McVeigh's 1995 bombing of the Alfred P. Murrah Federal Building in Oklahoma City, is a common response not only in the United States but in Islamic societies. But this episode of *Law and Order* constructs the plot in such a way as to swerve widely from such a conclusion. Instead, we learn that the young man believed his girlfriend, who worked at the professor's Center for Muslim Women, was being drawn away from her responsibilities as a submissive Islamic woman by her feminist work with the professor. In a jealous but also religiously motivated rage, he "smote" his enemy.

Cautious to protect itself against charges of insensitivity to Muslim Americans, *Law and Order* carefully disengages the young man from "true" Islam, but in much the same fashion that al-Qaeda has been distinguished in the popular U.S. news from "true" Islam: by condemning the "fundamentalist" irrationality of both, rather than making any substantive claims about the role of women in Islamic societies. In a decisive consultation between the prosecutors and a woman psychologist whom the prosecution will call as an expert witness, the psychologist concludes that Landen's primary motivation for murder was his sexual insecurity, reinforced by his difficult relationship with his parents and his desperate need to maintain absolute control over his girlfriend. I need hardly comment on how such a conclusion reduces to triviality all of the important ethical questions raised by this episode. To be sure, *Law and Order* does not argue that this young man represents all American Muslims, but it reinforces virtually every convention the West has used to distinguish its "civilization" from Islamic "barbarism" since Romantic Idealist philosophers like Hegel.

Talal Asad has argued in *Genealogies of Religion* that the "West" begins with the "project of modernization (Westernization)" that is inherently colonial and "defines itself, in opposition to all non-Western cultures, by its modern historicity. Despite the disjunctions of modernity (its break with tradition), 'the West' therefore includes within itself its past as an organic continuity: from 'the Greeks and Romans' and 'the Hebrews and Early Christians,' through 'Latin Christendom,' 'the Renaissance,' and 'the Reformation,' to the 'universal civilization' of modern Europeans."[33] Western imperialism, then, is a story that is told in countless different ways, media, and genres, but with surprisingly few variations when looked at in this light, which allows "otherness" to be internalized and rationalized, historicized, and civilized.

It perhaps should not surprise or even shock us that popular American television contributes to this narrative teleology in such transparently reductive ways. "Islam" is for a young American, like John Walker Lindh or the fictional character in this episode, merely "acting out" childish rebellion, a confirmation of the "undeveloped" features of those "backward cultures," which like Hegel's Africa are "without history." In a similar fashion, conservative politicians and the general public accepted antiwar activism in the Vietnam War era as "college hijinks," "adolescent rebellion," a "rejection of their fathers' America." What each of these historical moments—the Vietnam War and the current inchoate "war on terrorism"—have in common is a desperate desire to reaffirm national values by repressing utterly the history and reality of supposed "enemies" in Southeast Asia and the Islamic world. Few today would disagree, including such stubborn old hawks as General William Westmoreland, that the Vietnam War marked a historic moment in which the United States needed to change its foreign and domestic policies, its ties between government and corporation, its neglect of public opinion, and the changing political economies affecting these historical crises. If we are to learn the lesson of the Vietnam era, then we must learn to recognize, rather than repress, the complex, intertwined histories of Islam, its influence on the development of U.S. and other Western societies, and our dependence on the economic means it has provided to "modernize" and thus "Westernize," often at its own peril, the world. Before we can even begin to learn this lesson, however, we will have to read critically that other narrative of Western historicity Talal Asad has so cogently interpreted as dependent on a constant "assumption": "To make history, the agent must create the future, remake herself, and help others to do so, where the criteria of successful remaking are seen to be universal. Old universes must be subverted and a new universe created. To that extent, history can be made only on the back of a universal teleology. Actions seeking to maintain the 'local' status quo, or to follow local models of social life, do not qualify as history making. From the Cargo Cults of Melanesia to the Islamic Revolution in Iran, they merely attempt (hopelessly) 'to resist the future' or 'to turn back the clock of history.'"[34] It is time for us to think differently about how "history" is and has been made, to count the "local" as well as the "global," and to develop new institutions, not simply interpretive methods, to negotiate the inevitable conflicts of such histories. Without such critical knowledge, there is likely to be unending terror from all sides in a new era of global warfare only one stage of which is being enacted in the U.S. occupation of Iraq.

NOTES

1. Max Horkheimer and Theodor Adorno, *Dialectic of Enlightenment,* trans. John Cumming (New York: Continuum, 1988), 122

2. Horkheimer and Adorno, *Dialectic of Enlightenment,* 120.

3. See http//www.informationclearinghouse.info/article2842.htm.

4. Chalmers Johnson, *The Sorrows of Empire: Militarism, Secrecy, and the End of the Republic* (New York: Henry Holt and Co., 2004), 30.

5. "In Search of Al Qaeda," *Frontline,* PBS (original airing date November 21, 2002).

6. Anne Friedberg, *Window Shopping: Cinema and the Postmodern* (Berkeley and Los Angeles: University of California Press, 1993), 120.

7. Karl Marx, *Capital: A Critique of Political Economy,* trans. Ben Fowkes, vol. 1 (New York: Random House, 1977), 125–77; Georg Lukács, *History and Class Consciousness: Studies in Marxist Dialectics,* trans. Rodney Livingstone (Cambridge, Mass.: MIT Press, 1971).

8. Mark Poster, *What's the Matter with the Internet?* (Minneapolis: University of Minnesota Press, 2001), 20.

9. Anna McCarthy, *Ambient Television: Visual Culture and Public Space* (Durham: Duke University Press, 2001), 226–51.

10. Karl Marx and Friedrich Engels, *The German Ideology,* ed. C.J. Arthur (New York: International Publishers, 1988), 47.

11. Francis Fukuyama, *The End of History and the Last Man* (New York: Free Press, 1992).

12. Johnson, *The Sorrows of Empire,* 138–39, 217–18.

13. John Gallagher and Ronald Robinson, "The Imperialism of Free Trade," *Economic History Review,* 2nd series, 6 (1953), 1–25.

14. Johnson, *The Sorrows of Empire,* 31.

15. As quoted in John Carlos Rowe, *Literary Culture and U.S. Imperialism: From the Revolution to World War II* (New York: Oxford University Press, 2000), 132.

16. Today China is the source of the greatest imbalance in U.S. trade relations globally.

17. Robert Kagan, *Of Paradise and Power: America and Europe in the New World Order* (New York: Random House, 2003), 157–58.

18. John Carlos Rowe, *The New American Studies* (Minneapolis: University of Minnesota Press, 2002), 180–86.

19. Johnson, *The Sorrows of Empire,* 249.

20. Johnson, *The Sorrows of Empire,* 177.

21. Anthony Swofford, *Jarhead: A Marine's Chronicle of the Gulf War* (New York: Scribner, 2003), 210.

22. Jean Baudrillard, *La Guerre du Golfe n'a pas eu lieu* (Paris: Galilée, 1991); translated and introduced by Paul Patton as *The Gulf War Did Not Take Place* (Bloomington: Indiana University Press, 1995).

23. Lynn Spigel, "Entertainment Wars: Television Culture after 9/11," *American Quarterly* 56.2 (2004): 239.

24. One of my points in this essay and in *Literary Culture and U.S. Imperialism* is that when we view U.S. imperialism in its full historical scope, rather than as a recent "neo-imperialism" dating either from World War II or from the Spanish-American War, we see such features as U.S. Orientalism as relatively unchanged, except for the specific peoples employed. From the Barbary Pirates of nineteenth-century Tripoli, to the Philippine revolutionaries led by Aguinaldo in the Philippine-American War (1898–1902) who resisted U.S. annexation, to the Viet Cong and North Vietnamese Army regulars, and, more recently, to the Libyan, Palestinian, Iraqi, Iranian, and transnational al-Qaeda-style revolutionaries, diverse groups around the globe have been consistently Orientalized by the United States. For an interesting discussion of U.S. Orientalism in these contexts, see Christina Klein, *Cold War Orientalism: Asia in the Middlebrow Imagination, 1945–1961* (Berkeley and Los Angeles: University of California Press, 2003), 1–19.

25. I am indebted to Thomas LeClair of the University of Cincinnati for this interpretation of the Kurdish elements in the dissident group represented in *Three Kings.*

26. Lisa Lowe, "Imagining Los Angeles in the Production of Multiculturalism," in *Mapping Multiculturalism,* ed. Avery F. Gordon and Christopher Newfield (Minneapolis: University of Minnesota Press, 1996), 420.

27. Spigel, "Entertainment Wars," 235.

28. Spigel, "Entertainment Wars," 240–41.

29. The other two programs are *Law and Order: SVU (Special Victims Unit)* and *Law and Order: CI (Criminal Intent).*

30. Rowe, *New American Studies,* 170–71.

31. John Walker Lindh, "I Made a Mistake by Joining the Taliban," *Washington Post,* October 5, 2002, A1.

32. *Law and Order*, NBC, season 13, episode 1 (original airing date October 2, 2002).

33. Talal Asad, *Genealogies of Religion: Disciplines and Reasons of Power in Christianity and Islam* (Baltimore: The Johns Hopkins University Press, 1993), 18.

34. Asad, *Genealogies of Religion*, 19.

11. Metaphors of Sovereignty

Lisa Lowe

Two current U.S. national campaigns draw legitimacy from the definition of state sovereignty traditionally understood as the exclusive right of the modern nation-state to govern people and territories, a definition harking back to the time of the Treaty of Westphalia (1648) up through most of the twentieth century. Proponents of both proposed legislation to criminalize an estimated twelve million immigrants living and working in the United States, and the U.S. "war on terror," ranging from the invasion of Afghanistan and the occupation of Iraq to the policing of dissent against U.S. state militarism, seek to draw justification from these traditional understandings and to associate the measures with the securing of U.S. national security within the "new world order."[1] Both efforts view the nation-state as the primary political actor on the global stage and define the sovereignty of the nation-state in terms of its power to control its borders, as well as the populations within and outside of those borders. While this definition of sovereignty refers to a particular genealogy of academic political science, from an interdisciplinary feminist perspective the recent fortification of the U.S.-Mexican border appears less as a rational index of a *new* immigration crisis, and more an expression of a gendered transformation of the meaning of U.S. state sovereignty within the context of globalization. The operations that have prioritized transnational markets and gendered labor supplies have challenged the traditional autonomy of the U.S. state and rendered its coherence increasingly disaggregated; migrant flows that satisfy agribusiness and service industries simultaneously disorganize the Immigration and Naturalization Service and border patrols. In addition, as the U.S. government has withdrawn from its earlier role as the guardian of American citizens' social welfare, it has increasingly lost its former legitimacy; with this loss, the U.S. state after 2001 under George W. Bush struggled to maintain its authority by exerting juridical or military controls rather than by broadening its electoral base of support. In this sense, the U.S. war in Iraq has been from the outset *not* a political response to a traditional threat to territorial sovereignty, but the nation's attempt to occupy Iraq in order to gain political control of Middle Eastern petroleum reserves on which many industrialized nations depend; with the scarcity of oil, military occupation of the oil-rich region has been imagined as the means not merely to control the resource but to exert influence over the most economically productive competitors in the global system, including China and India.[2] It has become clear that the Iraq war provides neither answers to waning U.S. sovereignty nor restoratives for the country's economic anxiety; to the contrary, it has increasingly turned the international public against the United States, as it has destabilized the Middle East and incurred enormous financial debts. In this essay, I discuss the role of U.S. political science in shaping understandings of contemporary world governance; yet the mainstream discipline's ideas of state sovereignty are incommensurable with the practices that characterize globalization, and "gender" is one significant index in which we may "read" this incommensurability. Transnational modes of gender discipline within globalization articulate the shift from the Cold War management of third world nation-states to a *biopolitical governmentality* focused on bodies and populations that disrespects such borders. Not aiming to provide anything as exhaustive as a history of the field, I restrict myself to tracing how the dominant paradigm of U.S. political science has defined the study of the "political" in terms of the *nation-state*, a definition that has both produced and restricted knowledge about the present conditions of globalization and has provided the framework within which the "war on terror" and legislation of the "immigration crisis" are currently rationalized. I conclude with an examination of a cross-border feminist environmental campaign, representing a counter-politics that provides an alternative to the modern definition of sovereignty as inhering in the power of the state and its institutions.

The U.S. wars after September 2001 mark a particular stage in the global dialectic of political and economic priorities. The near unilateral militarism of the U.S. war on Iraq has been not only reminiscent of a much earlier era, but the hijacking of public fear, the enforcement of public patriotism, the breach of civil rights of prisoners held at Guantánamo—all these measures have demonstrated a supersession of "political freedoms" of U.S. citizens by corporate interests in "free trade," or what some call "free market fundamentalism," to denote the dogmatism that fervently subordinates interests in social justice or political equality to purely economic ones.[3] More to the point, the U.S. war in Iraq militates against longer term international institutions like the United Nations, the multilateral diplomacy of the North Atlantic Treaty Organization (NATO), and regional interests and coalitions like the European Union (EU), which political science over two decades ago had argued were commensurate with the neoliberal economics of globalization. "Keeping the world safe for capitalism" had in effect already been secured by the "Washington Consensus" during the Ronald Reagan, George H. W. Bush, and Bill Clinton presidencies in the 1980s and 1990s, and even officials who were inclined to expect little from international institutions had discovered their value in achieving American economic purposes.[4] Yet the global unilateralism of the U.S. invasion of Iraq not only broke with what political scientists call an "international regime"—the principles, norms, rules and governing arrangements that affect interstate interdependence—it broke with the international regime that had been in effect for at least three decades.[5] This national government has used the so-called war on terror to create an apparent crisis to justify the state's monopoly on both violence and power; it combines extreme military force in extraterritorial war with the state-supported suppressions of civil and political dissent to protect unimpeded progress of corporate capitalism.

"Small states often welcome international regimes as barriers to arbitrary abuse of power by the strong. But regimes can be equally valuable to great powers, such as the United States, that want to create, but are unable to dictate, the terms of a stable world environment," observed Robert Keohane and Joseph Nye in 1985.[6] Recalling key debates in political science will help us make sense of this contemporary contradiction in which the U.S. militarism employed to command the current global economy appears to hark back to political policies of an earlier isolationist nation. I briefly trace the neorealist and neoliberal debates in political science, characterizing the research methods of apparently opposed academic perspectives. Yet I argue that even in their disagreements, the two approaches actually confirm a normative notion of nation-state sovereignty, obscuring the effects of global governance for most of the world's population. Ultimately, I direct my discussion towards the exploration of feminist political forms that practice alternative notions of sovereignty. Where might we "read" these practices that are rendered illegible within the studies that privilege the normative politics of the western nation-state?

Modern political science emerged as a definable area of research in the United States and Europe within the general systematization of the social sciences in the twentieth century. Modern political theory built upon classical theories from Plato, Aristotle, and Thucydides and early-modern thinkers such as Hobbes, Machiavelli, and Montesquieu to discuss on what bases and principles social groups form political societies. Yet modern political science has been largely concerned with the theory and practice of liberty and sovereignty within the western nation-state; drawing from the liberal political philosophies of John Locke, Jean-Jacques Rousseau, and John Stuart Mill, it has been concerned with freedoms for the citizen within the nation-state as well as for sovereign nations themselves within the international system.[7] The liberal tradition defines sovereignty as the right of the state to exercise jurisdiction over its citizens, maintain internal order, and defend its territory. Sovereignty rests on an internal principle, not on the lineage of a dynasty or aristocracy, and in the concept of the *nation-state*, the political sovereignty of the state is broadened through constitutional enfranchisement and legitimized through a common national culture.[8] In principle, civil society integrates national culture, economy, and social order, and the distinction between civil society and the state is crucial to the emergence of the rational public sphere in which citizens speak and debate within the rule of law.[9] Yet this principle understates the degree to which control over the means of violence has proven to be the defining characteristic of state sovereignty; indeed, the more effectively a state *monopolizes* the use of force, the less frequent may be the resort to actual violence. Political science in the United States adopted this liberal definition of sovereignty, and the democratic nation-state has been presumed to be the *ideal type*, or the model of statehood, for participation in the international interstate system.[10] The result is that there is an underestimation of the contradictions within the nation-state, on the one hand, and between imperial nation-states and the formerly colonized world, on the other.

With respect to the contradictory inequalities within the nation, the state declares the universal extension of rights to all citizens, yet U.S. history has shown that the access to rights has always been unevenly distributed, requiring social movements that have called upon the state to establish liberties for subjects to whom they are guaranteed in theory. Conceiving the state as the grantor of rights, emancipatory and democratizing politics have often struggled to reform the state. For example, workers' struggles in the 1940s and civil rights movements for women and racialized minorities in the 1960s and 1970s are examples of popular efforts to extend equal rights and to make the state accountable for political liberties already promised in theory.[11] When rights have been suspended or curtailed in times of national security—as the rights of

Japanese Americans relocated to internment camps during World War II, or the rights of U.S. citizens imprisoned at Guantánamo Bay during the U.S. wars in Afghanistan and Iraq—struggles for justice on behalf of those denied civil rights have addressed the state. The growth of national industries exacerbated inequalities of property and political representation, and labor movements and trade unions have called upon the state to create certain controls on the "liberties" of factory owners and corporate profits. Of course, tensions between capital and labor have grown with the neoliberal globalization of the U.S. economy. The internationalization of production not only broke links between domestic producers and domestic labor, but transnational corporate imperatives aimed at reducing labor costs drove corporations to shift production to labor markets in the poorest countries, with the lowest wages and the fewest taxes and regulations.

The focus on the nation-state as the normative political unit also leaves unstudied the historical and structural inequalities between imperial nation-states and the nations of the formerly colonized world, most of which gained independence through decolonization movements in the mid-twentieth century. During the centuries of European rule, colonial administrations in Africa, Asia, Latin America, and the Caribbean extracted profits through imposed forms of economy, politics, religion, language, and culture, justifying rule through a "civilizing mission."[12] Colonialism included the capture and import of Africans for slave labor on colonial plantations, the destruction of indigenous peoples and brutal suppression of the colonized cultures, and the imposition of European education and social administration. Throughout the nineteenth century, native anticolonial movements sought to establish self-governing nations independent of their British, French, Dutch, and Spanish colonizers.[13] Anticolonial movements in most of the former colonies in Africa, Asia, and the Caribbean articulated their independence by the mid-twentieth century by becoming new states on the international stage.

Newly independent nations emerging from decolonization entered a world system in which the nation-state was the normative unit of sovereignty recognized by the postwar world. While scholars and statesmen have tended to cast postcolonial nationhood as the vehicle for third world "progress" and entry into the modern world of nations, statehood for the formerly colonized has rarely meant actual autonomy and self-determination.[14] After the establishment of "independence," the new national governments—often provisional, not yet "legitimate"—created new societies with difficulty; there were internal and external obstacles to the redistribution of sovereignty, land, and economic power necessary for actual decolonization.[15] Furthermore, the struggles of emerging independent formerly colonized nations converged with U.S. postwar economic interests in expansion and investment abroad; U.S. "development" and investment projects often created new dependency or reproduced old inequality for the new nations.[16] New postcolonial states have remained disadvantaged in the uneven distribution of both sovereignty and resources, and it is evident that what Francis Fukuyama called "the universalization of Western liberal democracy as the final form of human government" has hardly taken place.[17] Unfavored by a political economy of development organized around the interests of the industrialized nations, many formerly colonized countries were further beset by what Mahmood Mamdani has observed as the U.S. Cold War conduct of covert wars against left-leaning secular movements in areas from Mozambique and Angola to Nicaragua and Afghanistan.[18]

The United Nations was founded in 1945 to be the central institution for guiding and organizing international relations, yet however much the UN attempts to represent the larger community of nations, it has tended to be the circle of victors emerging from World War II who have held sway. The UN Charter framed abstract principles for international cooperation: sovereign equality, territorial integrity and political independence of states, nonintervention in internal affairs, equal rights—yet the Charter is not a constitution for international society, and it has no central authority to legislate nor does it possess the character of a government.[19] Multilateral organizations within the UN, such as the Non-Aligned Movement growing out of the 1955 Bandung Conference, sought to address the disparity of power between states, representing those not aligned with or against the major superpowers.[20] International non-governmental organizations, or INGOs, have sponsored forceful multilateral initiatives in the areas of human rights, war crimes, world health and environmental protection.[21] Yet comparative politics and international relations have only begun to explore the range of extra-state issues that accompany globalization, such as the politics of immigration or the growth of non-governmental organizations.

There have been two particular "schools" for understanding international politics, both presuming the *ideal type* of the nation-state. The "realist" school (sometimes called "neorealist" to indicate both its affinity with and distinction from earlier approaches) conceives the state as a sovereign, monolithic unit with little internal differentiation whose primary purpose is to defend the national interest; neorealists generally see, as did Thomas Hobbes, the conflicts among nations as necessarily aggressive, perpetual struggles for security and power.[22] What Hans Morgenthau called "political realism" gained a particular vigor after World War II and during the Cold War when the U.S. was engaged in a struggle with the Soviet Union for power in both the developed and developing worlds. Realism deployed the language of power and interests rather than of ideals and norms; it encompassed the propositions that states are the major actors in world affairs, that international anarchy is the principal force shaping states, that states in anarchy are predisposed toward conflict and competition, and that international institutions will only marginally affect the prospects for cooperation.[23] "The state among states . . . conducts its affairs in the brooding shadow of violence. Because some states may at any time use force, all states must be prepared to do so—or live at the mercy of their militarily more vigorous neighbors. Among states, the state of nature is a state of war," Kenneth Waltz wrote in 1979.[24]

The "liberal institutionalist" or "neoliberal" school challenged the realist assumption of anarchy and its utilitarian "state as actor" approach, and argued for international institutions of cooperation. If the "realist" tradition follows a particular understanding of Thomas Hobbes, the "liberal" one emerges out of the political theory of John Locke, and became embodied by Woodrow Wilson, John Dewey, and Franklin Roosevelt.[25] The "neoliberal" approach emphasized its distinction from "liberalism" by integrating realism's concern with interests and power, and it argues that increased global interconnection has transformed earlier meanings of state sovereignty and autonomy, and that international relations depend upon what Robert Keohane and Joseph Nye called "complex interdependence," or multiple channels and institutions of common interest and collaboration.[26] Neoliberals envision a global society that functions alongside individual states by means of regional treaties or hemispheric economic trade agreements, institutions such as the United Nations, and increasing numbers of international nongovernmental organizations addressing issues from environmental protection to human rights to nuclear deterrence. This latter "institutionalist" approach had come to represent the mainstream analysis in the political science of international relations in the two decades after the Cold War.[27] Since September 2001, however, the United States has pursued what must be termed not simply a "neorealist" but a "neoconservative" foreign policy that harks back to the political realist approach of the Cold War period. Indeed, neoconservatives like Donald and Frederick Kagan argue that the United States never should have reduced its military power after the Cold War, and that the aggressive unilateral stance in Iraq was the only way for the United States to recuperate its global stature.[28] Neoconservatives believe that U.S. nationalism should be vigorously institutionalized in both public and private institutions, such as in schooling and the family; they are antagonistic to international institutions, believing they undermine the authority of the U.S. state. This approach, exemplified by the "Bush Doctrine" of pre-emptive war, constitutes a radical departure from earlier U.S. foreign policy, effectively abandoning both the Cold War doctrine of deterrence and post–Cold War notions of multipolar collaboration.[29]

Where neorealists study factors in the individual nation-state to observe actions by states to defend themselves, neoliberals study diplomatic treaties, international institutions, and trade and development policies that represent common interests and cooperation. Neorealists see war as necessary in a world in which every state seeks to dominate others.[30] Neoliberals, on the other hand, contend that complex systems of "international regimes"—the norms, rules, regulations, decision-making procedures, and institutions that accompany global economic interdependence—have greatly diminished the necessity of military force; international regimes do not replace reciprocity and agreement but work to stabilize, reinforce, and institutionalize it.[31]

It should be clear that because the two dominant schools of American political science select and value different objects and processes, and ask different research questions of those objects and processes, they have different investments in definitions of political order and political change. The implications of their approaches for political policy and action seriously differ, as well. Yet the academic "dialogue" between neorealists and neoliberals collaborates in reinscribing particular absences in political science research, just as the apparently different philosophies of Hobbes and Locke constitute together the origins of modern Western political theory. Despite their apparent opposition, the two approaches share a *state-level* focus on international relations that refers to the liberal democratic nation-state as its normative *ideal type*. This focus defines "politics" in terms of states and excludes, on the one hand, the "politics" of popular social movements or workers' struggles beneath the level of the state or organizing transnationally, and, on the other, communist or socialist non-Western states like China or Cuba, or those newly independent nations in Africa, Asia, or the Caribbean whose narratives of political development diverge from the "modernization" model based on states in Europe or North America. Both the neorealist and neoliberal approaches employ a social-scientific method of comparison that constructs tests, gathers data, and assesses its findings in relation to the liberal democratic nation-state, even when the emphasis is on international regimes that integrate and supplement the interests of those states. A shared definition of "politics" as the activities of states and international regimes obscures an understanding of how government, interest, and power affect the lion's share of the nonelite world. The definition of sovereignty as inhering exclusively in the nation-state itself effects a normative notion of governance that obscures other modes of rule, as well as other modes of politics that specifically counter that rule. State-centric approaches to world governance presume that international cooperation is most possible among those modern nation-states that resemble one another in their structures and policies, or which show evidence of developing in the direction of the *ideal type.* State-centrism presumes an *isomorphism* of nation-state properties and measures these increasingly standardized properties across nation-states both old and new.[32] In effect, neofunctionalist, state-centric research effectively *produces* the conditions for "integration" among developing countries of relatively equal size, with symmetries of trade, level of development, governing institutions and ideologies, and per-capita income.[33]

In a sense, most political science continues to be organized in relation to a "phantom" model of the nation-state, even when it sets out to study how global interdependence challenges or reinforces the power of the nation-state. As studies investigate changes to the nation-state form, they also naturalize that form within the history of global development, without analyzing the inevitable variations of state viability depending on its geopolitical location within the global North or South. The maintenance of state-centric factors for study—from GDP/GNPs to the demographics of citizenship—ahistorically flatten the history of colonialism and the world system, and render illegible social actors like women, refugees, the poor, noncitizen migrants—who disappear within standardized categories of state-related and state-recognized activities.

Political science that places nation-state sovereignty at the center of its studies has left "understudied" a broad range of phenomena that nonetheless possess political significance, from sovereignty movements for self-determination by native indigenous peoples, to multilateral solidarities or international nongovernmental organizations that have sponsored initiatives in the areas of human rights, war crimes, world health and environmental protection, to transnational extrastate activities like the so-called antiglobalization movement.[34] Native American and indigenous sovereignty movements in North America, Latin America, Australia, and New Zealand are rarely studied by the mainstream discipline.[35] Political science has also consistently disregarded the Bandung conference, which in 1955 gathered a coalition of twenty-nine states organized by Indonesia, Burma, Ceylon, India, and Pakistan, representing more than half the world's population, promoting Afro-Asian economic and cultural cooperation and opposing colonialism or neocolonialism by the United States or the Soviet Union.[36] The Bandung conference led to the organization of the Non-Aligned Movement in 1961, which joined over one hundred states not formally aligned with or against either Cold War power bloc in a "declaration on promotion of world peace and cooperation," affirming their moral and practical solidarity with one another in their pursuit of independent sovereignty, territorial integrity, economic independence, and peace within the Cold War context.[37] Opening the 1955 conference, President Sukarno of Indonesia called for an end to colonialism, not only "the classic form which we of Indonesia, and our brothers in different parts of Asia and Africa, knew," but also stressed that political economic domination by the United States and USSR was "colonialism . . . in modern dress" and warned of war's absolute powers of destruction in an atomic age. Jawaharlal Nehru spoke about the importance for Asian and African nations to stand for peace in an era in which war between the United States and USSR could destroy the world. The final communiqué of the conference underscored the need for developing countries to become independent from the leading industrialized nations by forging an alternative path to development, with lateral technology exchanges among one another and the establishment of regional training and research institutes. Yet despite the powerful vision of African and Asian antiwar and anticolonial solidarity, the Bandung conference has been virtually forgotten by twentieth-century political science, illegible within its normative classifications. This "forgetting" of Bandung exemplifies a persistent disinterest in the study of the formerly colonized or developing world in U.S. political science. This blind spot continues and is reproduced within the discipline's concept of globalization; neither neorealist nor neoliberal approaches make visible indigenous peoples, minority groups, women and children, and poor migrant workers beneath the level of the state, or, more to the point, in neither approach are their deteriorating conditions within globalization made a priority as objects of research.

While neoliberal narratives of globalization assert that economic "integration" benefits all regions, increasing numbers of economists, policy makers, and activists charge that it is an economic program aggressively commanded by the United States and enacted directly through U.S. foreign policies and indirectly through institutions such as the World Bank, the International Monetary Fund, and the World Trade Organization.

Deregulation has only widened the disparities of wealth and life opportunity that already existed between core and periphery in the postwar period, between the industrialized G8 nations and the developing world, between the countries in the former "periphery" that industrialized after World War II and the rest of the former non-aligned countries, between these "third world" nations and the even more destitute Africa.[38] Academic disinterest in the 1955 Bandung conference is commensurate with both the powerlessness of the developing world in world governance and the complicity of social science research in the centralization of U.S. interests. Both demonstrate the urgent need for alternative forms of study, literacy, and interpretation, including feminist paradigms for understanding the politics (in the broadest sense) of globalized communities.[39] We must relinquish the presumption that all societies in the modern world system are organized in the same way, in order to take seriously the ample evidence that modernization has been a violently uneven process that has produced antagonisms and asymmetries in different regions and locales, and that neither exploitation nor the emergence of political subjects and practices can be thought only in terms of a single uniform collectivity, teleology, or narrative of development. In other words, the practice and the terrain of the *political* must be redefined and imagined differently in relation to different histories of uneven material conditions.

I began my discussion by linking the neoconservative American foreign policy of the U.S. war in Iraq with the anti-immigrant fortification of the U.S-Mexican border. Mainstream ideas of nation-state sovereignty used to justify contemporary militarism in Iraq and at the border misrecognize and misrepresent the material practices of globalization, and transnational "gender" is one significant index in which we may "read" this incommensurability. Transnational gender disciplines register the shift from the Cold War management of nation-states to a *biopolitical governmentality* focused on bodies and populations. An interdisciplinary feminist analysis can foreground the contradiction between political isolationism and economic globalism, between manipulations of racialized gendered labor in the production of an alleged "immigration crisis" and the dependence of U.S. middle-class consumer society on male migrant labor and female manufacturing labor in the export processing zones. Government-declared national "crises" appear to authorize the state's monopoly on violence and are used to justify the disrespect of laws and liberal political bodies and the overriding of civil rights. Recent cross-border feminist projects on the U.S.-Mexican border address these contradictions in a variety of ways: from workplace struggles to campaigns for environmental justice to migrant community protections. These movements constitute new forms of transnational politics that establish and practice an alternative meaning of "sovereignty" in domains that the social sciences have normally bracketed as "culture." By addressing issues of life and death in the workplace, community, and border regions, these feminist movements have named the power of the state to decide who lives and who dies; appealing to a transnational public sphere that includes both Mexicans and U.S. Americans, these cross-border movements have redefined *social justice* as the gendered exercise of sovereignty by the border communities themselves to end the state's arbitrary power over life. They have called for transformations in the responsibilities of states and corporations on both sides of the border toward the legal, economic, and environmental protection of border communities.

The contemporary production of an "immigration" crisis is only the most recent moment in a much longer U.S. history of peaks in anti-immigrant sentiment during periods of national insecurity, whether Chinese, Irish, Jewish, Mexican, and Russian, or even freed slaves migrating to Northern cities after the Civil War. In the last decade, Immigration and Nationality Service (INS) inspectors at checkpoints along the U.S.-Mexico border have reported increases in human trafficking and smuggling: they find people rolled inside carpets, sewn into car seats, stuffed into washing machines; at the Tecate Port of Entry, a five-year-old girl was discovered meticulously sealed inside a *piñata*.[40] Border enforcement projects, like Operation Gatekeeper, have added expensive fencing and militarized the urban border areas. As of this writing, amid active cross-border protests, the private military firm Blackwater is attempting to establish a training facility at the U.S.-Mexican border.[41] Meanwhile, the Border Patrol has unearthed dozens of elaborate underground tunnels straddling the border through which migrants and goods are smuggled. Yet while the increased militarization of the border has made "illegal" crossing more difficult and treacherous along the massively fortified twenty-mile border between San Diego and Tijuana, it has not reduced the numbers of people putting themselves at risk to work in the United States. Border officials suggest that the militarization of the border, which has made it dangerous and even fatal for male migrants to cross back and forth, has forced these men to work undocumented in the United States, and women and children to remain in Mexico or to pay expensive "coyotes" to smuggle them across. Yet this production of a contemporary "immigration crisis" absents the historically unequal relationship between the United States and Mexico, which reaches back to conquest and war in the nineteenth century, continued in the subordination and exploitation of Mexican residents in the United States as noncitizen workers, and is exacerbated by neoliberal globalization today.[42] The Mexican debt crisis of 1982 and Mexico's entry into the General Agreement on Tariff and Trade (GATT) and the North American Free Trade Agreement (NAFTA) decisively opened the country to global economic restructuring and reconfigured many border areas as export processing zones for multinational corporations. Peso devaluation and neoliberal reforms have resulted in even more dramatic cuts in Mexican state provisions for education and health care, sending greater numbers of people into poverty. All of the human traffic at the border takes place in the context of these longstanding global inequalities.

In other words, even as global conditions disaggregate state sovereignty, the state still continues to flex its muscles to exert a role in border and immigration policies, though its power is challenged by transnational corporations, regional treaties, and supranational organizations which actually promote transnational immigration to satisfy the demand for inexpensive labor. In this sense, the U.S. targeting of "illegal immigration" must be understood as a performance of narrow government power in the face of declining state sovereignty. Saskia Sassen has observed that with globalization, the scope of state competence has changed, narrowing the range within which the state's authority and legitimacy operates.[43] To focus on "illegal immigration" is to disavow the long, extensive relationship of conquest and exploitation between the United States and Mexico, which today includes enormous corporate profits both from undocumented labor in the United States and from the *maquiladoras* in Mexico. Since the 1970s, U.S. investors have profited greatly from the low cost of Mexican labor, whose wages are maintained by agreements between the Mexican state, unions, and corporations. With the end of the Bracero Program that had supplied mostly male labor to the United States, the Mexican government established *maquiladora* factories at the border, employing over 850,000 workers, more than 50 percent of whom are girls. Employing mostly girls and women exploits their structural vulnerability in family and society, and deepens and reproduces patriarchal gender relations in the workplace.[44] For Mexico's centralized government and the large state-run unions who view the *maquiladoras* as a strategy for national development, as well as for multinational corporations who set up factories to take advantage of tax holidays and a lack of labor or environmental laws, the profits are a disincentive to creating protections for the young women.

Within this context, cross-border organizing for social, economic, and environmental justice along the U.S.-Mexican border region can be understood as an international *counterpolitics* that contests mainstream definitions of political sovereignty. In addressing the transnational conditions of globalization, in which labor exploitation is deepened and eased by product design in one location, assembly in another, marketing and sales in yet another—the innovation of cross-border organizing is that it is likewise "transnational," a "politics" not aimed exclusively at rights within the nation-state. In creating a public discourse about industrial accountability for environmental health and safety, transnational feminist advocacy networks explicitly target the Mexican and U.S. states' collusion with the industries that expose workers to lethal chemicals and pollutants, and declare that those states exploit women and children at the border, as not merely instruments of labor, but as *disposable life*. Cross-border organizing to counter the deadly conditions for border communities constitutes a new form of political activism in light of the declining legitimacy of both the U.S. and Mexican national governments.

A 2006 documentary film by Vicki Funari and Sergio De La Torre, *Maquilapolis: City of Factories*, both exemplifies and depicts these new forms of transnational political activism. A unique collaboration between Latino filmmakers in the United States and women working in Mexico's *maquiladoras*, *Maquilapolis* depicts a group of women struggling for environmental justice in Tijuana, a major border site for electronics manufacturing in which over 80 percent of factory workers are women migrants from southern Mexico. The film's aesthetic is multivocal and multiperspectival, and the selection and organization of images, narrative, and sound are the result of collaborative decisions among the women. *Maquilapolis* is composed of video segments that the women themselves have filmed and narrated, in which each presents her own particular story within the history of the border's development as an export processing zone: arrivals at the border from rural Mexico, discoveries of toxic conditions in their workplace and in their *colonias*, decisions to take action and become *promotoras*, activists who educate other women in the community—these particular stories are enfolded within the growth of the *maquiladora* industry. The woman named Carmen begins: "My name is Carmen Durán . . . I have worked in nine assembly plants. I was thirteen years old when I arrived in Tijuana." Another woman, Lourdes, tells the viewer she is "turning on the camera" to show us the toxic river running through her neighborhood, placing her children and neighbors at risk for leukemia, cancer, and anencephaly; speaking directly into the camera, she points to the lesions on her own body. Carmen offers a tour through her daily routine: feeding and bathing her children in their house without running water, electricity, or sewage, which she built of discarded garage doors bought in the United States; going to work, explaining that because she is exposed to lead contamination in the factory she cannot wash her color-coded work smock with her children's clothes. At a neighborhood meeting of women advocates, she describes her transition from being unknowingly exposed to taking action: "You're a student, and then you become a teacher." "We see things differently," says another *promotora*.

This transformation of perspective is thematized throughout the film, in both narrative form and content: the women record the shift from being an object viewed as commodified yet disposable labor to becoming a subject who depicts oneself as an analyst of these conditions and as an activist working against them. For example, in one segment, Carmen films Lourdes as Lourdes films the U.S. side of the border through a space in the corrugated metal wall that divides the two countries: "I'm looking at the other side of the border," her voice-over explains, "This is something new for me." "I've lived here eighteen years and I've never been to it," adds Carmen. The segments, together, visually document various parts of the process through which the women—exposed to contamination in the workplace, raising their children amidst toxic pollution and waste—organize to make accountable the industries responsible for the environmental conditions causing disease and death in their communities. Contrary to state and industry discourses that represent the women workers as docile or passive, this environmental campaign is one of the many examples in which girls and women have engaged in struggles to transform the conditions in which they live and work.[45] Involved in what Melissa Wright has termed "a project of reversing the discourse of female disposability," they counter the regimes that subject their communities to death; they refuse to be treated as less than human.[46] In the last 35 years since the maquiladoras were established, women's struggles have ranged from work stoppages on the shop floors, to organized protests against factory shutdowns and withheld severance pay, to organizing against routine sexual abuse and harassment—all indices of the multiple modes and strategies employed by girls and women at the border to counter their treatment as dispensible life.[47]

In this sense, the *promotoras* in *Maquilapolis* suggest that specifically gendered violence on the U.S.-Mexican border gives rise to political practices that cannot be remediated through rights-based citizenship, and whose strategies necessarily reach beyond traditional state channels.[48]

The activists are mostly women who migrated from rural Mexico at a young age, with sole responsibility for raising children without extended family support.[49] While traditional labor unions would organize around the workplace issue of wages, of greater concern for these women are the health and safety of their children within the context of high incidences of birth defects in polluted communities, and the vulnerability of girls and women to sexual abuse and violence.[50] The film ends with the success of a decade-long campaign, in which their Chilpancingo Collective collaborated with the San Diego Environmental Health Coalition to publicly pressure the Mexican Procuraduria Federal de Proteccion Al Ambiente (PROFEPA), and the U.S. Environmental Protection Agency. International media coverage created enough pressure to obligate both to a joint cleanup of the lead waste in Chilpancingo. Ultimately, *Maquilapolis* depicts an alternative practice of "sovereignty" to counter state-sanctioned death in their border community. Yet Lourdes comments that with still hundreds of polluting factories, the future is uncertain. At present, the corporation responsible is involved in a lawsuit to suppress the circulation of the film itself.

Feminist organizing at the U.S.-Mexican border necessarily links processes and relations that are transnational and not exclusively managed by citizenship in the nation-state; furthermore, the women who become activists and filmmakers in *Maquilapolis* are a nontraditional population, often unrecognized by sociology, political science, or economics. *Maquilapolis* is a cultural *and* social project in which these women—who are simultaneously workers, mothers, advocates, and teachers—are political actors addressing not only the conditions of wage labor within an individual factory, but who identify a broader frame to describe the lethal assault on life chances within globalization, both in their gendered treatment as disposable workers to be exploited and thrown away, and in the destruction of their border community environment through the heedless dumping of industrial wastes. Their practices rearticulate the border as more than an export processing zone, and name it as a dehumanized social space, a gendered *necrospace*, one of complex and pervasively gendered violence to life. The women explicitly foreground the state's and capital's impunity as they dictate who is protected and who may be used up to the point of extinction, what Achille Mbembe has termed "necropolitics."[51] Their actions aim to stop the conversion of populations of border women and children into what Giorgio Agamben calls "the new juridical category of 'life devoid of value.'"[52] In refusing to be less than human life, the women contest the regime that presumes their lives to be readily available and easily dismissed. Contrary to formal exercises in political modernization that aim to universalize the *ideal type* of state-centered politics everywhere, collaborative aesthetic and political projects like *Maquilapolis* instead open spaces in a transnational public sphere to address who may live and who must die within the longer history of global inequality.

NOTES

An earlier version of this essay was previously published under the title "The Gender of Sovereignty" in the online journal *The Scholar and the Feminist*, vol. 6.3, summer 2008.

1. While the concept of a "new world order" harks back to Woodrow Wilson's League of Nations following World War I, its more recent coinage was in the speech given by President George H. W. Bush on September 11, 1990, titled "Toward a New World Order." The address describes a post–Cold War, U.S.-led world political governance in which the United States and Russia would cooperate to contain Third World instability, whether in the form of Asian economic challenges, Islamic movements, or Latin American social movements. At the time, the *New York Times* observed that many on the American left called this "new world order" a "rationalization for imperial ambitions" in the Middle East. Many charged that it was a unipolar political vision under the guise of multipolar collaboration. The term receded in the 1990s under the presidency of Bill Clinton, when liberal institutionalist policies dominated. After 2003, however, the term recurred to name the designs of President George W. Bush's U.S.-led "war on terror."

2. In 1999, China lifted the prohibition on foreign-private economic cooperation; as the world's seventh largest trading country, China joined the WTO in 2001, and by 2002 it had surpassed the United States as the most favored destination for foreign direct investment. Reports of U.S. trade deficits with China have grabbed headlines and fanned protectionist flames throughout the United States. For some time, China has been extremely competitive in labor-intensive manufacturing, but it has now moved ahead in sophisticated high technology and electronic design and innovation. The U.S. trade deficit with China topped $250 billion in 2008.

3. Joseph Stiglitz, *Globalization and Its Discontents* (New York: Norton, 2002), 12.

4. On the "Washington Consensus" and neoliberal assumptions held by the IMF, World Bank, and U.S. Treasury since the 1980s for developing countries in Latin America, Asia, and Africa, see Joseph Stiglitz, *Globalization and Its Discontents;* and Robert Pollin, *Contours of Descent: U.S. Economic Fractures and the Landscape of Global Austerity* (London: Verso, 2003).

5. Stephen Krasner, ed., *International Regimes* (Ithaca, N.Y.: Cornell University Press, 1983).

6. Robert O. Keohane and Joseph S. Nye, *Power and Interdependence* (Glenview, Ill.: Scott, Foresman, 1989), 271.

7. John Locke, in *Two Treatises of Government* (1689), wrote against the arbitrary rule of the absolute monarch, asserting that once man accumulated property it would necessitate a political society to protect property rights. Jean-Jacques Rousseau, in *The Social Contract* [Du contrat social] (1762), wrote that natural

rights are renewed and protected when individuals agree to enter into the social contract founding a political society, organized according to collective, rather than individual, "general will." Drawing upon these and other Enlightenment philosophers, classical liberalism stressed not only human rationality but the importance of individual property rights, natural rights, the need for constitutional limitations on government, and, especially, freedom of the individual from external restraint. In *On Liberty* (1859), John Stuart Mill, the major British theorist of political liberalism, synthesized the principles of representative government, the protection of civil liberties, and laissez-faire economics that were in force for much of the nineteenth century.

8. Benedict Anderson, *Imagined Communities: Reflections on the Origin and Spread of Nationalism* (London: Verso, 1983).

9. A crucial early formulation of this notion of public reason was Immanuel Kant's famous 1784 essay, "An Answer to the Question: What is Enlightenment?" [Beanwortung der Frage: Was ist Aufklärung?], reprinted in *What Is Enlightenment?* ed. James Schmidt (Berkeley and Los Angeles: University of California Press, 1996).

10. The sociologist Max Weber originated the *ideal type*, a heuristic proposition against which the difference, variance, or convergence of specific social and historical instances could be measured; this comparative mode of study continues to be influential in most of the modern social sciences, including political science. Weber is well known for having observed that social behavior in modern Western society of the early twentieth century had come to be dominated more and more by goal-oriented rationality and instrumental reason, and less by traditional values and forms of sociality. This *ideal-typical* construction of "pure rational action" presumed the individual within the context of modern Western industrial society, and measured the *different* degrees of rationalization as "deviations," by comparing concrete social instances to this normative regulatory type. Weber, *Economy and Society: Volume I* (1922; New York: Bedminster reprint, 1968).

11. Michael Omi and Howard Winant, *Racial Formation in the United States: From the 1960s to the 1990s* (New York: Routledge, 1994).

12. Eric Hobsbawm, *The Age of Empire, 1875–1914* (New York: Pantheon, 1987); Edward Said, *Culture and Imperialism* (New York: Knopf, 1993).

13. On anticolonial nationalisms, see Amilcar Cabral, *Return to the Source: Selected Speeches of Amilcar Cabral* (New York: Monthly Review Press, 1973); Frantz Fanon, *The Wretched of the Earth*, trans. Constance Farrington (New York: Grove, 1963); Aimé Césaire, *Discourse on Colonialism* (1955), trans. Joan Pinkham (New York: Monthly Review Press, 2000); Partha Chatterjee, *Nationalist Thought and the Colonial World* (London: Zed, 1986); and P.O. Esedebe, *Pan-Africanism: The Idea and the Movement, 1776–1991* (Washington, D.C.: Howard University Press, 1994).

14. See Mortimer Sellers, ed., *The New World Order: Sovereignty, Human Rights, and the Self-Determination of Peoples* (Oxford: Berg, 1996).

15. For the most lucid discussion of the challenges to decolonization after the capture of the state by the national bourgeoisie, see Fanon, *Wretched of the Earth*.

16. For excellent critiques of the discourse of development and the impact of development policies in Latin America, see Arturo Escobar, *Encountering Development: The Making and Unmaking of the Third World* (Princeton, N.J.: Princeton University Press, 1995); and Maria Josefina Saldaña-Portillo, *The Revolutionary Imagination in the Americas and the Age of Development* (Durham: Duke University Press, 2003).

17. Francis Fukuyama, *The End of History and the Last Man* (New York: Free Press, 1992).

18. Mahmood Mamdani, *Good Muslim, Bad Muslim: America, the Cold War, and the Roots of Terror* (New York: Pantheon, 2004).

19. Adam Roberts and Benedict Kingsbury observe that the UN has proven to be much more successful as an international forum for debating and declaring principles than as a body capable and powerful enough to govern or legislate war, peace, crime, or violations of human rights. See *Presiding Over a Divided World: Changing United Nations Roles, 1945–1993* (Boulder, Colo.: Lynne Rienner, 1994).

20. See http://www.nam.gov.za/.

21. Since 1850, more than 25,000 nonprofit, nongovernmental organizations with an international focus have been established, most after World War II; roughly 6,000 from 200 countries have been recognized by the Union of International Associations. Regarding issues like medical aid for the world's poor, human rights violations, women's rights, and the prevention of environmental and biological destruction, global social movements and international nongovernmental organizations (INGOs) have been much more effective on these issues than either individual nation-states or the United Nations. See John Boli and George Thomas, "World Culture in the World Polity: A Century of International Non-Governmental Organization," *American Sociological Review* 62, no. 2 (1997): 171–90; and John Keane, *Global Civil Society* (Cambridge: Cambridge University Press, 2003).

22. Thucydides, Machiavelli, and Hobbes are often cited as intellectual ancestors of political realism. See Thomas Hobbes, *Leviathan* (1651; Oxford: Blackwell reprint, 1967); on the legacy of Hobbes for international relations, see Robert O. Keohane, "Hobbes's Dilemma and Institutional Change in World Politics: Sovereignty in International Society," in *Whose World Order? Uneven Globalization and the End of the Cold War: Perspectives on World Politics*, ed. Hans-Henrik Holm and Georg Sorenson (Boulder, Colo.: Westview, 1995).

23. See Hans Morgenthau, *Politics among Nations: The Struggle for Power and Peace* (1948; New York: Knopf, 1973).

24. Kenneth Waltz, *Theory of International Politics* (Reading, Mass.: Addison-Wesley, 1979), 96. Waltz's work has been regarded as the paradigmatic work of neorealist international relations. See Robert O. Keohane, ed., *Neorealism and Its Critics* (New York: Columbia University Press, 1986).

25. The liberalism of Woodrow Wilson, John Dewey, Franklin Roosevelt, and others was a part of the era of globalization that came to an end with World War I, the Treaty of Versailles, the collapse of the gold standard, and the Great Depression. "Neoliberalism" is associated with the subsequent era of globalization, beginning after World War II with Bretton Woods and the founding of the World Bank and International Monetary Fund and continuing today; it favors international institutions while deemphasizing government intervention, advocating the reduction of local regulations and barriers to commerce, corporatism, and the privatization of state-run enterprises.

26. See Keohane and Nye, *Power and Interdependence;* and David A. Baldwin, *Neorealism and Neoliberalism: The Contemporary Debate* (New York: Columbia University Press, 1993), 284.

27. See, for example, Robert O. Keohane, Joseph S. Nye, and Stanley Hoffman, eds. *After the Cold War: International Institutions and State Strategies in Europe, 1989–1991* (Cambridge, Mass.: Harvard University Press, 1993).

28. The neoconservative position is well represented by Donald Kagan and

his sons Frederick and Robert. In *While America Sleeps: Self-Delusion, Military Weakness, and the Threat to Peace Today* (New York: St. Martin's Press, 2000), Donald and Frederick Kagan draw an analogy between the post–Cold War United States' vulnerability to "terrorism" and the situation of Great Britain between the two world wars. They characterize Britain as having ignored international realities and crippled itself by cutting military forces, thereby arguing for greater U.S. military spending. Robert Kagan argued for U.S. unilateralism in Iraq despite European opposition ("Power and Weakness," *Policy Review* 113 [June 2002]) and for greater military force in Iraq ("Do What It Takes in Iraq," with William Kristol, *Weekly Standard* 8, no. 48 [September 2003]).

Neoconservatives return not only to Thucydides and Hobbes, and to the anticommunist political realism of the Cold War, but also to the work of Leo Strauss. Strauss brought to American neoconservatism the ideas of Carl Schmitt, the German legal scholar and political philosopher of the 1920s–30s whose ideas were largely suppressed in the United States due to Schmitt's Nazi association. Yet Strauss was engaged with Schmitt's thought in the 1930s and wrote the concluding notes to Schmitt's 1932 *The Concept of the Political,* trans. George Schwab (Chicago: University of Chicago Press, 1996). See Heinrich Meier, *Carl Schmitt and Leo Strauss: The Hidden Dialogue,* trans. J. Harvey Lomax (Chicago: University of Chicago Press, 1995); and Nicholas Xenos, "Leo Strauss and the Rhetoric of the War on Terror," *Logos* 3.2 (2004), available at http://www.logosjournal.com/xenos.htm.

Schmitt argued that the "concept of the political" is founded on the ineliminable role of power in an ongoing state of war epitomized in the distinction between "friend" and "enemy." Schmitt's vehement critique of liberalism, pluralism, and liberal process charged that they "depoliticized," or hid, this condition. "The political entity presupposes the real existence of an enemy and therefore coexistence with another political entity. As long as a state exists, there will thus always be in the world more than one state. A world state which embraces the entire globe and all of humanity cannot exist" (*The Concept of the Political,* 53). In *Political Theology: Four Chapters on the Concept of Sovereignty* (1922; Cambridge, Mass.: MIT Press, 1985), Schmitt wrote that the state should have the sovereign power to declare the state of exception, if necessary, to override liberal political bodies and laws to maintain the authority and power of the state.

29. The other moment in U.S. history in which the use of force could be considered analogous to this "pre-emptive" move might be the atomic bombing of Hiroshima and Nagasaki under Truman. Certainly not "pre-emptive" in the sense of acting *before* an actual attack (however, this sense in our current world is equally debatable), the bombing that followed the surrender of the Japanese government during World War II could have been calculated to deter future contestations of U.S. power by any other powers. See Robert J. Art and Kenneth Waltz, eds., *The Use of Force: International Politics and Foreign Policy* (Boston: Little Brown, 1971). Indeed, in his September 2, 2004, acceptance speech at the Republican National Convention, framing the nation's foreign policy in sweeping terms, George W. Bush likened himself to Truman after World War II, restructuring U.S. national security to meet a transcendent new threat.

30. Art and Waltz, eds., *The Use of Force.*

31. Stephen Krasner, ed. *International Regimes;* and Celeste A. Wallander and Robert O. Keohane, "An Institutional Approach to Alliance Theory" (Cambridge, Mass.: Center for International Affairs, Harvard University, 1995). See also Keohane, Nye, and Hoffman, eds., *After the Cold War.*

32. Though within the subfield of sociological institutionalism, a good example of this approach might be John Meyer, John Boli, George Thomas, and Francisco Ramirez, "World Society and the Nation-State," *American Journal of Sociology* 103, no. 1 (1997): 144–81. Meyer et al. argue that a causally significant world culture creates incentives for countries to conform to the modern nation-state model in order to integrate into world society; alternative models have little legitimacy and find it difficult to survive if they do not assume the legitimized form.

33. Among the most important postwar theories of European integration were Leon N. Lindberg, *The Political Dynamics of European Economic Integration* (Stanford, Calif.: Stanford University Press, 1963); and Ernst Haas, *Beyond the Nation-State: Functionalism and International Organization* (Stanford, Calif.: Stanford University Press, 1964). Current studies include Andrew Moravcsik, *The Choice for Europe: Social Purpose and State Power from Messina to Maastricht* (Ithaca, N.Y.: Cornell University Press, 1998); and Wolfgang Wessels et al., eds., *Fifteen into One? The European Union and Its Member States* (Manchester: Manchester University Press, 2003).

34. Much U.S. political science employs a top-down perspective on nation-states as the privileged unit of government and action; women, poor, nonelites, indigenous peoples, and international nongovernmental organizations (INGOs) are largely invisible in most of these studies. Those INGOs that are the most bureaucratized are the most legible for study.

35. Native sovereignty refers to the authority of native peoples to determine and govern themselves. See David E. Wilkins and K. Tsianina Lomawaima, *Uneven Ground: American Indian Sovereignty and Federal Law* (Tulsa: University of Oklahoma Press, 2002); and Paul Chatt Smith and Robert Allen Warrior, *Like a Hurricane: The Indian Movement from Alcatraz to Wounded Knee* (New York: New Press, 1997). In Canada, indigenous peoples are referred to as First Nations peoples; in other contexts, native peoples are considered "Fourth World." The Hawai'ian sovereignty movement is a coalition of groups seeing self-determination for native peoples and redress of the U.S. government for military occupation and appropriation of lands beginning in 1893. See Haunani Kay Trask, *From a Native Daughter: Colonialism and Sovereignty in Hawai'i* (Honolulu: University of Hawai'i Press, 1999); and Jocelyn Linnekin, "Indigenous Sovereignty scenarios in Latin America and Hawaii: Parallels and Possibilities," *Journal of Latin American Anthropology* 1, no. 2 (spring 1996): 152–63. Aboriginal peoples in Australia have struggled for sovereignty; most recently the 1992 Mabo Case declared the long-held *terra nullius* to be invalid and recognized Aboriginal land claims before British settlement, and subsequent legislation established native title claims. See Ann Curthoys, *Freedom Ride: A Freedom Rider Remembers* (Crow's Nest, New South Wales: Allen & Unwin, 2003). For an important collaboration that brings together native and Pacific discussions of indigenous cultures, see Vicente Diaz and J. Kehaulani Kauanui, eds., *Native Pacific Cultural Studies on the Edge*, a special issue of *The Contemporary Pacific* (13, no. 2, fall 2001).

36. The Asian-African Conference, convened upon the invitation of the Prime Ministers of Burma, Ceylon, India, Indonesia, and Pakistan, met in Bandung in April 1955. In addition to the sponsoring countries, the following twenty-four countries participated: Afghanistan, Cambodia, People's Republic of China, Egypt, Ethiopia, Gold Coast, Iran, Iraq, Japan, Jordan, Laos, Lebanon, Liberia, Libya, Nepal, Philippines, Saudi Arabia, Sudan, Syria, Thailand, Turkey, Democratic Republic of Vietnam, State of Vietnam, and Yemen. The Asian-African Confer-

ence considered problems of common interest and concern to countries of Asia and Africa and discussed ways and means by which their people could achieve fuller economic, cultural, and political cooperation.

37. The Ten Principles of Bandung were:

1. Respect for fundamental human rights and for the purposes and principles of the Charter of the United Nations.
2. Respect for the sovereignty and territorial integrity of all nations.
3. Recognition of the equality of all races and of the equality of all nations large and small.
4. Abstention from intervention or interference in the internal affairs of another country.
5. Respect for the right of each nation to defend itself singly or collectively, in conformity with the Charter of the United Nations.
6. (a) Abstention from the use of arrangements of collective defense to serve any particular interests of the big powers. (b) Abstention by any country from exerting pressures on other countries.
7. Refraining from acts or threats of aggression of the use of force against the territorial integrity or political independence of any country.
8. Settlement of all international disputes by peaceful means, such as negotiation, conciliation, arbitration or judicial settlement as well as other peaceful means of the parties own choice, in conformity with the Charter of the United Nations.
9. Promotion of mutual interests and cooperation.
10. Respect for justice and international obligations.

38. Samir Amin, *Capitalism in the Age of Globalization: The Management of Contemporary Society* (London: Zed, 1997).

39. The so-called antiglobalization movement—manifested in popular demonstrations at the Seattle WTO meetings and at the World Social Forum in Porto Alegre, Brazil—has yet to capture the attention of most political science, although sociologists have begun to ask if "antiglobalization" may constitute a new transnational social movement. Best understood as "counter-capitalist" or "anticorporatist," the antiglobalization movement protests the excesses of unregulated global corporate capitalism and includes single-issue groups focused on local agriculture as well as larger-scale transnational coalitions for global environmentalism; at this point it even includes groups whose imperatives may appear naturally at odds, e.g., U.S. trade unions who object that their jobs are undercut by corporations moving their manufacture to locations with tax holidays and lower wages, and labor groups asking for greater protection of labor rights and human rights for workers in *maquiladoras* or export processing zones. Yet a common target of protest supersedes the inconsistencies among individual groups: the presumption of economic integration that demands the merging of all countries within a single model of development and into a single, centralized system. See James Harding, "Counter-Capitalism: Globalisation's Children Strike Back," *Financial Times*, September 2001; and Vandana Shiva, "Ecological Balance in an Era of Globalization," in *Principled World Politics: The Challenge of Normative International Relations*, ed. Paul Wapner and Lester Edwin J. Ruiz (Lanham, Md.: Rowman and Littlefield, 2001).

40. Leslie Berestein, "Girl in Piñata Found during Border Check," *San Diego Union Tribune*, November 12, 2005.

41. "Southern California Residents Gear Up for New Fight to Stop Secretive Expansion by Military Firm Blackwater," *DemocracyNow.org*, May 2, 2008. On Blackwater, see Jeremy Scahill, *Blackwater: The Rise of the World's Most Powerful Mercenary Army* (New York: Nation Books, 2007).

42. The principle of Manifest Destiny was invoked to justify the nineteenth-century westward expansion, the U.S. war with Mexico, and the 1848 Treaty of Guadalupe Hidalgo that ended the U.S.-Mexican war and appropriated from Mexico the lands that are now California, Arizona, Nevada, Utah, Wyoming, Colorado, Kansas, Oklahoma, and New Mexico. Despite being granted equal protection under the law by the Treaty of 1848, for decades following the annexation most former Mexican citizens occupied subordinate social and economic positions. Anglo-American domination over local economies created an environment in which the annexed Mexican population lost political influence. See Reginald Horsman, *Race and Manifest Destiny: The Origins of American Anglo-Saxonism* (Cambridge, Mass.: Harvard University Press, 1981).

In the 1910s–20s, new immigration from Mexico was met with fervent opposition. Anti-immigrant factions represented Mexicans as a threat to the racial, cultural, and social integrity of the United States. Restrictionists cast Mexicans as a "foreign menace" that threatened the homogeneity of U.S. society. Proponents of immigration represented Mexicans as a tractable labor force to be exploited. But with the Great Depression, Mexican workers were singled out as scapegoats; nativists charged that they committed crimes and displaced U.S. workers. In the 1930s, repatriation campaigns sought to force workers to return to Mexico; the largest, most publicized campaign was in Los Angeles. As many as 350,000 Mexicans repatriated during the 1930s. See David G. Gutiérrez, *Walls and Mirrors: Mexican Americans, Mexican Immigrants, and the Politics of Ethnicity* (Berkeley and Los Angeles: University of California Press, 1995).

43. Saskia Sassen, *Globalization and Its Discontents* (New York: New Press, 1998).

44. Girls and women routinely work within conditions and restrictions that are specifically "feminized": from color-coded smocks under the surveillance of male supervisors to unwanted physical advances, pregnancy testing, unhealthy or unsafe work, and intrusive questions about their sexual activities. See Patricia Fernandez-Kelly, *For We Are Sold, I and My People: Women and Industry in Mexico's Frontier* (Albany: SUNY Press, 1983); Susan Tiano, *Patriarchy on the Line: Labor, Gender and Ideology in the Mexico Maquila Industry* (Philadelphia: Temple University Press, 1994); and Leslie Salzinger, *Genders in Production: Making Workers in Mexico's Global Factories* (Berkeley and Los Angeles: University of California Press, 2003).

45. Rosa-Linda Fregoso observes that industry recruitment, newspapers, and popular stereotypes construct *border femininity* as docile, abject, and sexually improper. Fregoso, *MeXicana Encounters: The Making of Social Identities on the Borderlands* (Berkeley and Los Angeles: University of California Press, 2003).

46. Melissa W. Wright, "A Manifesto against Feminicide," *Antipode* 33, no. 3 (July 2001): 550–66, 564.

47. Organizing strategies that emerge from specifically gendered discrimination imply neither the dispersal of struggle nor the passivity of exploited workers, but recognize a new subject impacted by forms of domination that are political, economic, regional, and cultural, and gendered within both national and inter-

national frameworks. With the feminization of work and preferences for women laborers in assembly and manufacture, different strategies for organizing have emerged. These mixed strategies go beyond traditional approaches that focus exclusively on wages or on state remediation. See Norma Prieta, *Beautiful Flowers of the Maquiladoras: Life Histories of Women Workers in Tijuana*, trans. Michael Stone and Gabrielle Winkler (Austin: University of Texas Press, 1997); Lisa Lowe, "Work, Immigration, Gender: New Subjects of Cultural Politics," *The Politics of Culture in the Shadow of Capital*, ed. Lisa Lowe and David Lloyd (Durham: Duke University Press, 1997); and Grace Kyungwon Hong, *The Ruptures of American Capital: Women of Color Feminism and the Culture of Immigrant Labor* (Minneapolis: University of Minnesota Press, 2006).

48. The women activists are "nonstate actors" operating as a transnational advocacy network to publicize human rights violations. The "norms-socialization" literature on international human rights suggests that such advocacy groups aim to establish human rights norms so that they may be internalized by national states who will implement changes; such norms define a category of states as "liberal democratic states," which respond quickly to such norms, and "authoritarian" or "norm-violating states" (e.g., China, Cuba) which do not; moral consciousness-raising by the international human rights community often involves "shaming" of the norm-violating states as "pariah states who do not belong to the community of civilized nations." See Thomas Risse, Stephen C. Ropp, and Kathryn Sikkink, eds., *The Power of Human Rights: International Norms and Domestic Change* (Cambridge: Cambridge University Press, 1999), 15.

To the contrary, however, the cross-border environmental campaigns I discuss here are not aimed at creating international norms of individual rights to create such hierarchical classifications to discipline "norm-violating" states, but rather they consider *all* states as "violating" life at the border, in effect targeting the *governmentality*—the larger set of social disciplines that includes state institutions, corporate industry, media discourses, border policing, and social norms themselves—that results in the treatment of the border as a zone of disposable life.

49. Prieta, *Beautiful Flowers of the Maquiladoras.*

50. More than a decade of feminicides in Ciudad Juárez constitute the most publicized example of this gendered violence. See especially Rosa-Linda Fregoso, *MeXicana;* Alicia Schmidt-Camacho, "Ciudadana X," *The New Centennial Review* 5, no. 1 (spring 2005): 255–92; Melissa W. Wright, "The Dialectics of Still Life: Murder, Women and the Maquiladoras," *Public Culture* 11, no. 3 (1999): 452–74; and the documentary *Señorita Extraviada* (2001, dir. Lourdes Portillo).

51. Achille Mbembe, "Necropolitics," *Public Culture* 15, no. 1 (2003): 11–40.

52. Giorgio Agamben, *Homo Sacer: Sovereign Power and Bare Life* (Stanford, Calif.: Stanford University Press, 1998), 139.

12. On Humanitarian Intervention

A New World Order Dilemma

Richard Falk

POINTS OF DEPARTURE

When the United Nations was established in 1945 the UN Charter was careful about respecting the sovereign rights of states despite remembering that liberal democracies watched from the sidelines while the Nazi movement pursued its campaign of persecution that culminated in the Holocaust. This deference to sovereignty was offset by the public realization that peace was indivisible and, also, that retaining territorial space as a privileged sanctuary for genocide and crimes against humanity was no longer acceptable. In response, the architects of world order after 1945 did what diplomats usually do: they obscured the tension by endorsing contradictory norms.

On the sovereignty side was the Charter provision declaring that the UN could not intervene in matters of "domestic jurisdiction," which is a legalistic way of exempting whatever goes on within territorial space, including oppression and governmental abuse, from external accountability. But the exemption is subject to a qualification that can operate as a loophole, namely, if the internal circumstances are viewed as a sufficient threat to international peace and security, then the Security Council has the authority to impose "enforcement measures." In a fundamental sense, the normative tension is shifted to a political level of resolution, respecting sovereign rights unless the Security Council decides upon a protective intervention. But the shift is itself complicated and confused by the veto power vested in the five permanent members of the Security Council. In effect, any of these states, which in the decades following World War II generally pitted the United States against the Soviet Union, could block a response to humanitarian catastrophes by the United Nations and thereby nullify the capacity for response by the organized international community.

On the interventionary side were several offsetting developments. The UN Charter at several places affirms a commitment to promote "universal respect for, and observance of, human rights." The Universal Declaration of Human Rights set forth a comprehensive framework of norms that were supposed to shape governmental policy in sovereign states. Such a framework was deliberately phrased in promotional and aspirational language to avoid encroaching upon sovereign prerogatives, but it was nevertheless deeply subversive in relation to these prerogatives. It provided political actors with an agreed normative foundation from which to challenge the legitimacy of internal governmental policies and practices in foreign states. Because of the onset of the Cold War, such challenges seemed absorbed in the propaganda struggle between the liberal West and the socialist East, and they did not appear to challenge sovereign prerogatives in any principled manner.

The Nuremberg judgment is also relevant. It had convicted leading German civilian and military leaders of war crimes, including crimes against humanity if linked to the finding of aggressive war. This imposition of accountability on such leaders overrode the Westphalian idea that the sovereign state was the source of the highest law. Although Nuremberg was an instance of "victors' justice," it did set the stage for establishing a broader framework of responsibility upon individuals who act on behalf of sovereign states. Prosecutors at Nuremberg made a promise that the legal norms relied upon to convict the German defendants would in the future be applicable to all public officials who acted on behalf of sovereign states. As with human rights, the Nuremberg impulse was long stymied by the Cold War confrontation in which the "crimes" of one side were the "just causes" of the other side. It was impossible to agree upon responses that transcended this ideological divide.

The same kind of commentary can be associated with the Genocide Convention, adopted as an expression of the European pledge of "never again," but not capable of generating any meaningful political commitment that might credibly challenge extreme domestic wrongdoing by sovereign states. As genocidal events in Vietnam, Tibet, Cambodia, Bosnia, Rwanda, and elsewhere confirmed, the efforts to protect vulnerable peoples were far too feeble to overcome the primacy of geopolitics, including the insulation of most sovereign states from the normative claims embedded in international law. Note that there are two intertwined obstacles: the deference given to territorial sovereignty and the reinforcement of this deference by geopolitical concerns of the major political actors that give priority to strategic alignments and ideological affinities over humane governance. Thus, the Soviet bloc had little trouble reconciling its claims of liberating the peoples of the world with the realities of its own oppressive rule over an array of nations held captive in the Soviet Union and East Europe. Similarly, yet less crudely, the American-led West had little difficulty overlooking the authoritarian excesses of its ideological friends while claiming to lead the "free world."

Yet the picture was not quite as disappointing as these observations suggest, essentially for two reasons. First of all, and the focus of this chapter, civil society forces took seriously the normative claims implicit in the intergovernmental commitment to human rights and the closely related idea of holding governments responsible for violations of international law. These features of the global setting led many governments to adopt a more principled approach in their foreign policy that began to move these concerns from the domain of piety to the domain of politics. American adoption of a high-profile human rights diplomacy in the aftermath of defeat in Vietnam during the early years of the Carter presidency represented an attempt to restore national morale. The superpower status of the United States meant that this official emphasis on human rights had a momentum of its own with a variety of intended and unintended reverberations.

The anti-apartheid movement in the 1980s demonstrated that support for certain human rights goals could in special circumstances transcend the ideological fissures of the Cold War era. Adding to this turn toward international human rights in the same time frame were the nonviolent resistance movements in East Europe that had been inspired and legitimated by the call for implementation of the human rights norms that these governments had cynically, yet formally, subscribed to; the Soviet Union also helped dig its own grave partly by striking a bargain with the United States in which it stabilized its borders in East Europe in exchange for submitting annual reports on internal human rights that were then internationally scrutinized for conformity to norms (the so-called Helsinki Process).

Second, the Cold War came to an end, opening space for the promotion of human rights in an atmosphere where geopolitical inhibitions were greatly weakened. Furthermore, the salience of economic globalization and the impact of information technology (IT) blurred the boundaries between internal and global political space. This chapter considers, against such a background, the debate on humanitarian intervention that emerged in the 1990s, reaching an initial climax in relation to the Kosovo war of 1999, but later controversially confused by the attempt of the Bush presidency to validate the Iraq war in the post-9/11 atmosphere as an instance of humanitarian intervention. Just as geopolitics could block the implementation of humanitarian norms, so too could the manipulation of these norms provide geopolitical actors with pretexts for waging aggressive wars that cause great havoc and large-scale suffering, victimizing the very people that were supposedly being protected as well as undermining authentic calls for humanitarian intervention

THE GLOBAL SETTING

No issue has proved more divisive in global civil society since the end of the Cold War than the morality and politics of humanitarian intervention. In many respects the 1990s represented the golden age of Westphalian geopolitics: with the completion of the process of decolonization (including the collapse of the Soviet empire), the major premise of a world order based on the universality of territorial authority under the control of independent sovereign states belonging to the United Nations was substantially realized for the first time; there was no serious prospect of a major international war between states; the peoples of East Europe, the Soviet Union, and South Africa had been unexpectedly liberated from oppressive rule without accompanying violence; the ideological tensions that had underpinned the Cold War disappeared; information technology and personal computers were empowering individuals and groups to participate in an increasingly networked world; the Nuremberg idea of holding leaders accountable for crimes of states was dramatically revived with respect to such dictators as Pinochet and Milosevic, leading to the establishment of ad hoc international criminal tribunals that, in turn, surprisingly gave rise to a successful movement to establish a permanent International Criminal Court; and historic wrongs, long ignored, were acknowledged, producing apologies, remembrances, and even remedies, as with the recovery of the gold confiscated from Holocaust victims or by offering compensation for the ordeals of forced labor in Europe and Asia.

Along these lines, also, redress was sought for wrongs associated with the recent and distant past, leading to the formation of many commissions of peace and reconciliation, in countries undergoing transitions from dictatorial rule to democracy; serious efforts were made by representatives of indigenous peoples and by descendants of African-American slaves to develop arguments seeking reparations; also, the European experiment in world order established itself as the most successful effort to combine the practical benefits of cooperation among states with the transformation of the most afflicted war zone on the planet into an area of intergovernmental relations where the prospect of durable peace has become a virtual certainty; the international protection of human rights moved from the shadow lands of world politics toward a terrain of greater policy prominence; civil society actors became increasingly acknowledged as subjects of history to be included in any credible identification of the elements of world order; and under UN auspices world policy conferences were held on such matters as the environment, human rights, the status of women, population, and social well-being, and in their unfolding, became impressive experiments in *global democracy* due primarily to the participation and impact of civil society actors. In view of these developments, it was no longer acceptable to rely on a statist framework of inquiry and interpretation that regarded *only* sovereign states, and their interactions, as worthy of attention. At the same time, the building blocks for a hopeful future based on the rule of law, global justice, and the absence of international warfare seemed misleadingly present. Alongside these developments of the 1990s, there emerged what was described by its supporters as "humanitarian diplomacy." This development has many overlapping and conflicting explanations: as a natural incident of the rising attention given to human rights; more cynically, as a means of sustaining military budgets and national security establishments in a global setting that lacked strategic threats or as a moral rationale for postcolonial imperialism; as an expression of human solidarity responsive to the "CNN factor" that conveyed in real time the unfolding of humanitarian disasters; and as a relatively inexpensive means to divert criticism of neoliberal globalization as a heartless, capital-driven restructuring of global economic relations. The centerpiece of this humanitarian diplomacy was the use of force, with the formal blessings and participation of the United Nations, as a means employed to protect victimized peoples, a dynamic discussed and debated in various concrete circumstances under the rubric of "humanitarian intervention."

The 1990s gave rise to several instances of humanitarian intervention that generated sharp debate in civil society circles and much academic commentary in connection with Somalia, Rwanda, Bosnia, East Timor, and especially Kosovo and later Iraq. The debate focused on two kinds of concerns: was the intervention under discussion legally, morally, and politically justified, and was it feasible from cost and risk perspectives? Did a refusal to intervene in the face of a humanitarian catastrophe expose a serious weakness in the structure of world order and the quality of global leadership?

What seems interestingly relevant from the perspective of normative assessment is the extent to which the voices of civil society clashed on the interpretation of facts and norms pertaining to humanitarian intervention. This clash was reflected in relation to core questions of interventionary claims, but also in relation to their implementation. It first surfaced in a serious way after the high-profile reversal of the American approach to Somalia in 1993–94, particularly the refusal of the Clinton presidency to sustain its dominant role in peacekeeping efforts after armed resistance had inflicted a small number of American combat deaths. While Clinton had earlier promised by way of an embrace of "muscular multilateralism" to go beyond the George H. W. Bush approach in Somalia, eighteen American deaths in Mogadishu led to a domestic backlash in the United States and a hasty retreat. This retreat spilled over in tragic ways to discourage an international response in 1994 to an unfolding massive genocide in Rwanda. This seemed particularly lamentable, as reliable observers insisted that a small international commitment by way of humanitarian intervention in Rwanda under UN auspices might have saved the lives of several hundreds of thousands of Tutsis. This attitude of reluctance also accounted for the meagerness of the UN effort to oppose Serbian ethnic cleansing in Bosnia that culminated in the Srebrenica massacre of several thousand Muslim males in 1995. In relation to all three of these instances, the UN had formally acknowledged its responsibility to protect and in each there was a demonstrated humanitarian emergency. The failures to protect effectively arose from the weakness of political will on the part of major states, especially the United States, exhibited by an unwillingness to make troops and logistical capabilities available for peacekeeping or to offer the needed financial resources.

These cross-cutting issues assumed a much more contested form in relation to Kosovo in the late 1990s. Kosovo was technically a subdivision of Serbia, or, more accurately at the time, subject to the sovereignty of the government of the former Yugoslavia. Russia and China were geopolitical opponents of a humanitarian intervention authorized by the Security Council, and therefore no basis existed in international law to use force to protect the Albanian majority population in Kosovo from an imminent threat of ethnic cleansing, a threat made credible by the events in Bosnia a few years earlier and as a result of several violent incidents in Kosovo. In the Kosovo context the United States, in conjunction with the countries of Western Europe, possessed the political will and the logistical means to act effectively on behalf of the threatened Kosovars who made up about 90 percent of the population. The strength of this political will was not primarily an expression of a deeper humanitarian commitment in one instance rather than another, but seemed to reflect mainly an American geopolitical motivation to reestablish Atlanticist solidarity in the aftermath of the Cold War, and to show that NATO, then approaching its fiftieth anniversary, could have a new life after the death of the Soviet Union. Additionally, the European locus of the humanitarian crisis, combined with a certain guilty conscience about the failures to avert ethnic cleansing in Bosnia, ensured that the response to the situation in Kosovo would not depend only on the vagaries of international altruism. The success of the American-led coalition in the first Gulf War created a belief in Washington that the Kosovo war could be won quickly and decisively from the air without risking the level of casualties that had discredited the UN peacekeeping mission in Somalia. Finally, entrusting the operation to NATO rather than to the UN pleased American conservatives who never wanted to provide the UN with the sort of capabilities required to be effective in situations where the territorial sovereign would not give consent for peacekeeping.

CLEAVAGES IN CIVIL SOCIETY

The Kosovo debate illuminated some deep divisions in civil society that were brought to the surface before, during, and after the Kosovo war. On the interventionist side were those who primarily identified with the endangered civilian population in Kosovo and considered the humanitarian imperative of providing security for these potential victims and the invalidation and criminalization of the Serbian leadership in Belgrade that was allegedly responsible for such dire happenings as had earlier occurred in Bosnia. For these advocates of intervention, their main goal was a timely and effective operation, and considerations of auspices and legality were distinctly secondary. Some argued that the UN Charter framework for the regulation of force had long since broken down, and Charter norms had lost their authoritative status, making a "coalition of the willing" an adequate legal grounding for a humanitarian intervention.

On the anti-interventionist side were two sorts of civil society actors. First, there were those who believed that international uses of nondefensive force without a mandate from the Security Council would establish a bad and dangerous precedent that could jeopardize the sovereignty and independence of weaker states in the future, as well as allow strong states to evade the constraints on the use of force embedded in the UN Charter. Others argued that entrusting NATO with such an undertaking was to embrace "military humanism" of a highly questionable variety. In effect, by extending NATO's writ beyond what was permissible by reference to the UN Charter, or even to the NATO treaty itself, a new instrument of hegemonic geopolitics was taking shape under the public-relations banner of humanitarianism. It was on this basis that China and Russia let it be known that if this kind of coercive initiative were to seek the blessings of the Security Council, they would use their veto. The United States reacted to such a prospect by circumventing the Security Council, thereby avoiding the need to defy UN authority. The Kosovo war commenced on February 14, 1999, and continued for seventy-four days, ending with a ceasefire agreement. During this period Slobodan Milosevic was indicted for crimes in Bosnia and Kosovo by the ad hoc International Criminal Tribunal for the Former Yugoslavia (ICTY). This tribunal had been set up in 1992 under the authority of the Security Council and was largely funded by and awkwardly receptive to informal U.S. pressures. The war was conducted from the air by NATO, and several civilian targets were selected for air strikes in Kosovo and Serbia. At the same time, the war had the effect of freeing Kosovo from oppressive Serb rule and a likely onslaught of ethnic cleansing. It also induced most of the refugees who had fled the country prior to or during the NATO attacks to return to Kosovo.

The supporters and critics focused on different aspects of the Kosovo experience. The supporters argued that only this NATO undertaking had the means and the will to protect the civilian population of Kosovo, and that this was a successful example of humanitarian intervention. The critics alleged that the bombing from high altitudes constituted a major violation of the laws of war that should have been punished as a war crime. Further, they argued that the UN presence in Kosovo after the fighting had stopped did not act promptly to ensure the safety of the now-endangered Serbian minority, which resulted in what some observers called "reverse ethnic cleansing." Critics also contended that Kosovo was not truly "liberated," but was made into a NATO protectorate that includes a large, semipermanent American military base, and that insufficient reconstruction aid was made available, which makes the situation in Kosovo verge on anarchy: widespread unemployment and crime, as well as interethnic tensions, especially between the now dominant Albanian Kosovars and the 10 percent or so who constitute the Serbian minority. The contested character of the Kosovo war encouraged assessments that could recommend a future course of action. The most influential assessments were made by independent groups of prominent individuals who investigated the issues in controversy, issuing reports summarizing their conclusions. Such groups performed as "independent commissions," appointed on the initiative of governments that funded the inquiry, whose goal was the preparation of a report to be presented to the Secretary-General of the United Nations. The main idea was to provide a normative framework for humanitarian intervention in the future. The process is itself suggestive of a norm-creating role for civil society actors operating in a new space that is neither purely statist nor fully situated in civil society. The commission is itself a hybrid actor that has come to prominence in this historical period where various modifications of the Westphalian framework of statist diplomacy are taking place before our eyes.

The first of these commissions was the Independent International Commission on Kosovo. It was chaired by Richard Goldstone, a member of the South African Constitutional Court and the first prosecutor at the ICTY, and was funded by various governments, but mainly by Sweden. Its final report (*Kosovo Report: Conflict, International Response, Lessons Learned,* 2000) was submitted to the Secretary-General. The commission's main undertaking was to find an adequate way to deal with the controversy surrounding the intervention. The report relied on drawing a distinction between "legality" and "legitimacy." The main argument relied upon was that the facts justified the apprehension of an impending humanitarian catastrophe, but that there was no *legal* means to intervene without obtaining a prior Chapter VII mandate from the Security Council. At the same time, the urgency of the situation combined with the availability of an effective means to protect the endangered Kosovar population meant that the moral and political grounds for intervention were present, making the operation *legitimate.* The report also recommended efforts by the Security Council to close this gap either by suspending the veto in circumstances of humanitarian emergency or by acknowledging a residual right of the General Assembly or regional institutions to authorize humanitarian intervention if the Security Council is gridlocked.

A second effort along similar lines was stimulated by the Canadian government, which took the form of the International Commission on Intervention and State Sovereignty, chaired by Gareth Evans, a former foreign minister of Australia, and by Mohamed Sahnoun, a prominent diplomat and international civil servant from Algeria. Its report (*The Responsibility to Protect,* 2001) focused more on the generic problems posed by the Kosovo debate than on evaluating the Kosovo experience itself. It made a creative linguistic move to minimize the challenge of humanitarian intervention to the idea and reality of state sovereignty by shifting the policy emphasis to the international community, positing that "the responsibility to protect" exists in the event of an impending humanitarian catastrophe. Such a responsibility to protect creates a duty of the organized international community that, in effect, takes precedence over the sovereign right of a state to withhold its consent with respect to intrusions on its territory. Such a normative shift makes sovereignty conditional on protecting people within territorial boundaries, and repudiates views of sovereignty that have historically provided a haven for the commission of "human wrongs." The Security Council has been influenced by this report, accepting the normative reorientation as a part of the reform package recommended by the Secretary-General's High-Level Panel on Threats, Challenges and Change, and then formally endorsing the responsibility to protect norm in several Security Council resolutions, including its approach to the Darfur crisis in Security Council Resolution 1706.

Civil society actors made two major contributions: first, to illustrate very clearly the fault lines of disagreement when it comes to specific instances of humanitarian intervention in which the territorial sovereign withholds consent and the Security Council is gridlocked, yet where the political will and logistical means are available to achieve urgent humanitarian goals, thereby averting massive human suffering; and second, to provide various normative guidelines for future responses, taking into account the Kosovo experience, and in this regard prefiguring a normative approach by way of law, morality, and politics that seeks to protect vulnerable peoples confronting an impending humanitarian catastrophe without undermining international law and the authority of the Security Council. My purpose here is not so much to argue the substantive merits of recasting the humanitarian intervention argument in the aftermath of Kosovo, but to show how civil society actors engaged in the debate both prior to and subsequent to the Kosovo war. A further observation is that the pre-intervention debate involved civil society activists and organizations, while the post intervention process was dominated by initiatives that relied on civil society elites with close and credible ties to the Westphalian system.

POST-KOSOVO: 9/11, IRAQ, AND DARFUR

Even before the 9/11 attacks, the Republican turn in American political life had meant that the dynamics of normative globalization, so prominent in the 1990s, would no longer be benefited by and subject to American leadership. The Bush presidency from its outset in January 2001 signaled its opposition to both humanitarian diplomacy and UN peacekeeping operations. It was signaled from the outset of this new leadership that from now on

American foreign policy would emphasize strategic priorities as defined by the entourage of neoconservative advisers at the White House and Pentagon. Tangibly, this meant an increased defense budget, an unwillingness to constrain discretion in the domain of weaponry by arms control treaties, a greater readiness to use force to resolve international disputes, and a preoccupation with restructuring the politics of the Middle East. These features of American foreign policy were reinforced by the U.S. response to the 9/11 attacks. This dramatically altered global setting had a major impact on the practice of diplomacy relevant to humanitarian intervention, including the civil society debate.

There was some support among liberal hawks for extending the Kosovo precedent to Iraq in the lead-up to the invasion. Most notably, Michael Ignatieff, Christopher Hitchens, and to a lesser extent Anne-Marie Slaughter supported the invasion of Iraq on partially humanitarian grounds and were willing to overlook the absence of a UNSC endorsement. Slaughter, in particular, relied on the distinction in the Kosovo Commission Report that stressed the legitimacy/legality reasoning. She argued that the intervention could be legitimized after the fact and was provisionally legitimate due to the oppressive leadership and international criminality of the Baghdad regime as personified by Saddam Hussein. The official American emphasis prior to the invasion was on the strategic threat posed by Iraq due its possession of weapons of mass destruction (WMD), its supposed links to international terrorism, and only incidentally its dictatorial and brutal governing process. After the invasion, as it became clear that there were no WMD to be found in Iraq and no significant Baghdad links to terrorism, the official rationale in Washington shifted markedly to the promotion of democracy and human rights by way of military intervention and occupation. And after years of denial, President Bush would eventually acknowledge that oil was a factor, and that if the United States were to withdraw from Iraq it would lose control over Iraqi oil pricing, which might drive the world price up to $300–400 per barrel. This attempted application of the legal/moral rationalization for the Kosovo war to the circumstances of the Iraq war was uniformly rejected by civil society actors throughout the world. The American effort to mobilize international support for its invasion at the United Nations and elsewhere gave rise to a worldwide antiwar movement that was completely unpersuaded by the alleged humanitarian benefits of the proposed American-led intervention. On February 15, 2003, a few weeks before the invasion, there took place the largest expression of globalized antiwar sentiment in world history, with some 12 million demonstrators displaying their sentiments in 80 countries and some 600 cities. These demonstrations also expressed the overwhelming outlook of public opinion, especially in the European democracies. Even in countries whose leaders were prepared to support American policy, such as the United Kingdom and Spain, an overwhelming majority of the citizenry was opposed to the Iraq war from its inception.

Of course, there was an abstract humanitarian justification for seeking regime change in Iraq, but the means chosen illustrate the dangers of humanitarian intervention being used as a pretext for aggressive warfare. Furthermore, even if UN support had been forthcoming, military action of a nondefensive sort in the absence of any immediate threat of a major humanitarian catastrophe would have resulted in an outcome not very dissimilar from what has resulted. Humanitarian intervention may be effective as an emergency measure to protect a vulnerable population or minority, but it is rarely able to impose a new political structure on a country, given the realities of postcolonial world order. This should have been a lesson of Somalia—as soon as the humanitarian effort morphs into a political restructuring operation, nationalist energies tend to be effectively mobilized to resist the foreign presence. The Iraq experience should be interpreted throughout civil society to impart this lesson: In the absence of a humanitarian emergency, intervention is most unlikely to achieve humanitarian goals at an acceptable cost. Of course, Iraq was an extreme case, given the relative stability of political rule at the time of the invasion, considering the unwillingness of the UN to give its blessings, and in view of the near universal opposition to the proposed war throughout global civil society.

This civic opposition to the invasion and occupation of Iraq has, of course, continued during the long and bloody occupation of Iraq. It has taken several forms, perhaps most notably a world tribunal process. In at least twenty countries, civil society initiatives organized a people's tribunal composed of citizens who passed legal judgment on the invasion and occupation, concluding that the American and British leaders were criminally responsible for violating international law and should be held personally accountable. The culminating expression of this initiative was the World Tribunal on Iraq (WTI) held in Istanbul in June 2005, with a distinguished panel of world citizens and presided over by the Indian novelist Arundhati Roy, issuing a Declaration of Conscience that concluded that the Iraq war was a war of aggression and that its perpetrators and their facilitators were indictable under international criminal law. The WTI heard testimony from fifty-four expert witnesses, including several Iraqis, as well as international law specialists and high-ranking former UN officials. Although this antiwar consensus in civil society was ineffectual in altering American policy, it did contribute to a climate of *illegitimacy* associated with the continuing occupation of Iraq. A main lesson of the Iraq war (reinforcing the lesson of the Vietnam War) is that a strategic intervention is likely to fail even if supported by a strong political will that can mobilize impressive military capabilities; the UN will not ratify the outcome, civil society will oppose, and nationalist forces will resist.

If Iraq shows that political will is insufficient to liberate an oppressed people, the persisting humanitarian crisis in Darfur, already accounting for between 200,000 and 400,000 deaths, with more than two million others displaced and at risk, shows that a requisite political will is necessary to fashion an effective response. Security Council Resolution 1706 accepts the mandate of the "responsibility to protect" norm, but absent the consent of the government of Sudan and without the deep commitment of the United States, the deepening ordeal endured by the people of Darfur resembles the experience of Rwanda in 1994, except that the mass lethality takes place this time in slow motion. Civil society is almost as unified as in relation to Iraq, but it lacks the capacity to transform its moral and political commitment to safeguard the Darfurians into a political project. The required participation of the main geopolitical forces is absent. As East Timor shows, where a geopolitical consensus is present, and a regional actor is sufficiently engaged, the humanitarian mission can be effectively implemented.

It seems clear that the "responsibility to protect" norm is becoming accepted as part of customary international law, but its implementation in specific instances remains dependent on mobilizing the political will of states, usually the globally dominant states, although the engagement of regionally dominant state(s) is sometimes sufficient. At present, such a political will is not likely to be supportive of humanitarian intervention unless it happens to coincide with significant strategic interests. Also, where the territorial sovereign refuses consent, even geopolitical actors often cannot translate their interventionary commitment into viable political projects. To some extent, the failure to implement the responsibility to protect norm in Darfur is a result of the refusal of the government of Sudan to give its consent to have international forces on its territory.

As far as the role of civil society actors is concerned, the legitimacy/legality matrix is instructive: where legitimacy and legality factors overlap, civil society will lend support to humanitarian intervention (as in Rwanda, Darfur, East Timor); where legitimacy supports a call for humanitarian intervention but legality inhibits, civil society actors will be split (as in

Kosovo); where legitimacy factors are ambiguous and legality inhibits, then civil society will be overwhelmingly opposed to military forms of intervention (as in Iraq). Because humanitarian intervention in emergency situations will often depend on the threat and use of force, it must rely on states and international institutions, at both the regional and global levels.

Civil society actors play significant roles, but at the margins of policy making and policy implementation. Aside from significant contributions by way of relief activities, the main contributions of civil society actors has been to reframe the normative debate around legitimacy/legality considerations, as well as with respect to the conditions surrounding a proper implementation of the responsibility to protect norm. Also, civil society activism, as in relation to the Iraq war, does influence perceptions as to the legitimacy of recourse to threats and uses of force, especially in circumstances where the Security Council has withheld authorization. The civil society role can be one of mobilizing support for intervention, as is currently the case with respect to Darfur (e.g. George Clooney at the UN), as well as making an effort to build opposition as has been true with respect to Iraq ever since the prewar debate

A CONCLUDING REFLECTION

This ebb and flow within the last several decades on the question of the limits of sovereignty and the extent of interventionary responsibility is likely to persist. The globalization of moral consciousness and media awareness, combined with the network of civil society actors and transnational activists, ensures attention to these issues. At the same time, the political will to rescue peoples facing humanitarian catastrophe, absent strategic incentives, is not very strong. The UN lacks independent capabilities. Even oppressive governments can often mobilize nationalist resistance to outside intervention. Except in circumstance of genuine emergency, the costs and risks of armed intervention almost always seem to outweigh the benefits that will likely be secured. The fog of war is never thicker than in contexts where humanitarian and strategic interests overlap. At this stage, the defense of sovereign rights protects not only oppressors but also weak states. For this reason there is great reluctance to shift the locus of an interventionary decision outside the halls of the United Nations, or even to feel comfortable about UN authorizations of intervention. At the same time, as the developments in the Balkans, Rwanda during the 1990s, and more recently Sudan and Myanmar dramatized, it is unacceptable for the world's political actors to stand by as spectators while ethnic cleansing or genocide takes place.

The world order dilemma can be expressed in a very simple form: neither geopolitical passivity nor geopolitical activism are morally acceptable in relation to humanitarian crises internal to sovereign states. Resolving the dilemma is not likely to take place until the Westphalian world order of states is replaced by some operative form of regional or global governance that takes on the challenge of responding to severe infringements of human rights. In the interim, the best we can hope for is more benevolent geopolitical leadership from major states, especially the United States, as well as a vibrant civil society presence that pushes hard for timely humanitarian responses and a heightened role for the United Nations that is made more credible than at present by the establishment of independent financial and peacekeeping capabilities. The realities of moral globalization underscore the fundamental irrelevance of national boundaries when peoples are subject to systematic abuses by a territorial government while the realities of political, ethnic, and religious fragmentation ensure that many boundaries are likely to remain highly relevant, and may be given a more symbolic and physical role through the construction of walls.

Contributors

EILEEN BORIS is chair and Hull Professor in the Feminist Studies program at the University of California, Santa Barbara. Her publications include *Art and Labor: Ruskin, Morris, and the Craftsman Ideal in America* (1986); and *Home to Work: Motherhood and the Politics of Industrial Homework in the United States* (1994). She has also co-edited numerous volumes, including *Major Problems in the History of American Workers* (2003); and *The Practice of U.S. Women's History: Narratives, Dialogues, and Intersections* (2007). She is currently completing a book, co-authored with Jennifer Klein, entitled *Caring for America: How Home Health Workers Became the New Face of Labor.*

RICHARD FALK is Milbank Professor of International Law Emeritus at Princeton University and, since 2002, visiting professor of Global Studies at the University of California, Santa Barbara. He serves as chair of the board for the Nuclear Age Peace Foundation and since May 2008 has been the Special Rapporteur on Occupied Palestine for the United Nations Human Rights Council. His most recent books are *The Costs of War: International Law, the UN, and World Order After Iraq* (2008) and *Achieving Human Rights* (2009).

GILES GUNN is professor and chair of Global and International Studies and professor of English at the University of California, Santa Barbara. He is the author of *F. O. Matthiessen: The Critical Achievement* (1975); *The Interpretation of Otherness: Literature, Religion, and the American Imagination* (1979); *The Culture of Criticism and the Criticism of Culture* (1987); *Thinking across the American Grain: Ideology, Intellect, and the New Pragmatism* (1992); and *Beyond Solidarity: Pragmatism and Difference in a Globalized World (2002);* as well as various essays on American and modern literature, critical theory, and intellectual and cultural theory.

CARL GUTIÉRREZ-JONES is professor in the English department and director of the Chicano Studies Institute at the University of California, Santa Barbara. He is the author of *Rethinking the Borderlands: Between Chicano Narrative and Legal Discourse* (1995); and *Critical Race Narratives: A Study of Race, Rhetoric, and Injury* (2001); as well as numerous articles on literature, film, legal studies, and cultural theory. He is currently writing a book that examines the literature of human rights.

MARK JUERGENSMEYER is professor of sociology and of Global and International Studies and director of the Orfalea Center for Global and International Studies at the University of California, Santa Barbara. He is the author or editor of twenty books on religion and society, including *The New Cold War? Religious Nationalism Confronts the Secular State* (1993); *Terror in the Mind of God: The Global Rise of Religious Violence* (2000); and the *Oxford Handbook of Global Religion* (2006).

LISA LOWE is professor of Comparative Literature and Cultural Studies in the Literature department at the University of California, San Diego, and visiting professor in American Studies at Yale University. She is the author of *Critical Terrains: French and British Orientalisms* (1991); and *Immigrant Acts: On Asian American Cultural Politics* (1996); and co-editor of *The Politics of Culture in the Shadow of Capital* (1997). A forthcoming book, *Metaphors of Globalization,* discusses the politics of knowledge of neoliberal globalization. Her current research concerns the legacies of colonial slavery, indentured labor, and immigration within modern concepts of humanism, political freedom, and social justice.

SIMON ORTIZ is professor of English at Arizona State University at Tempe. A Native American writer of the Acoma Pueblo tribe, he is one of the key figures in the second wave of what has been called the Native American Renaissance. He is one of the most respected and widely read Native American poets. He has published dozens of books in a wide variety of genres. These publications include *From Sand Creek: Rising in This Heart Which Is Our America* (1981); *Fightin': New and Collected Stories* (1984); *Woven Stone* (1992); and *The Good Rainbow Road: Rawa Kashtyaa'tsi Hiyaani (A Native American Tale in Keres)* (2004).

DAVID PALUMBO-LIU is professor of Comparative Literature at Stanford University. His publications include *The Poetics of Appropriation: The Literary Theory and Practice of Huang Tingjian* (1993); *The Ethnic Canon: Histories, Institutions, Interventions* (1995); *Streams of Cultural Capital: Transnational Cultural Studies* (1997); and *Asian/American: Historical Crossings of a Racial Frontier* (1999); as well as numerous book chapters and articles in journals such as *Poetics Today; diacritics; differences: a journal of feminist cultural studies; New Literary History; New Centennial Review; Cultural Critique; Public Culture, boundary 2,* and others. Palumbo-Liu's current research includes studies of border art; notions of affinity in literature; race, media and visuality; culture and public policy; and the aesthetics and ethics of globalization.

LISA PARKS is associate professor of Film and Media Studies at the University of California, Santa Barbara. She is the author of *Cultures in Orbit: Satellites and the Televisual* (2005); and of the forthcoming *Coverage: Media, Space and Security after 911;* and is co-editor of *Planet TV* (2003) and the forthcoming *Down to Earth: Satellite Technologies, Industries and Cultures.* She is currently working on another book called *Mixed Signals: Media Infrastructures and Cultural Geographies.*

DONALD PEASE is professor of English, Avalon Foundation Chair of the Humanities, and chair of the Dartmouth Liberal Studies program. He is the author of *Visionary Compacts: American Renaissance Writings in Cultural Context* (1987) and of over seventy articles on figures in American and British literature and the culture of United States imperialism. He is the editor or co-editor of nine volumes, including *American Renaissance Rediscovered* (1985); *Cultures of United States Imperialism* (1993); and *The Futures of American Studies* (2002). He is also general editor of a series of books by Duke University Press called "The New Americanists."

WADE CLARK ROOF is the Rowny Professor of Religion and Society and director of the Walter H. Capps Center for the Study of Ethics, Religion and Public Life at the University of California, Santa Barbara. He is the author of eight books, including *A Generation of Seekers* (1993) and *Spiritual Marketplace: Baby Boomers and the Remaking of American Religion* (2002); and is currently engaged in research on the 2008 presidential election and prospects for progressive religion in the United States.

JOHN CARLOS ROWE is USC Associates' Professor of the Humanities in the departments of English and American Studies and Ethnicity at the University of Southern California. He is the author *of Henry Adams and Henry James: The Emergence of a Modern Consciousness* (1976); *Through the Custom-House: Nineteenth Century American Fiction and Modern Theory* (1982); *The Theoretical Dimensions of Henry James* (1984); *At Emerson's Tomb: The Politics of Classic American Literature* (1997); *The Other Henry James* (1998); *Literary Culture and U.S. Imperialism: From the Revolution to World War II* (2000); and *The New American Studies* (2002). He is currently working on post–World War II culture and U.S. imperialism and multicultural literature and the new democracy.

GABRIELE SCHWAB is Chancellor's Professor of English & Comparative Literature at the University of California, Irvine. Her books in English include *Subjects without Selves: Transitional Texts in Modern Fiction* (1994); and *The Mirror and the Killer-Queen: Otherness in Literary Language* (1997). She has published in the fields of literary studies, critical theory, reader-response theory, cultural criticism, psychoanalysis, literature and anthropology, and literature and science, as well as English, Irish, American, French, German, and Japanese literatures. Her work in-progress includes a theoretical book on the cultural unconscious and another book on the anthropological turn in literary studies titled *Imaginary Ethnographies.*

RONALD STEEL is professor emeritus of International Relations at the University of Southern California. He has written several books on American foreign policy, including *Pax Americana* (1967) and *Temptations of a Superpower* (1995). In addition, he is author of the award-winning biography, *Walter Lippmann and the American Century* (1980), as well as a biography of Robert Kennedy (2000). Among his fellowships are those from the Carnegie Endowment, the Woodrow Wilson Center, the Guggenheim Foundation, the Council on Foreign Relations, the Institute for Advanced Study in Berlin, and the American Academy in Berlin. He is a regular contributor to the *New York Review of Books* and other publications.

www.ingramcontent.com/pod-product-compliance
Lightning Source LLC
Chambersburg PA
CBHW020347270326
41926CB00007B/339

* 9 7 8 0 5 2 0 0 9 8 7 0 1 *